The Peace Corps
in **Cameroon**

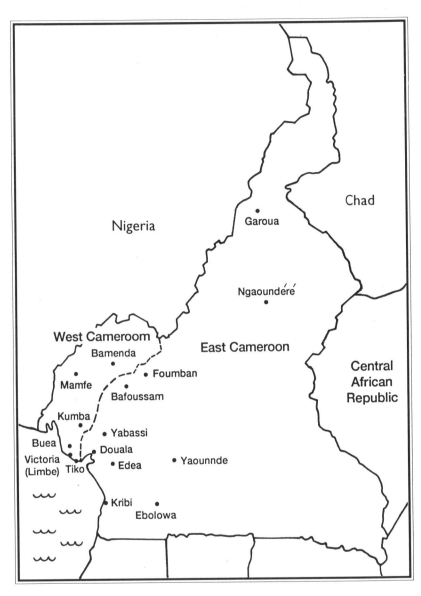

Map of Cameroon showing the main towns of Peace Corps services.

The Peace Corps in Cameroon

Julius A. Amin

The Kent State University Press

Kent, Ohio, and London, England

© 1992 by The Kent State University Press
Kent, Ohio 44242

All rights reserved
Library of Congress Catalog Card Number 91-29956
ISBN 0-87338-450-4
Manufactured in the United States of America

Library of Congress Cataloging-in-Publication Data
Amin, Julius Atemkeng.
    The Peace Corps in Cameroon / Julius Amin.
        p.   cm.
    Includes bibliographical references and index.
    ISBN 0-87338-450-4 (alk. paper) ∞
    1. Peace Corps (U.S.)—Cameroon—History.   I. Title.
HC60.5.A76   1992
361.6—dc20   91–29956

British Library Cataloging-in-Publication data are available.

Contents

Acknowledgments

Several people contributed in the writing of this book. My greatest intellectual debt goes to Professor George Q. Flynn of Texas Tech University. Professor Flynn read and made critical comments on several versions of the manuscripts. His suggestions enormously improved the substance and mechanics of the study. At various points I benefited from the suggestions of Professors Alwyn Barr, James Harper, Robert Hayes, Otto Nelson, and Edward Steinhart, all of Texas Tech University.

I owe a very special debt to the returned Peace Corps volunteers from Cameroon, Ghana, and Guinea. They completed a nine-page questionnaire, shared their personal letters, diaries, and Peace Corps papers with me. They are the forgotten people in the history books, and this book is partly their story. Very special thanks are due Professors Roy P. Fairfield, Carl Denbow, and Gilbert Schneider. All were associated with the early Peace Corps-Cameroon project. They provided me with hundreds of pages of Peace Corps documents and also granted me interviews. My continuous phone calls at odd times of the day never bothered them. Without their assistance I would have been imprisoned in this study.

My sincere thanks go to all those I interviewed in Cameroon. They shared with me their perspective on the Peace Corps in the most forthright manner. It was always a pleasure to listen to them talk about Peace Corps services and other issues in Cameroonian affairs.

At the Peace Corps Office in Washington, D.C., I always counted on the assistance of Bill Strassberger and John Von Rynn. While Bill ensured that I obtained all the photographs I needed, John acted promptly each time I submitted a request to obtain documents through the Freedom of Information Act.

My appreciation goes to the staffs of the various archives I visited for research. Their kindness, courtesy, and willingness to help made my work in the archives more enjoyable.

Roberta Alexander, chairperson of the History Department at the University of Dayton, assigned a student assistant to me each semester and also allowed the department to mail some of my questionnaires. John Heitman, my colleague in the department, commented on some chapters of the manuscript. Linda McKinley, the department typist, generously typed portions of the manuscript.

The Research Institute at the University of Dayton granted me a Summer Fellowship that enabled the completion of the revisions of the manuscript. Robert L. Leach of the Inter-Library Loan department at the university diligently processed my mounting requests and was always able to get what I wanted.

Special thanks go to my editors at the Kent State University Press—Julia Morton, Linda Cuckovich, and Joanna Hildebrand. They spotted many errors and insisted that the corrections be made promptly.

My wife, Brenda, and my daughter, Lori Ann, made many sacrifices. Brenda typed and retyped several versions of the manuscript. Lori kept her smile, and her frequent words of "da da" were very encouraging. This book is as much theirs as it is mine.

My parents, Sylvester T. and Anastasia A. Amin, always assured me that I could get it done. Their support and encouragement have never faltered.

The people listed above are not responsible for any shortcomings in the book. Any errors are mine.

This book is dedicated to the memory of my late brother and sister, Magnus and Gladys Amin. Their words of encouragement and love will never be forgotten.

Introduction

In 1960, John F. Kennedy accused President Dwight Eisenhower's administration of allowing America to lose momentum in the Cold War. Under the Republican administration, he said, the country had grown conservative, fat, and lazy. There were many problems: Sputnik, a missile gap, Castro's Cuba, and the neglect of the Third World countries. These problems, Kennedy noted, resulted from reacting to Soviet activities instead of initiating new policies. Kennedy promised "to get the country moving again" by offering new directions in foreign policy.

As president, Kennedy acted on his promise when, on March 1, 1961, he signed Executive Order 10924 establishing the Peace Corps. This agency quickly became part of U.S. governmental support for Third World development.

The Peace Corps, though a major innovation of the Kennedy administration, is often ignored in the Kennedy literature. The few studies that focus on the Peace Corps expound on it as an example of American idealism.[1] While not rejecting the idealism theory, I hope to show that more pragmatic thinking was at work when the Peace Corps was established. Additionally, I have been able to go beyond the agency's mere creation to examine the performance of the volunteers in Cameroon, West Africa. I have covered the period from the establishment of the Peace Corps in 1961 to 1966, when Sargent Shriver, the agency's first director, was appointed to other functions. (After 1966 the volunteers were no longer trained in the United States; they received their training in the host country.)

The reasons for focusing on Cameroon are varied. Like most African countries, Cameroon had an ocean of postindependence problems to deal with. It was, in addition, the only bilingual country in Africa after independence. Moreover, the Maquisards, a pro-Communist terrorist group, was active in Cameroon during the 1960s. And finally, as a Cameroonian citizen who studied under Peace Corps volunteers and later taught with them as a colleague in a high school in Cameroon, I had access to documents on both sides of the Atlantic.

Several questions were posed at the beginning of this study, including: What were the pragmatic origins of the Peace Corps Agency? What problems did Cameroon face in the immediate postindependence era? How did the training of the volunteers adequately prepare them for work in Cameroon? How did the volunteers perform in their teaching and community development work? Did they make a difference? How did the volunteers adjust to life in Cameroon? How did Cameroonians evaluate the work of these new Western visitors? What is the importance of this study? This book is a response to those questions and more.

My hope is that this study will add something to the interpretations of the Peace Corps, demonstrating the agency's importance in post–World War II American foreign policy and illustrating the rocky path the early Peace Corps volunteers traveled in executing their duties. Finally, I wish to encourage other studies of the Peace Corps in action.

Much of this study is based on previously uncited documents. I examined the responses to a nine-page questionnaire completed by fifty returned Peace Corps volunteers from Cameroon. (Returned Peace Corps volunteers from Guinea completed a similar questionnaire.) Also, returned volunteers from Cameroon, Guinea, and Ghana gave me personal Peace Corps notes and papers, diaries, and letters. Professors Roy P. Fairfield, Carl Denbow, Gilbert Schneider, and Jack Carmichael, all faculty at Ohio University and associated with Peace Corps-Cameroon during these early years, provided hundreds of pages of documents that were unavailable in the major archives, including the Peace Corps Library. I also conducted interviews in Cameroon on Peace Corps services there and obtained a vast number of documents through the Freedom of Information Act. All the documents collected and used in this study will be deposited at the John F. Kennedy Library in Boston, Massachusetts. On their request, the identities of some of the sources remain anonymous.

1

The Beginning

The news was received with shock, despair, uncertainty, and frustration. The tragic assassination of President John F. Kennedy on November 22, 1963, seemed to mark the end of an age. The Peace Corps volunteers felt cheated. Their hero had been snatched away from them. So thought the youth in America and in the Third World.

> The death of President Kennedy, a first-class international figure, fills me with shock and sorrow.
> Africa and the World at large have lost a truly noble, energetic liberal minded man. Africa will NEVER forgive Texas and its allies in the Deep South. . . . Will the Peace Corps programme end?[1]

> On November 25, 1963, the American community of Monrovia, Liberia, gathered in a union with the American family the World over, to mourn the death of its President. Shocked, hurt, and uncertain, the Americans huddled together, longing to be in the bosom of their own family and their own country in this hour when so much that was central to their lives had been wrenched away. The young . . . Peace Corps volunteers . . . gathered at the capitol building in Monrovia . . . where the government of Liberia . . . would hold its memorial tribute to the American President. . . . The Americans felt shame in the presence of the chiefs [Liberian Chiefs]. They listened to the Liberian President's eulogy for their own President, and knew [what] grief expressed. . . . They began to realize that the American President did not . . . belong to the American people alone.[2]

Many Third World leaders remembered Kennedy's good humor, charm, and manners. Some talked of his infectious smile. And there was a sense of betrayal. The Nigerian president, Nnamdi Azikiwe, a graduate of an American university, expressed his emotion on the loss in a stinging note to the American government. He stated that the

killing of Kennedy was "a setback for those who believed in fair play and social justice for the black race all over the world. . . . Perhaps Nigeria would begin to look elsewhere for its foreign aid." He added, "I once called the U.S. God's country. . . . I hope my countrymen will forgive me for being so simpleton."[3] Azikiwe seemed to have spoken for most Third World leaders. The future of their countries was suddenly covered with a "gust of cloud and smoke."[4]

The thousand days Kennedy spent in the White House were important. More than any former American president, Kennedy was able to persuade the emerging nations of the Third World to "start to look to America, to what the President of the United States is doing, not . . . Krushchev or the Chinese Communists."[5] In 1961 Kennedy hailed Kwame Nkrumah, the president of Ghana, for quoting Thomas Jefferson in a speech at the United Nations. "The disease of liberty is catching," Kennedy remarked. Nkrumah, a leading African nationalist, had been dismissed as a Communist by Kennedy's predecessor, Dwight Eisenhower.[6]

Kennedy understood the strategic importance of the Third World for American foreign policy. He denounced Eisenhower for lacking a well-coordinated policy for countries of Latin America, Asia, and Africa. Kennedy criticized this and remarked that, under Eisenhower, American foreign policy was "being starved on a diet of negatives." Kennedy believed that Eisenhower's policy of reacting to Soviet initiatives through "military pacts and alliances" had crippled American foreign policy. In Pennsylvania and Kentucky, Kennedy exhorted that "across the face of the globe freedom and communism are locked in a deadly embrace. At this moment and during the past few months and years, the Communist expansion has been on the move. We see it beginning to move."[7]

Kennedy dismissed such Cold War dogmas as "godless communism," "Soviet master plan," and the "liberation of the enslaved people" by stating that a "total solution is impossible in the nuclear age." Later he requested that Americans "must move forward to meet communism, rather than waiting for it to come to us and then reacting to it."[8] Kennedy had summoned Americans to take the initiative in the Cold War. To do this, the United States therefore needed a pragmatic Third World policy. The Third World had become the new battleground for the ideological struggle, Kennedy insisted.

As president, Kennedy took the initiative when, on March 1, 1961, he signed Executive Order 10924 establishing the Peace

Corps.[9] This agency became a major part of United States governmental support for Third World development. The idea of the Peace Corps was not totally new, however. The United States had begun in the post–World War II era to use political, economic, and military means to resist the spread of Communist influence. It is in this background that the origin of the Peace Corps is to be found.

Following World War II, United States policy planners arrived at several conclusions about the conduct of American foreign policy. Such past events and policies as appeasement, the rise of Hitler, and the bombing of Pearl Harbor dealt a severe blow to previous American notions of noninvolvement and isolation. It was "the greatest revolution the world has ever known," Charles de Gaulle remarked of World War II in 1940. The impact of the war was indeed severe. The war marked the "end of Europe" as the center of power; overnight, European nations were turned into secondary powers. Economically, Europe was devastated, and in 1945, "like a whale left gasping on the sand, Europe lay rotting in the sun," wrote one observer. Winston Churchill later described Europe as a "rubble-heap, a charnel house, a breeding-ground of pestilence and hate." The war's end also led to the disintegration of colonial possessions. Following World War II, European colonies in Asia and Africa were ready to break away. More important, two superpowers, the United States and the Soviet Union, emerged in 1945. In fact, it was on these superpowers, no longer the British or any other empire, that the sun did not set. In the period after 1945, the United States and the Soviet Union struggled to extend their "spheres of influence." The intense struggle for ideological domination by the superpowers gave birth to the Cold War. "Competitive interaction" between Moscow and Washington was comparable to "two big dogs chewing on a bone," Senator J. William Fulbright said.[10]

The post–World War II era was very different from the period following World War I. America had come to learn that in order to prevent another "Munich" or Hitler, it must remain committed in world affairs. Exactly what role America was to play in the world was vague and largely undetermined in 1945. On April 12, 1945, President Franklin Roosevelt, who had led the grand alliance to victory against the dictators, died, and his vice president, Harry S. Truman, immediately stepped into the presidency. Compared to Roosevelt, Truman was naïve, uninformed, and uneducated on foreign policy issues—yet he was suddenly put in the position of having to address the complexities of the world, which were, of course, monumental, and the stakes were exceedingly high. As vice president, Truman played a limited role in foreign policy issues. He knew little about the Yalta agreements. He had firm ideas and impressions about Communist Russia. As president, Truman had never met Churchill or Joseph Stalin. In fact, "the world came tumbling in on Harry Truman" during a critical moment in history. There was so much to learn and so little time.[11]

Topping Truman's agenda was relations with the Soviet Union. America had forged an alliance with the Soviet Union against Hitler during World War II, but problems between the two countries had emerged following the Yalta Conference. Washington officials described Joseph Stalin as a "liar and a crook." He had refused to allow free elections in Poland and had proceeded to create satellite states in Eastern Europe. According to Truman, such actions violated the Yalta agreements. Such were the issues Truman was to discuss at the Potsdam Conference in July 1945. Uncertain as to how to respond to Soviet actions, Truman was constantly reminded by Churchill that Stalin's Russia had an expansionist appetite and had to be stopped. Truman's lack of diplomatic craftsmanship complicated matters. In diplomacy, Truman's style was the direct opposite of Roosevelt's. "Where Roosevelt improvised . . . Truman stuck closely to positions worked out in advance," Charles Bohlen stated. Churchill admired Truman's zeal and determination but added that "he takes no notice of delicate ground, he just plants his foot down firmly upon it." Whatever impressions the world held of Truman, his first year in office was destined to be what he would later call a "year of decisions."[12]

At the Potsdam Conference, Truman met and talked with Churchill and Stalin for the first time. The conferees achieved little, but the two Western leaders returned with even firmer beliefs about Stalin. Truman remained cautious, but events moved quickly. Stalin consolidated his authority over Eastern Europe and was not prepared to stop Soviet incursions into Iran. Truman had hoped that the atomic bomb and the threat to cut off aid to Russia would reverse Stalin's expansionism, but both attempts failed.

By 1946, Truman had grown impatient with Stalin's behavior. In January he wrote, "Unless Russia is faced with an iron fist and strong language another war is in the making. Only one language do they understand. . . . I'm tired of babying the Soviets." For Truman it was time to "tell the Russians where to get off." Despite the "tough line" in rhetoric, Truman remained indecisive in actions because the American public still supported cordial relations with the Soviet Union. All this changed on March 5, 1946. On this day, speaking at Westminster College in Fulton, Missouri, Winston Churchill lashed out at Soviet actions. "From Stettin in the Baltic to Trieste in the Adriatic, an iron curtain has descended across the continent," Churchill said. Russia's appetite to expand beyond the "iron curtain" was insatiable, Churchill warned. The only way to stop Russia was the establishment of a "special relationship between the British Commonwealth and Empire and the United States." He called for the formation of a "fraternal association" between Britain and the United States.[13]

Churchill's "iron curtain" speech persuaded the American public that Russia was no ally. An opinion poll taken in 1946 showed that more than 70 percent of the American public supported Truman's tough diplomacy against the Soviet Union. For the Soviet Union the iron curtain speech was "a dangerous act calculated to sow the seeds of discord among the Allied Governments."[14] The speech dissolved all lingering illusions about cooperation with the Soviet Union. After the speech, the American public made up its mind: Russia was a more dangerous enemy than Nazi Germany. In fact, Churchill's speech had raised the Western curtain on the Cold War age; that it came in words made it no less definitive than the Soviet land seizures. After 1946, American officials became more determined to contain Communist expansion.

By 1947 the United States had concluded that the struggle between democracy and communism was permanent. On March 12, 1947, President Harry Truman, in a blunt message to Congress, declared the goals of American foreign policy:

> I believe that it must be the policy of the United States to support free peoples who are resisting attempted subjugation by armed minorities or by outside pressures. . . . I believe that our help should be primarily through economic and financial aid which is essential to economic stability and orderly political progress.[15]

The Truman Doctrine, as the message became known, formally committed the United States in the Cold War. The doctrine established ground rules for American foreign policy in the succeeding years. It directed the Communists to stay behind the iron curtain.

The speech rejected any form of revolution, because such upheavals represented an "assault on individual liberty and private property." These ideas were deeply rooted in the traditional American belief that revolutions rarely produced "orderly liberty."[16]

It was in the year of the Truman Doctrine that John F. Kennedy, at age thirty, took his seat in Congress. Kennedy fully endorsed this hard-line policy and later cited Truman as one of his heroes.[17] People often learn from their heroes, and Kennedy was no exception. His ideas on how to deal with the Russians were molded by Harry Truman and his administration.

Another development among policymakers in 1947 was the acceptance of George F. Kennan's dictum that "World Communism is like a malignant parasite which feeds only on diseased tissue." During this time Europe was the "diseased" zone. The United States responded with the Marshall Plan, designed to eliminate hunger and poverty. The plan, it was believed, would rescue Europe from a collapse into communism. Truman later stated that the plan and his doctrine were "two halves of the same walnut."[18]

Perhaps the most significant contribution of the Marshall Plan to the development of the Cold War was that it accelerated the rigid polarization of Europe. Russia tongue-lashed the United States for the plan and established the Molotov Plan. It created Cominform (Communist Information Bureau) to replace the defunct Comintern (Communist International). With these developments, the ideological division of Europe seemed complete. The superpowers wooed and waited for the rest of the world to take sides in this new war.

In the aftermath of the 1948 presidential election, Truman, now president in his own right, concluded that the new battleground for the Cold War was the underdeveloped areas of the Third World. This region was the warehouse of economic hardship. His beliefs were confirmed by the report of the National Security Council Paper 20/4 (NSC 20/4) of November 23, 1948. "Present intelligence estimates attribute to Soviet armed forces the capability of overrunning in about six months all of continental Europe and the Near East as far as Cairo," the report documented. The message was clear. The mention of Cairo indicated that the "Communist disease" was about to infect the entire Southern Hemisphere. The authors of the document concluded that Russia was seeking nothing short of world domination.[19]

The impact of NSC 20/4 was evident in Truman's inaugural address in 1949. This time the brickbats were not limited to the Soviet system. He proposed a new program for the Third World. Truman called on the United States "to embark on a bold new program for making the benefits of our scientific advances and industrial progress available for the improvement and growth of underdeveloped areas." He requested that the United States "help the free peoples of the World, through their own efforts, to produce more food, more clothing, more materials for housing, and more technical power to lighten their burdens."[20] This program became known as Point Four because it was ranked fourth on Truman's foreign policy list. It was Truman's "bold new program."

Point Four was unique. It placed American assistance to the underdeveloped areas in the context of the Cold War, something succeeding presidents continued. Methods varied, but the goals remained unchanged. The program would destroy the "seeds of communism" by eliminating hunger, poverty, and economic chaos. According to Truman,

> The Point Four program was a practical expression of our attitude toward the countries threatened by communist domination. It was consistent with our policies of preventing the expansion of Communism in the Free World by helping to insure the proper development of those countries with adequate food, clothing and living facilities.[21]

Though the program stressed the "distribution of knowledge rather than money," it was also designed to enhance the continuous productive capacity of American industries. "Common sense told me that the development of these countries would keep our industrial plant in business for untold generations," Truman wrote.[22] The underdeveloped countries contained mighty reserves of untapped resources needed by American industries.

The Point Four Program materialized on June 5, 1950, when Truman signed an act to "provide foreign economic assistance," the Act for International Development.[23] Of the $34.5 million Truman requested as funding for the program, only $26.9 million was appropriated. The Act for International Development and the founding of the North Atlantic Treaty Organization (NATO) in 1949 demonstrated in the most vivid manner the endorsement by Washington of these new tactics to wage the Cold War.

Despite the determination to enforce the new foreign policy, the United States in 1949 faced some major setbacks. Russia tested the atomic bomb and Mao Tse-tung took control of mainland China. Also, Truman realized that American conventional forces were in short supply to wage the Cold War.

The events of 1949 helped form John F. Kennedy's view of the Cold War. Though he supported the Truman Doctrine, he still expressed "ambivalence" and uncertainty on foreign policy, a traditional, normal attitude for most new recruits on Capitol Hill.[24] But he learned fast. He quickly became an arch-apostle of the hard-line policy. He swelled the ranks of the Cold War "hawks." At times he expressed dissatisfaction with Truman for not being tough enough.

Kennedy and his colleagues lashed at Truman for the loss of China. "What our young men have saved, our diplomats and our President have frittered away,"[25] Kennedy stated. His foreign policy education by this time seemed complete. The passage of time would produce minor adjustments, but the policy of going all the way against the Communist threat remained unreversed.

Few doubted the impact the failures of 1949 had on Truman. In the light of the setbacks, he requested that the State and Defense departments prepare a Cold War policy paper. This document was ready by the spring of 1950. Its recommendations were sent to Truman under the title of National Security Council Paper 68 (NSC 68).

NSC 68 became a significant Cold War document. The document reiterated the aggressive intentions of the Soviet Union. "The gravest threat to the security of the United States . . . stems from the hostile designs . . . of the U.S.S.R., and from the nature of the Soviet system," the paper warned. To effectively defend itself and the free world, the paper called on the United States to muster its political, military, economic, and social strengths for the task.[26] The advent of the Korean War paved the way for the realization of NSC 68.

The war, according to Truman, showed that the Russians would use any means to expand their influence. He informed the American public that Korea's freedom and independence was overdue. His supporters rallied and declared that Pyongyang, the capital of North Korea, would be returned to the Western alliance system. More important, the war proved to Truman that the security of the free world was at stake. He seized the opportunity and signed into law a series of Cold War measures against Russia and its Communist allies. The Korean War reinforced the notion of monolithic communism. Washington made no more attempts to separate communism in

China and Indochina from Russian communism. Any brand of communism was dangerous, Washington concluded.[27]

In 1951 Congress passed the Battle Act (Mutual Defense Control Act). The act stated:

> The Congress of the United States, recognizing that in a World threatened by aggression the United States can best preserve and maintain peace by developing maximum national strength by utilizing all its resources in cooperation with other free nations, hereby declares it to be the policy of the United States, to apply an embargo on the shipment of arms, ammunition . . . to any nation or combination of nations threatening the security of the United States.

In the same year Congress, in order to "coalesce the economic, military and technical programs," passed the Mutual Security Act. In signing the act, Truman declared that

> the United States will continue to participate in the great collective defense effort of the free nations and to assist free peoples around the World who want to develop and safeguard their freedom and maintain the peace. . . . The peoples of the underdeveloped areas of the World want desperately to take fuller advantage of their human and natural resources. We are . . . to help them achieve these aspirations.[28]

All these laws did not satisfy the extreme Cold Warriors, who, with their new complaints against the administration, inhibited Truman's ability to conduct foreign policy. Joseph McCarthy, the young junior senator from Wisconsin, led this group with a new wave of charges that the Truman administration was infested with pro-Communists. A close friend of the Kennedy family, McCarthy escalated his witch-hunt to include Americans from all walks of life in the early 1950s. Following the presidential election in 1952, McCarthy became chairman of the Permanent Subcommittee on Investigations of the Senate Government Operations Committee. Promptly McCarthy named Robert Kennedy as his assistant minority counsel. With the Kennedy name on his side, McCarthy struck terror into the lives of hundreds of Americans. Those who criticized his anticommunism crusade were tagged as "egg-sucking phony liberals." The early years of the Eisenhower presidency were the peak of the American red scare. The Kennedys' association with McCarthy was to haunt them later in their political lives, for at a time when the Kennedy

brothers were expected to be shrewd and courageous, in their dealings with McCarthy they failed. Though McCarthy was later cen-
sured and discredited for misleading the nation, John Kennedy and
his brother Robert did not repudiate his charges and methods.[29]

Walter Lippmann, the doyen of American liberal columnists at
the time, initially rejected Kennedy's nomination as a presidential
candidate because of his dealings with McCarthy. "I had grave reservations about him [Kennedy], both because of my knowledge of
his father, and because of his own record in the McCarthy affair,"
Lippmann wrote.[30] John F. Kennedy never condemned McCarthy.
McCarthyism and its advocates showed in the most vivid manner
the climate in which foreign policy of the time was made. All the
Communists would be hunted down.

McCarthyism was not the only issue that plagued the final years
of the Truman administration. Earlier Kennedy had criticized
Truman for not doing enough in the defense department. Kennedy
believed the fifty-five groups demanded by the secretary of defense,
Louis Johnson, were insufficient. Kennedy wanted the Air Force to be
expanded to seventy groups. Later, in 1952, Kennedy warned that
"the most serious deficiency in our military strength is our weakness
in the air."[31] In fact, Kennedy and the Cold War hawks continued to
criticize Truman for not being tough enough on communism.

Despite criticism, the Truman years had prepared the way for a
national stance; the United States would stand up to the Communist
threat. For all the setbacks caused him by the McCarthyists, the China
lobby, and the extreme Cold Warriors, Truman had started a new
chapter in the annals of American foreign policy. His vision of the
world would be amended to allow for flexibility, but the cardinal objective of confining communism behind the iron curtain remained.

The Marshall Plan, the Point Four Program, the Battle Act, the
McCarran Act, and the Mutual Security Act, all endorsed by John F.
Kennedy, represented a firm foundation for his presidential policies
in later years. Kennedy watched Truman pave the way for a large defense budget. By 1950 he had learned quickly that the defense of
Africa, Latin America, and the Far East was important for the defense of the free world.

As the new administration took office, Kennedy waited and
watched to see whether President Dwight Eisenhower would reverse
Truman's goals in foreign policy. President Eisenhower inherited the
containment policy from his predecessor. Though more restrained in

practice, the rhetoric of his administration emphasized the good-versus-evil view of the world. Little room existed for any dissent and neutrality. Additional laws were passed to enhance United States performance in the Cold War.

In 1954 the Mutual Security Act was amended. Section 400 of the act made available to the president an amount of $100,000 which could be used to defend American security at any time without consulting Congress. That same year, Truman's disciples in the Senate, led by Hubert Humphrey, pushed through the Communist Control Act, which outlawed the Communist party in the United States.

Just as important was the development of Eisenhower's Third World Policy in the 1950s. Eisenhower had entered the White House with preconceived notions about people in the southern regions of the world. These people were "non-white," "funny," "backward," "non-English-speaking" and consequently could not govern themselves, Eisenhower believed. He feared that it would be dangerous to set the "non-white" population free because they would immediately be engulfed by communism. The peoples of Asia and Africa were "dependent peoples" of the world. As a result, they needed a long period of Western paternalism, the White House believed. Continuous European domination in Africa would prevent what Eisenhower called "chaos" from running "wild" in that region. Eisenhower's racial views were shared by many in Washington. When he referred to Africa, he talked of "primitive people," "restless and militant population in a state of gross ignorance."[32] Such views shaped Eisenhower's Third World policy.

Eisenhower believed that former imperialist members of NATO, such as England and France, should be left to handle the affairs of their Asian and African colonies as they saw fit. English and French people were white and were what he called his "right arm." They would properly equip the "natives" to resist communism, Eisenhower believed. Consequently Eisenhower relegated much Third World responsibility to them. To assist his European allies, Eisenhower promoted the Central Intelligence Agency (CIA) into a major instrument of foreign policy. The CIA carried out covert action, the so-called "dirty work," in the developing nations. Third World leaders suspected of being communistic were either overthrown or eliminated or had their governments destabilized.[33]

Such an approach undermined the Point Four Program Truman had initiated for the Third World. Eisenhower's knowledge of Third

World development and the changes taking place in that part of the globe was embarrassingly poor. He compared the independence movement in the region to a "destructive hurricane." He supported his assistant secretary of state, C. Burke Elbrick, whose assessment of the development in Africa was that "premature independence and irresponsible nationalism may represent grave dangers to dependent peoples."[34] The Eisenhower administration failed to realize that by relying on a cheap policy of CIA disruption in the Third World, it created a situation easily exploited by Soviet and Chinese Communists.

Leading African nations criticized the United States for the policy of supporting imperialism. Ghana (under Kwame Nkrumah), Guinea (led by Sekou Touré), Congo (led by Patrice Lumumba), and other nations turned to Communist countries for support. These countries felt that the United States had failed to identify with their aspirations. At the United Nations the United States' position confirmed their worst fears. The record indicates that

> the last act of the Eisenhower Administration on the colonial question was to vote against the colonial declaration of December 1960 in the U.N. That declaration was a general statement upholding the rights of all peoples to self-determination. Under tense British pressure, President Eisenhower personally ordered the American representative in the U.N. to vote "no." That vote strengthened the impression prevalent in many anticolonial states that the United States was very much a supporter of the West European Hegemonists.[35]

But not all in Washington shared the Eisenhower-Dulles policy toward the Third World. John F. Kennedy became one of the most severe critics of this policy. The Korean War proved beyond any doubt that the Third World was the new battleground for the Cold War. Kennedy believed that the United States had to align itself with the forces of nationalism in order to prevent a Third World collapse into communism. Such an alignment would show these countries that the United States sympathized with their struggles. Therefore, Eisenhower's policy was drastically wrong and shortsighted.

Returning from the Far East in 1951, Kennedy pointed to "the fires of nationalism . . . now ablaze. . . . Colonialism is not a topic for tea-talk discussion; it is the daily fare of millions of men." Following his trip to Indochina, Kennedy became quite critical of British and French imperialism in that region, and he concluded that the Communists had exploited the situation to their advantage. Years later, Kennedy informed Americans about the changes taking place in Africa. "Call it nationalism, call it anti-colonialism, call it what you will. . . . Africa is going through a revolution," Kennedy stated. Additionally, he cautioned that "the word is out—and spreading like wildfire in nearly a thousand languages and dialects—that it is no longer necessary to remain forever poor or forever in bondage."[36] Though Kennedy advised against supporting France in Indochina, the Eisenhower administration failed to take him seriously. Indochina was a French problem, Eisenhower believed. After the Suez crisis of 1956, Kennedy talked of the "Eisenhower mess" in Egypt. He pointed to the high price the United States paid for reversing its desire to finance the Aswan Dam. Later, he did not limit his criticism to Eisenhower. He realized that France's imperial designs continuously frustrated America's goals in the Third World.

In 1957, Kennedy dropped a bombshell on France. On July 2, he took to the Senate floor and, in an address entitled "Facing Facts in Algeria," fiercely denounced French imperialism in Algeria. To France he warned, "Whether France likes it or not, admits it or not, or has our support or not, . . . their overseas territories are eventually going to break free and look with suspicion on Western nations who impeded their steps to independence."[37]

The immediate response to the speech was critical but welcomed. President Eisenhower resented the idea of "young men getting up and shouting about things." Dean Acheson noted, "Nothing could be more injudicious [than] that [Kennedy's] proposal." John Foster Dulles responded that "if anyone is interested in going after colonialism, there are a lot of better places to go after than the case of France." Robert Lacoste, then French minister in Algeria, responded that "the United States ought to solve its Negro problem before telling France how to get along with the Moslems."[38] Such criticism did little to scare Kennedy.

On July 8, 1957, Kennedy answered his critics. He reaffirmed his position by stating that

> the sweep of nationalism is the most potent factor in foreign affairs today. We can resist it or ignore it but only for a little while; we can see it exploited by the Soviets with grave consequences; or we in this country can give it hope and leadership, and thus improve immeasurably our standing and our security.[39]

Eisenhower chose to ignore it. Though the State Department established a Bureau of African Affairs in 1957, many African nationalist leaders and their supporters viewed the department with suspicion. Even the move by Congress in July 1958 to establish the post of assistant secretary of state for African affairs did not alter their impression. These leaders ignored the bureau and quickly looked to Kennedy as their hero. Later, such presidents as Leopold Senghor (Senegal), Moktar Ould Daddah (Mauritania), and Ahmadou Ahidjo (Cameroon) were convinced of Kennedy's sympathies for Africa after the Algerian speech. Kennedy repeatedly requested that Americans support the crusade for freedom taking place in Africa and urged that Americans must not "think of Africa in terms of Europe."[40]

Kennedy's interest in the tide of nationalism and Africa soon paid off. In 1959 he became chairman of the African subcommittee of the Senate Foreign Relations Committee. As chairman, he warned that the United States had to support the African countries struggling to destroy the roots of imperialism. Such support was important to the security of the free world, he noted. Though Kennedy called relatively few meetings on Africa, he continuously stressed that the United States had to assist the economic and educational development of the continent.

Simultaneously, Kennedy was angry with the sorry image of the United States in the Third World. American diplomats in the developing regions created an exclusive world for themselves in these countries. In 1958 William J. Lederer and Eugene Burdick surprised the nation with the shocking revelations of a significant novel on American diplomats in the Third World. In *The Ugly American* they wrote:

> The American Ambassador is a jewel. He keeps his people tied up with meetings, social events, greeting and briefing the scores of Senators, Congressmen, generals, admirals, undersecretaries of state and defense, and so on, who come pouring through here "to look for themselves." He forbids his people to go "into the hills," and still annoys the people of Sarkhan with his bad manners.[41]

Such representation of the United States by its diplomats was contrary to what Kennedy expected. In contrast to the American diplomats, the Communists had a dynamic approach; their means of recruiting in the Third World was never "so restricted." The

Communists organized schools in which they taught a variety of courses. They learned the dialects of the peoples with whom they had contact. No wonder Southeast Asians were "enthusiastic about the Chinese communists."[42] Thus, the Communists understood more than Americans the craft of spreading doctrine. Unlike the Communists, who sent their agents to the rural areas to live and toil with the common people, the American ambassadors confined their activities to the capital cities and abandoned the interior.

The Ugly American exposed the shame of American Third World policy. America had a "sorry record" in its dealings with the developing countries, Senator Fulbright wrote in 1958. American diplomats in the developing world were untrained in languages and totally ignorant of the cultures of the countries in which they served. They were "arrogant" snobs and concentrated their activities in the "golden ghettos." Understandably, foreign service officials were critical of the novel, but Secretary of State Christian Herter "found a good deal of good" in the book. Senator Hubert Humphrey said that it was his view that "*The Ugly American* has served to strengthen our foreign policy in Southeast Asia."[43] A significant consequence of this book was that America had to recognize the changes taking place in the developing world and also learn that the old tactics of diplomacy were no longer sufficient. Kennedy became one of the leading men in Washington to realize that the United States had to incorporate the local people in the Third World into its policy.

The years Kennedy spent in the Congress in the 1940s and 1950s were years of learning and mastering the facts of foreign policy. His ideas on foreign policy had evolved from "ambivalence" to specifics. He realized quickly that after the 1940s the action of the Cold War had shifted to the southern half of the globe. The United States should initiate policies to win this region, Kennedy often insisted during the 1950s.

Though Kennedy's concern for the Third World also originated from his dislike of British imperialism, his primary objective during this time was to check the spread of communism in this region. Like Harry Truman and Dean Acheson, Dwight Eisenhower and John Foster Dulles, Kennedy was a committed Cold Warrior; but unlike them he preferred acting over reacting, flexibility above dogma. He wanted speed instead of watchful waiting, and he encouraged boldness in policy making. The establishment of the Peace Corps in 1961 showed the combination of these qualities.

John F. Kennedy was not alone on Capitol Hill in suggesting assistance for the developing countries. In 1957, the year of the first Russian Sputnik and the Eisenhower Doctrine, Senator Hubert Humphrey introduced a bill in Congress to assist the development of the Third World. The bill suggested the use of "talented young men and women in an overseas operation for education, health care, vocational training and community development." Humphrey's bill received little support as "traditional diplomats quaked at the thought of thousands of young Americans scattered across their world."[44]

On June 5, 1958, Senator Richard L. Neuberger of Oregon, in a debate to amend the Mutual Security Act, called on the United States to help educate the people of the Third World. Congressman Henry Reuss of Wisconsin soon joined the chorus when in July he suggested the creation of a Point Four Youth Corps. Reuss's proposal rejuvenated Truman's Point Four Program. Returning from Southeast Asia in 1957, Reuss concluded that the ugly image of the United States had to change. His proposal "linked a volunteer corps with the nation's foreign aid program." Both Congressman Reuss and Senator Neuberger were determined to see their idea of a youth corps become a reality. In 1960 they introduced bills for the study of the possibility of establishing such a program. These bills were accepted and became part of an amendment of the Mutual Security Act, requiring the government to prepare a policy paper on the "advisability and practicality of a Point Four Youth Corps, under which young U.S. citizens would be trained to serve abroad in programs of technical cooperation."[45] The paltry sum of $10,000 was allocated for this preliminary study, which was to be conducted at Colorado State University.

In June 1960, Hubert Humphrey introduced Senate Bill 3675, designed to provide for the immediate establishment of the Peace Corps. The bill stated that the Peace Corps should be established

> to develop a genuine people-to-people program in which
> talented and dedicated young American men will teach basic
> agricultural and industrial techniques, literacy, the English lan-
> guage and other school subjects, and sanitation and health pro-
> cedures in Asia, Africa and Latin America.[46]

Humphrey's bill did not receive much Senate support at the time, but it was significant. It gave congressional members the opportunity to study the program before the next session, and Humphrey, by introducing the bill, became one of the "founding fathers" of the Peace Corps.[47] Also, it attracted more public support for the program. But the person who most enhanced the popularity of the Peace Corps in 1960 was John F. Kennedy.

While the debate on the Peace Corps continued on Capitol Hill, Kennedy in 1960 seized the opportunity and turned the idea into a major campaign issue. The Eisenhower years were "seven lean years of drought and famine. . . . Too many Americans have lost their way, their will and their sense of historic purpose," Kennedy said. Kennedy assailed the Eisenhower administration for the neglect of the Third World. He described the Eisenhower era as "eight years of drugged and fitful sleep." Repeatedly he said, "we are going to do better," and he told his audience that "the theme of this campaign is going to be action . . . action abroad to meet the challenge of our adversaries. I believe the American people elect a President to act." In one speech after the other, Kennedy reminded the voters:

> The reason Franklin Roosevelt was a good neighbor in Latin
> America was because he was a good neighbor in the United
> States. . . . I want people in Latin America and Africa and
> Asia to start to look to America . . . what the President of the
> United States is doing, not . . . Khrushchev or the Chinese
> Communists. . . . Can freedom be maintained under the most
> severe attack it has ever known? I think it can be and I think in
> the final analysis it depends upon what we do here. I think it's
> time America started moving again.[48]

Kennedy's mastery of foreign policy in the 1940s and 1950s proved to him that things had to be different in the 1960s. In September 1960, he told a New York audience that "I think to be an American in the next decade will be a hazardous experience. We will live on the edge of danger." Earlier, he had told his supporters in Maine that they "must make people feel that in the year of 1961 the American giant began to stir again, the great American boiler to fire again, this country began to move ahead again." Also, Kennedy reiterated that the real battleground for the Cold War was the Third World. It was in this region that the United States had to fulfill its obligation to freedom. "Our responsibility is to be the chief defender of freedom at a time when freedom is under attack all over the globe," Kennedy announced.[49] Rarely had a presidential candidate requested that all Americans perform such important functions.

For the first time in an American presidential election, Africa became a conspicuous issue. Before the campaign was over, Kennedy had made 479 references to Africa. He told his opponent, Richard Nixon, that "we have lost ground in Africa because we have neglected and ignored the need and aspiration of the African people." With specific reference to the failures of Eisenhower's African policy, Kennedy noted:

> After the key African State of Guinea, now voting with the Soviet Union in communist foreign policy, after it gained its independence, a Russian Ambassador showed up the next day. Our Ambassador did not show up for 9 months. Today, we do not have a single American diplomat in residence in six new countries of Africa which are now members of the United Nations, not a single American diplomat in residence in any of the 6, and of the 16 new African countries which were admitted to the United Nations, do you know how many of them voted with us on the admission of Red China? None. There are only 26 Negroes in the 6,000 of our Foreign Service officers, and yet Africa contains one-quarter of all the votes in the General Assembly. I think we can do better.[50]

Kennedy's reference to Guinea was not mere campaign rhetoric. Guinea had been dismissed in 1960 by the Eisenhower administration as just another Soviet satellite.

To fill the gap of American ambassadors, Kennedy appealed to youth to serve America's interest in the Third World, suggesting

> a Peace Corps of talented young men and women, willing and able to serve their country in this fashion for 3 years as an alternative or as a supplement to peacetime selective service . . . well qualified through rigorous standards, well trained in the languages, skills, and customs they will need to know, and directed and paid by the ICA point 4 agencies.

Another problem Kennedy attacked in 1960 was the official representation of the United States in the Third World. "Many have shuddered at the examples in *The Ugly American*," Kennedy told a group in San Francisco on November 2, 1960. During the Eisenhower era many American ambassadors chosen were too often "ill-equipped and ill-briefed," Kennedy said. Additionally, he stated that

> men who do not even know how to pronounce the name of the head of the country to which they are accredited . . . have been

sent to important countries, essential countries in the struggle between East and West. How can they compete with communist emissaries long trained and dedicated and committed to the cause of extending communism in these countries? . . .

It was reported last month that 70 percent of all new Foreign Service officers had no language skill at all last year. Only 3 of 44 Americans in our Embassy in Belgrade could speak Yugoslavian. In Athens only 6 of 79 Americans spoke the modern language of Greek. In New Delhi, not a single American could speak an Indian dialect fluently.[51]

The Peace Corps volunteers would solve these problems. They would be trained in foreign languages, solve problems in Third World villages, and establish friends for America in that part of the world. With the Peace Corps Kennedy would show Khrushchev that America was on the move again.

The youth responded positively to Kennedy's suggestion. In November 1960, a group of students meeting at a conference at Princeton University gave overwhelming support to the Peace Corps idea. The group met at The Conference to Discuss the Challenge to American Youth from the World's Emerging Nations, organized by the Whig Cliosophic Society. The participants at the conference agreed that the Peace Corps would "fight communism" and also "rekindle American idealism."[52]

Responding to the charges of *The Ugly American* and the behavior of American diplomats, most agreed that the Peace Corps would change the "image of the United States immeasurably." The popularity of the Princeton conference accelerated the emergence of other groups and committees in support of the idea. Groups such as Americans Committed to World Responsibility sprang up and enhanced the morale of enthusiasts through seminars.[53] Rarely has a presidential candidate attracted so many youth to his side.

Despite widespread positive response to Kennedy's suggestion, Richard Nixon and his colleagues attacked the idea. President Eisenhower mocked the idea of the Peace Corps, ironically calling it a "juvenile experiment." Nixon, who had dismissed a similar idea after it was suggested to him by an official in the Bureau of African Affairs, called the Peace Corps a "haven for draft dodgers." Nixon said, "Mr. Kennedy . . . would develop a cult of escapism." Others ridiculed the Peace Corps as "Kennedy's Kiddie Corps" and the "Children Crusade." Cartoonists had a field day with the Peace Corps idea, and some joked that whereas Franklin Roosevelt had established the Civilian Conservation Corps (CCC), John Kennedy would create the Draft Dodger's Delight (DDD).[54]

Such criticism did little to slow the momentum of the crusade Kennedy was launching—and this crusading metaphor emerged repeatedly. He would send "a new generation of Americans [who will] serve the cause of freedom . . . as communists work with their system."[55] Kennedy's triumph in the election was also a triumph of the Peace Corps.

The Peace Corps idea was a political asset for John F. Kennedy in 1960. But it also showed Kennedy's commitment to the defense of the free world. He was definitely a Cold War Warrior; being around when the Cold War began, Kennedy had studied and understood the mechanics for waging it. Shortly after dawn on November 9, 1960, Kennedy knew it was time to "get the country moving again." His New Frontier, in which the United States would challenge "unsolved problems of Peace and War, unconquered pockets of ignorance, and prejudice, unanswered questions of poverty and surplus,"[56] was about to be given a chance.

2

The Establishment of the Peace Corps

President Kennedy took to Washington a sophisticated team. He moved quickly to replace Eisenhower's soft, dull, businesslike administration with men who were young and tough, aggressive, and full of style and courage. They came from the right families, attended the right schools, and received the right degrees. They had seen a "lot of war and diplomacy" during their early years. They liked to be identified as World War II veterans and called themselves "hard-nosed realists." They "dazzled the nation by intellectual brilliance and social swank," wrote Joseph Kraft. And like Kennedy, they had a mission, a sense of purpose. They had gone to Washington in 1961 "to get the country moving again."[1]

These men shared the Cold War view that freedom was facing "the most severe attack it has ever known," and they had to defend it. The keynote to the administration was a set of challenges in the New Frontier and inaugural speeches. The United States "shall pay any price, bear any burden, meet any hardship, support any friend, oppose any foes, in order to assure the survival of liberty." At least one analyst has called the speeches "brilliant . . . moving . . . [but] dangerous." Repeatedly, Kennedy warned about the Communist threat to freedom in the Third World. On March 22, he told Congress: "We live at a very special moment in history. The whole southern half of the world—Latin America, Africa, the Middle East, and Asia—are caught up in the adventures of asserting their old ways of life. . . . Without exception they are under communist pressure. In many cases, that pressure is direct and military."[2]

Flexibility, urgency, activism, and courage became the main commandments of the new frontiersmen. They were determined to overhaul a State Department Kennedy had compared to "a bowl of jello." Diplomats in the New Frontier administration had to be "reform minded missionaries of democracy who mixed with the people, spoke the native dialect, ate the food, and involved themselves in local struggles against ignorance and want." They were told that their shortcomings and mistakes must be disguised from the public.[3]

Communism was the greatest peril of the 1960s, Kennedy informed Congress. On January 30, 1961, he added, "Each day the crises multiply. Each day their solution grows more difficult." It was as though Kennedy had invented these crises to test his mettle. "Each day we draw nearer the hour of maximum danger . . . the tide of events has been running out and time has not been our friend," he continued.[4]

Significantly, Kennedy indicated that the United States "ought to" and should "affect events around the globe." America would "intervene anywhere" to check Communist aggression, a strategy that became known as flexible response. The policy was designed "to act at all levels" to reverse the tide of communism.[5]

To fulfill this objective, Kennedy accelerated the building of conventional weapons. He trained a counterinsurgency force, the Green Berets, "to torture and destroy" suspected communists. He established the Alliance for Progress, an assistance package for Latin America; it reminded these countries that the United States was still a "good neighbor" and was geared to check Castroism. To the newly independent nations "struggling to break the bonds of mass misery," Kennedy responded with the Peace Corps. The Peace Corps would help to correct the situation described in *The Ugly American* and restore America's credibility. The agency would "help less fortunate nations improve themselves" and also "polish America's image abroad."[6]

All these programs set the tone for the Kennedy administration. The agenda for the programs was as inflated as the inaugural speech. Only America's most talented people and "pragmatic realists" could transform them into action. Each program seemed urgent. Each policy had a task force. Everything seemed new. Even the Cold War seemed to have just started. It was as though Russia had launched the Cold War to challenge the new frontiersmen.

And these new frontiersmen were always in a rush to keep their promise to freedom. They were in "a constant hurry, taking last minute corrections at last minute meetings, making last minute corrections to last minute statements, as if they were always trying to catch up with events, or with each other, or even each with himself." Joseph Kraft painted a vivid picture when he wrote that Kennedy was at all times in "motion, smoothing his hair, adjusting his tie, fiddling with his belt, clicking a pen against his teeth, slipping his hands in and out of his pockets." Robert Kennedy summed it all up when he remarked that "those were the days [early 1960s] when we thought we were succeeding because of all the stories of how hard everybody was working."[7]

In launching the Peace Corps, Kennedy drew upon the thinking of the new frontiersmen to transform ideas into action. The task of establishing the Peace Corps was entrusted to Sargent Shriver, Kennedy's able brother-in-law. Shriver had excellent credentials within the Kennedy team and family. He was in every way a new frontiersman: young, tough, vigorous, idealistic, determined, and always ready to face new challenges. "He is a man of action who finds it hard to stand still," a journalist said in describing Shriver.[8]

A Yale graduate and a World War II veteran, Shriver was in his element in Washington. He occasionally boasted of his World War II experience. "I got the kicks you're supposed to get. . . . We sank some Jap ships," Shriver said. After World War II, Shriver was rather briefly an employee of *Newsweek,* and in the fall of 1946, he became an employee of Joseph Kennedy, Sr. Later he married Eunice, Joseph and Rose Kennedy's oldest daughter. Shriver's efforts promoted Joseph Kennedy's Merchandise Mart from a small infant industry into an efficient and gigantic money-making corporation.[9] In 1955, Shriver became president of the Chicago Board of Education, a position he held until 1960.

Following Kennedy's victory in the election, Shriver became head of the talent hunt for Kennedy's "best and brightest." As the "big game hunter," Shriver convinced many that Washington was the place to be in the 1960s. Notable was Shriver's ability to woo Robert McNamara to abandon his well-paid position as president of the Ford Motor Company and become Kennedy's secretary of defense.[10]

January 21, 1961, was a busy day for Kennedy and Shriver. Tense but excited, Kennedy was in the office before 9:00 A.M. By 10:30, he had signed the first executive order of his administration. The order increased the quantity of food available to the needy. Later on the same day, Kennedy asked Shriver to create a task force "to report how the Peace Corps could be organized and then organize it." Privately, Shriver responded to Kennedy's request by stating, "This could be either the worst boondoggle in history or a real going outfit. I'll just try to make it a going outfit."[11]

Wasting no time, Shriver telephoned Harris Wofford, a young and distinguished law professor from the University of Notre Dame who had served as one of Kennedy's advisers during the presidential campaign. In the call, Shriver said to Wofford, "You thought you were going to have a vacation, didn't you? The President just asked me to set up a Task Force to see whether this Peace Corps makes sense. When shall we have our first meeting?"[12] The Peace Corps began at that moment.

Three days later, Shriver and Wofford met at the Mayflower Hotel in Washington for the first task force meeting. They spent most of the time recruiting more people. Shriver's directions to each person he spoke to were, "come as you are," "come quickly," and "we need you in a hurry."[13] Shriver and Wofford would not wait.

Among those in the first group they recruited were Gordon Boyce, from Experiment in International Living; Al Sims, from the Institute of International Education; Arthur Adams, of the American Council of Education; George Carter, a brilliant civil rights worker; Father Theodore Hesburgh, president of the University of Notre Dame; Louis Martin, a newspaper editor; and Franklin Williams, a civil rights attorney with an interest in African affairs. Shriver wanted "brains" for his task force. He explained, "My style . . . was to get bright, informative, creative people and then pick their brains."[14]

Meanwhile the president had turned over to Shriver copies of the reports of Max Millikan of the Massachusetts Institute of Technology and Samuel Hayes of the University of Michigan and a preliminary study on Henry Reuss's proposal from Colorado State University. These reports created a base for Shriver's task force. Later Shriver and Wofford also received another seminal paper, "The Towering Task," prepared by Warren Wiggins and William Josephson, both of the Far Eastern Bureau of the International Cooperation Administration (ICA).[15]

Wiggins and Josephson had the necessary credentials. Wiggins had participated in the administration of the Marshall Plan in Western Europe, and Josephson was in the Far Eastern regional bureau of ICA. These two were familiar with previous American policies in the Third World, and they had lamented over the existence of the "golden ghettoes" established there by American diplomats. Both believed a change was needed. The title of their paper came from a speech in which Kennedy stated:

> Our role is essential and unavoidable in the construction of a
> sound and expanding economy for the entire non-communist
> world, helping other nations build the strength to meet their

own problems, to satisfy their own aspirations—to surmount their own dangers. The problems in achieving this goal are towering and unprecedented—the response must be towering and unprecedented.[16]

"The Towering Task" was an illustrative document that discussed the need for the establishment of the Peace Corps. The idea had public support, the authors declared, and it was a "program that will allow the United States to move faster in many situations." The authors of the document rejected the suggestion of skeptics who preferred that the program begin at a very low level. A "small cautious National Peace Corps may be worse than no Peace Corps at all," the authors wrote. The paper called on the American government "to consider initiating the program with several thousand Americans participating in the first 12 to 18 months—say 5,000 to 10,000." Utilizing the Philippines as a case study, the authors showed how 5,000 volunteers could serve and make a positive impact in that country. The Philippine example could be duplicated in countries such as Nigeria, India, and more, the authors wrote. "The Towering Task" was the kind of document Shriver needed, especially during these times of "sleepless nights" because he "couldn't come to grips with the thing [Peace Corps]."[17] The document would serve as a significant framework for Shriver's task force.

"The Towering Task" had enormous influence on Shriver and Wofford. Excited after reading the paper, Wofford called Shriver at 7:00 A.M. on February 6 and informed him about it. But Wofford was "a little late." Shriver, after reading the paper, had already invited Wiggins and Josephson to attend the Peace Corps task force meeting at 9:00 A.M. on the same day.[18]

Very quickly Wiggins and Josephson became the "engine room of the Peace Corps," and their paper provided the "philosophy" for the agency.[19] Their arrival hastened the pace of things in the Peace Corps office. Kennedy was equally anxious to move ahead with the Peace Corps, which also contributed to this last-minute rush.

An early draft on the Peace Corps, dated February 20, 1961, asserted that the agency will help in "the creation of stable and self-reliant . . . communities capable of withstanding the stress of modern life." The Peace Corps would assist in the creation of "modern democratic societies." Additionally, the draft stated that the Peace Corps would check the "influence and appeal of Castroism" in Latin America. After this draft, the pace of the work more than doubled.

The final draft was the combination of many. While some wrote the "basic copy," others "rewrote it." Wofford did the "final rewrite," and Wiggins dashed "back and forth between rooms . . . delivering pieces of papers along the chain."[20]

These were the new frontiersmen in action. Though the final draft was ready by February 22, it was not given to the president until February 28. "The Report to the President on the Peace Corps" began: "Having studied at your request the problems of establishing a Peace Corps, I recommend its immediate establishment." Shriver's report recommended "an Executive Order establishing the Peace Corps within the Mutual Security Act." Also, it requested that the Peace Corps should be divorced from previous programs that had failed. It stated that "the Peace Corps should be a semi-autonomous entity with its own public face. This new wine should not be poured into the old ICA bottle." The new agency must be synonymous with success.[21]

In defining the purpose of the agency, the report stated that the Peace Corps

> can contribute to the development of critical countries and regions. It can promote international cooperation and good will toward this country. It can also contribute to the education of America and to more intelligent participation in the world.

The report also stressed that the Peace Corps would "demonstrate . . . American values" and "make many friends" for the United States.[22]

Explaining the reasons for the immediate establishment of the Peace Corps, Shriver noted that for the agency to succeed it had to "recruit the best people from this year's graduating classes." Like the members of his task force, Shriver wanted "brains" for Peace Corps service. Shriver wanted action, not waiting around for bureaucrats to place Peace Corps recruitment in their organizational chart. The problems of the world were "towering and unprecedented" and required a similar response.[23]

On March 1, 1961, Kennedy signed Executive Order 10924 establishing the Peace Corps. By signing the executive order, Kennedy utilized the authority granted to the president in the Mutual Security Act. The order established the agency on a temporary pilot basis financed by the president's contingency funds. It placed the Peace Corps under the State Department.[24]

Kennedy acted quickly to capitalize on his election momentum. His popularity was high in early 1961. His "style and sophisticated courtesy" and his tough "personality and charisma" not only earned him support but also showed that he had the capacity "to move a nation."[25] He used these personal assets to attract many to join the Peace Corps, in which "they [could] do something for America."

Wiggins said the executive order "hit us like a thunderclap." He added, "We had been prepared to wait for a few days. . . . Shriver knew Kennedy was prepared to go the executive-order route, but no one guessed it would happen so fast. Talk about morale—we were sky-high." The reaction of the country's youth was also positive. Their immediate response "caused the switchboard at Peace Corps head-quarters to jangle endlessly; it could not handle the thousands of calls from volunteers and inquirers."[26]

Explaining the reaction to the executive order, Mitzi Mallina, one of the earliest Peace Corps employees, recalled the excitement of the time. People called and offered their help to the Peace Corps. Some offered free desks, typewriters, and so on. Everything was moving.[27]

It was a time of high hopes. Even Bill Moyers, Lyndon Johnson's most able and trusted aide, left the vice president's office. Moyers wanted to be where all the excitement was. Johnson anguished that "this boy here . . . cajoled and begged and pleaded and convinced and threatened and politicked to leave me to go to work for the Peace Corps. For the life of me I can't imagine him doing that to go to work for the foreign aid program. . . . If you want the Peace Corps to work, friends, you'll keep it away from the folks downtown who want it to be just another box in an organizational chart."[28]

Numerous applicants wrote and inquired about the agency. "I want to serve my country. Tell me what to do," thousands wrote. In-quiries came from all segments of society. "I'll go wherever I can help. I'll do whatever I can," a college student informed Shriver. A high school student showed his interest in the program when he wrote, "I don't care about a salary. This is something I want to do for my coun-try." A farmer wrote, "If you can use my plow, it is ready. If you can use me, I am ready, too." The Peace Corps was a "great, fine, beau-tiful idea," and several thousands wanted to be part of it. A Gallup Poll taken between January 12 and 17, 1961, showed that 71 percent of the public supported the Peace Corps Agency, 18 percent opposed it, and 11 percent had no opinion. Another poll conducted during the same period showed that 66 percent would encourage their chil-dren to serve in the Peace Corps. An opinion poll taken in April 1961 was quite favorable; 68 percent of the public endorsed the Peace

Corps and 32 percent opposed it. The Peace Corps was a popular program on college campuses. A survey of American university presidents showed an overwhelming support of the program. By March 6, the agency had received more than 4,500 applications and letters of inquiries.[29]

The new Peace Corps spirit celebrated a break with past policies. Many were delighted with the promises the Peace Corps held for future American foreign policy. Even Eugene Burdick and William Lederer, authors of *The Ugly American,* were optimistic as they wrote in later editions of their book that "President Kennedy's Peace Corps is the answer to the problem raised in this book."[30] Peace Corps volunteers were expected to live and serve in the rural areas. The golden ghettoes were about to be dismantled.

Peace Corps activities were planned along the lines of President Kennedy's new view of diplomacy. Soon after taking office, Kennedy informed all American ambassadors that "we are living in a critical moment in history" and urged them to "travel extensively outside the nation's capital." Kennedy requested that they make friends with the local people and pointed out that in order to achieve this they must understand the whole country, not just the capital.[31]

By creating the Peace Corps under the authority of the Mutual Security Act of 1954, President Kennedy integrated the agency into previous Cold War policies.[32] The Mutual Security Act, as signed by Truman in 1951, was designed to enhance America's Cold War policy. The passage of time did not alter this cardinal objective.

The Peace Corps was "similar in intent" to the Green Berets and the Alliance for Progress. During the campaign in 1960, John F. Kennedy lashed out at Republican candidate Richard Nixon for the existence of a Communist Cuba in America's backyard. To prevent further Communist incursions in the region, Kennedy suggested an Alliance for Progress for Latin America, an economic package designed to stimulate economic growth in the region. In March 1961, Kennedy signed a bill implementing the Alliance for Progress. The program committed the United States to spend $10 billion within a ten-year period. Based on the Kennedy thinking, economic growth would repel communism in the region. The Alliance for Progress became a "weapon to fight [Communist] revolutions in Latin America."[33]

A university official who spent several years with the Peace Corps volunteers noted that the agency was ideologically inclined.

"American PCVs [Peace Corps volunteers'] presence did influence" their respective countries, he remarked. Supporting this contention was Gilbert Schneider, a member of the Peace Corps training staff in the early 1960s, who stated that "the presence of the volunteers influenced the minds of the local people."[34] The volunteers were the "doers" and "operators" of the new foreign policy.

Returned Peace Corps volunteers Freeman T. Pollard, who served in Cameroon in the early 1960s, placed the objectives of the Peace Corps in the broad setting of American foreign policy. "President Kennedy was painfully aware of the grievous mistakes in foreign policy because Americans were so ignorant of international affairs and peoples of other cultures," Pollard wrote. He added, "I believe that he [President Kennedy] thought the Peace Corps would produce a cadre of better educated people for the future with a world view that would be broader than his own or previous generations . . . I believe that, in part, has happened."[35]

As "good ambassadors of democracy," the volunteers were assigned the task of developing the economies of host countries. A by-product of their achievement would be the "abdication of communism" by these countries.[36] Thus the Peace Corps Agency added a new dimension to Truman's Point Four Program and was part of Kennedy's solution to the Communist menace of the 1960s.

Though the executive order established the Peace Corps, the agency still required congressional approval for permanent funding. Between March 1 and the passage of the final Peace Corps Act in September 1961, the agency struggled to establish a firm foundation. During this interim period, the agency made and corrected its mistakes. It struggled to obtain support from foreign countries. More importantly, the agency recruited, selected, trained, and sent overseas its first group of volunteers.

Three days after the executive order, Kennedy appointed Sargent Shriver as the agency's first director. Shriver, notwithstanding his excellent credentials for the job, wondered why Kennedy took such a move. He wrote, "President Kennedy picked me to organize the Peace Corps, I was told, because no one thought the Peace Corps could succeed, and it would be easier to fire a relative than a political friend." At a March 6 press conference, Shriver commented on his appointment as director: "The New Frontier, it seems, is full of surprises. The last thing I expected when I resigned from the Presidency of the Board of Education in Chicago a few months ago was that I would go from the frying pan of a big city's public school system propelled into the fire of this new worldwide venture, the Peace Corps."[37]

As director, Shriver began the urgent search for a staff. "Nice guys don't win ball games," Shriver said, often sounding like his brother-in-law. He told workers at the Peace Corps office to bypass the time-consuming State Department "channels." "Do the job first. Worry about the clearance later," Shriver told his employees.[38] On March 30, 1961, a Peace Corps National Advisory Committee was established. The creation of this board cleaned the slate of the recommendations made in Shriver's report to the president.

Simultaneously, Shriver struggled to keep the Peace Corps independent from the foreign aid organizational chart. It was at this point that Lyndon Johnson performed his greatest role during these early days. He secured from the president a mandate to keep the agency independent from the Agency for International Development (AID) box chart. This was hardly a surprise, because Kennedy also adhered to the motto that "there were things in life more important than the symmetry of organization charts."[39]

During the early days, Shriver's new staff worked hard, but, unlike Shriver, they never stopped complaining. To them, the Peace Corps office in the early days was comparable to "a campaign headquarters on the eve of a national election." One worker complained that "when you join the Shriver team you put yourself in line for an ulcer, a heart attack, or a nervous breakdown." "Anyone who wanted a kindly father-figure as a leader found out that this wasn't the place . . . Shriver mercilessly drains people. He won't take 'tomorrow' for an answer," an employee stated.[40]

Shriver labored hard to enhance the popularity of the Peace Corps. He became a regular keynote speaker at business meetings, commencement ceremonies, churches, and philanthropic groups' meetings. Extracts from his speeches and his articles appeared in daily and weekly newspapers around the country. Wherever he spoke, his message was similar: Shriver defined the Peace Corps and explained why Americans should sign up for service and the rewards for such services. Shriver told an anxious group on March 24, 1961:

> The Peace Corps is a Georgia lawyer who left his practice to come to Washington—at his own expense—to serve as our counsel—to work on a case that will be heard before the bar of the world. But the Peace Corps is more. . . . The Peace Corps is part of our effort to help make that leap forward a success. It is

part of our effort to help in the world-wide assault against poverty, hunger, ignorance and disease—a grass roots, rice roots volunteer effort of free men.

On June 7, 1961, Shriver took his message to De Paul University. Speaking at the commencement ceremony, Shriver said to the graduates:

Is America qualified to head the free world? Why are they asking it? Why is there evidence? Because . . . Americans have gone soft. . . . The president of one of our largest universities says we are beset by "spiritual flabbiness." I recently heard it said that we are producing a strange new kind of human being—"a guy with a full belly, an empty mind, and a hollow heart." . . . Americans are not alone . . . in doubting the intellectual and spiritual fiber of modern America. I encountered these doubts all around the world on my recent trip. . . . Do you think young Americans possess the spiritual values they must have to bring the spirit of that revolution to our country? Your Peace Corps must touch the idealism of America and bring that to us. Can you do it . . . ? Let me tell you that a world is waiting for you, and there is plenty to do. . . . One after another the leaders of Africa and Asia not only welcomed the idea of the Peace Corps, but they requested Peace Corps volunteers to serve in their countries.[41]

The year 1961 was quite busy for Shriver. On July 24, he took his Peace Corps message to Nashville, where he told his audience that the response to the Peace Corps had proved skeptics wrong. Additionally, Shriver stated:

When President Kennedy launched the Peace Corps earlier this year, many people in and out of the administration labeled his action "an act of faith"! . . . Then there were the critics who said we as a nation were not up to an idea like the Peace Corps, that our luxuries were too precious, that the demands of our society were so lax that we had gone soft. They joined with those who thought only fuzzy idealists with beards and sandals would join the Peace Corps. They classified anyone who would give up a good job to work two years in the bush country as a little "sick." . . . To date, I am happy to report the American people have responded in a way to surpass our expectations. More than eleven thousand Americans have volunteered to serve and the applications are coming into the headquarters at a rate of almost one hundred a day.[42]

Recruitment, selection, and training of the volunteers were equally important. Shortly after the executive order, the Peace Corps received more than 25,000 letters and telephone calls from prospective volunteers inquiring about the agency. The agency itself also sent out thousands of application forms to various institutions, including colleges and universities.[43]

Volunteers were specifically told that invitation to participate in the training sessions did not mean that they would be sent overseas. The Peace Corps office instructed the volunteers: "Do not sell your home, furniture or car, or cut your ties completely, when you accept an invitation for training." Repeatedly Shriver told applicants that Peace Corps services would not be easy. "I'd like to guarantee anybody who is thinking of coming in that it won't be a picnic, nor will it be a children's crusade. Nor will it be an International Boy Scout and Girl Scout operation, good as those things are," Shriver said during a press conference.[44] The selected volunteers were subjected to psychological testing and psychiatric interviews. Previous and current employers of the volunteers were also interviewed. Several cases were referred to the Federal Bureau of Investigation for full field investigations. Later, to J. Edgar Hoover, Shriver wrote, "In my judgment, the role the Federal Bureau of Investigation plays in this process is critical." He added, "I wanted to make sure you know how much we value and support and respect its efforts."[45]

Equally demanding was the training. Volunteers were expected to be "doers" and "operators" by the time the training was over. They were trained in various subjects, but it was policy to emphasize "the study of American principles of governments, democratic life and also tactics of communist agitators."[46]

Trainees resented the constant scrutiny they were kept under. Moritz Thomsen, a former trainee, lamented that the trainees were "studied and appraised like a bunch of fat beeves, about to be entered in the State Fair." Also, the training was designed to enable the volunteers to meet "mental and physical challenges" while executing their functions. Their Outward Bound training consisted of "rock climbing with ropes, long jungle treks in the rain forest, drownproofing . . . and community participation."[47] To some volunteers, it was a nightmare.

American universities and college campuses were utilized as training grounds. Universities hosting the training were subjected to rules from Washington. Professors were used as instructors in the training, and in the process they had to shelve some of their academic freedom. During the training of volunteers for Cameroon, one of the professors, perhaps the American with the longest practical experience in that country, was originally rejected as a Peace Corps training instructor by Peace Corps agents in Washington. "Faulty data from the field [Cameroon] and international politics" caused the Peace Corps to reject a highly qualified professor selected by the university. It was only after continuous insistence that there was no one more qualified on Cameroon that Peace Corps-Washington reversed its original decision.[48]

Books selected for the training had to be carefully screened in order not to violate the guidelines and regulations from Washington. Racially segregated institutions, especially those located in the South, were denied the opportunity to host Peace Corps training. Experts in certain subjects were denied access to Peace Corps training classrooms because of their views on international politics.[49]

As the selection and training went on, Shriver and his associates lobbied through the spring of 1961 for the passage of a permanent Peace Corps bill. Shriver engaged in personal lobbying. Such tactics were not new in Washington, but his were perhaps the most intense and elaborate. His methods included hotel breakfasts with congressmen, telephone calls, courtesy visits, and personal correspondence. Once a management official informed Shriver, "You guys had a good day today. . . . You broke fourteen laws." The congressional breakfast was an effective tactic used by Shriver. Those were the days when Shriver and his aides arrived at the Capitol building in the early morning to meet congressmen for breakfast. The daily breakfasts were turned into occasions when Shriver convinced congressmen of the importance of the Peace Corps and also asked for their support in the House and Senate. Shriver also listened to congressmen's ideas and feelings on the program. Such exchanges of opinion gave Shriver the advantage of preparing answers to possible questions he could be asked on the congressional floor during the deliberation over the Peace Corps bill. During these breakfasts, Shriver made appointments to visit and discuss the Peace Corps program with congressmen. Shriver referred to his tactics as "saturation bombing." By the time the Peace Corps bill was passed, Shriver had seen more than 363 senators and representatives in less than four months. Congressional critics who described the Peace Corps as "terrifying" resented

Shriver's frequent visits to Capitol Hill and charged that the breakfast sessions were illegal.[50]

Shriver and his aides were aware of the significance of obtaining support from congressmen before the bill went to the congressional floor. As a result, correspondence from congressmen was considered urgent. Peace Corps employees were informed that phone calls and letters "received from a congressional office and . . . any requests made via this means were to receive immediate action." Letters and memoranda from congressmen were identified by a "special red tag and the notation that the letter[s] must be answered, approved by the department head, and be returned to the office of the executive secretary within three days." Following the breakfast sessions and visits with congressmen, Shriver wrote several letters of appreciation to them. Letters of appreciation were brief and to the point. On March 15, 1961, Shriver wrote House Speaker Sam Rayburn that

> it was very good of you to spend so much time with Bill Moyers and me this morning. I am personally very grateful to you for sharing with us your thinking on the Peace Corps. We think we have a wonderful program that will mean a great deal to American foreign policy and to the development of a better world for all people. The problem, of course, as you pointed out, is to carry it out in such a way that will be constructive and beneficial to everyone concerned. We want it to be a down-to-earth, people-to-people approach that will avoid waste and unnecessary expense, and I was glad to get your thinking along these lines. I am enclosing a list of the names of some of the people who are helping us get the Peace Corps underway. I thought you would be interested in knowing that we have the benefit of many years of experience and much sound thinking as we undertake this significant challenge.[51]

Other congressmen received similar letters. Shriver's tactics were geared toward dismantling any form of unified action from Capitol Hill against the Peace Corps before the bill got there. The planning was shrewd and skillful; it showed Shriver's mastery of the Washington scene. For a man who had made a difference each time he had headed an agency in the past, failure was unthinkable. Shriver channeled his energy toward ensuring that the Peace Corps bill passed through Congress. He was the optimistic, courageous, and hardworking administrator the Peace Corps Agency needed during those early days when the whole program was still an experiment. It was a very busy time, Shriver later recalled; "He [was] never very far from the Peace Corps," Eunice Shriver said.[52]

On May 30, 1961, Kennedy sent a draft bill to Congress requesting the establishment of a permanent Peace Corps Agency. In his bill, Kennedy asked for an initial budget of $40 million for the agency. He wanted the bill to pass before the end of the year, hoping it would help rebuild his prestige, which had suffered after the Bay of Pigs fiasco in April. Moreover, Ghana and other Third World countries had been promised dozens of Peace Corps volunteers by August 1961.

Hubert Humphrey and William Fulbright introduced Kennedy's bill S. 2000 in the Senate on June 1, 1961. The bill was immediately supported by many of their colleagues, including Claiborne Pell, Joseph Clark, Albert Gore, Sr., Jacob Javits, and Paul Douglas. In the House, the bill was introduced by Thomas E. Morgan, the chairman of the Foreign Relations Committee. Thus, the bill was introduced by senior legislators, respected men on Capitol Hill, some of whom were among the original proponents of the Peace Corps. Deliberations on the bill were surprisingly brief. Shriver was the main Peace Corps spokesman. He knew the details and had effectively utilized "saturation bombing." Additionally, he had the advantage of being the president's brother-in-law.

A recurring theme in the Senate and House hearings was the potential of the Peace Corps as an instrument of the American policy of containment. A surprising number of politicians accepted Kennedy's complaint that America was not doing nearly enough in the Cold War. Many had read *The Ugly American;* all were witnesses to the various threats America was facing in the world. The Cuban and Berlin crises made vivid impressions. To many on the Hill, the Peace Corps represented one of America's new responses to the challenges posed by a rapidly changing world. The Peace Corps would "add a positive and constructive 'new dimension' to U.S. foreign policy," several in Congress believed.[53]

Equally appealing was the cost of the program. The Peace Corps was cheaper than a "rocket or bomber."[54] The $40 million requested for the agency was less than the money necessary to buy spare parts for a rocket. The United States had troops in South Korea, West Germany, and other parts of the world to reassure weak nations of a U.S. willingness to contain Soviet aggression. The Peace Corps might have a similar impact in the Third World. A majority on the Hill saw the Peace Corps as something to show the Third World what a "free society can do for itself."

Thanks to the climate of public opinion and backstage maneuvering, the debate over the Peace Corps bill was brief. Within four months Congress gave Kennedy the key items he requested in his bill. On August 10, 1961, the Peace Corps bill, S. 2000, was passed unanimously in the Senate Foreign Relations Committee. Penny-pinchers who had hoped to limit the agency's first-year budget to $25 million were disappointed when that amendment was rejected. The committee did accept an amendment from liberal Republican senator Kenneth B. Keating requiring that Congress evaluate the Peace Corps' progress by 1963 in order to "determine whether it was coordinated with American Foreign Policy and met goals established in S. 2000." Conservative Republican senator Bourke B. Hickenlooper's amendment requesting that volunteers be trained in "communist philosophy, strategy and tactics" was also endorsed.[55]

In September, H.R. 7500 was passed in the House Foreign Relations Committee. Following a brief deliberation, the bill was amended and passed in the House by a 288-to-97 roll-call vote on September 14. The following day, the bill was successful in the Senate and later was sent to a conference report. On September 21, it was declared that the bill passed in the House by a 253–79 roll-call vote and by a voice vote in the Senate. The Peace Corps bill had received bipartisan support on Capitol Hill. On September 22, 1961, President Kennedy signed the Peace Corps Act as Public Law 87-293.[56]

The passage of the act represented one of Kennedy's major achievements and restored his confidence. He correctly "paid tribute to Shriver" by calling him "the most efficient lobbyist in the Washington scene." The act was not much different from Kennedy's draft legislation. Its purpose was stated in the opening lines:

> The Congress of the United States declares that it is the policy of the United States and the purpose of this Act to promote world peace and friendship through a Peace Corps, which shall make available to interested countries and areas men and women of the United States qualified for service abroad and willing to serve, under conditions of hardship if necessary, to help the peoples of such countries and areas in meeting their needs for trained manpower, and to help promote a better understanding of the American people on the part of the peoples

served and a better understanding of the other peoples on the part of the American people.[57]

The act placed the agency under the direction of the secretary of state. More significant was section 4(c) of the act, which requires the secretary of state to ensure that "Peace Corps activities are effectively integrated both at home and abroad." Also, the act stated that "the President shall make provision for such training as he deems appropriate for each applicant for enrollment." The trainees were required to understand the "philosophy, strategy, tactics and menace of communism." Finally, Section 18 of the act required the president to apply the Mutual Defense Assistance Control Act (Battle Act) of 1951 to the Peace Corps.[58] These portions of the Peace Corps Act, and particularly the focus on Communist tactics in volunteer training, reveal the pragmatic considerations at work at the time the Peace Corps was established. The agency, whatever its idealism, was also intended to serve the American policy of containment. No wonder Shriver's initial targets for volunteers were the so-called strategic countries.

Indeed, Shriver's "Report to the President" came close to assuring the president that the Third World was desperately inviting and awaiting the Peace Corps volunteers. But this was not the case. Shriver's hands were tied. Despite the continuous flow of applications from prospective volunteers, fairly few countries (less than a dozen in the Third World as of March 6) had shown interest in the program.[59]

Following Kennedy's executive order establishing the Peace Corps, independent African countries responded with a wait-and-see attitude toward the agency. These countries had other, more urgent, problems. They had to deal with internal subversion, budgetary problems, Nkrumah's call for the formation of a Union of African States, and more. But the policy of watchful waiting did not last long. Angered at the previous U.S. record on colonial issues, African political and union leaders at the All-African People's Conference in Cairo in March 1961 passed "resolutions . . . condemning the [Peace] Corps as a tool of neo-colonialism." The conference disapproved of Kennedy's Peace Corps as a "so-called volunteer corps for peace set up by the American government to reconquer and economically dominate Africa." The African public, while suspicious of the intentions of the Peace Corps, saw the agency as a unique opportunity to help dispel the myths about Africa promoted by Hollywood movie directors in films, such as in the Tarzan movies. As one newspaperman put it, the

Peace Corps volunteers, whether effective or not, would help "explode some of the myths put about by Hollywood."[60]

Complicating the situation was the Bay of Pigs disaster of early April. To many of the developing countries, the crisis showed that the United States could not be trusted. For the African nations represented at the All-African People's Conference in Cairo, the Bay of Pigs incident confirmed their worst fears. Third World leaders became quite suspicious of Kennedy. The first bold venture of his administration had failed. Realizing the problem, Shriver invited himself to Third World countries to sell the Peace Corps. On April 22, 1961, he left Washington for Africa and later proceeded to Asia. He was accompanied by Harris Wofford, Ed Bayley, Bill Kelly, and Franklin Williams. Shriver's team did not underestimate its task of selling the Peace Corps to Third World leaders. The team had prepared answers to questions on the Bay of Pigs.

In planning the trip, Shriver's team decided to target the so-called "strategic countries." These were countries that had the capacity to move and influence the smaller countries. The initial countries included Ghana, Nigeria, Tanzania, Pakistan, Burma, Malaysia, India, and the Philippines; later Guinea and Cameroon were among others added to the list. Ghana and Guinea were particularly important. In 1957, Kwame Nkrumah had defeated the British imperialists and secured independence for Ghana. This move set off a chain reaction that climaxed in 1960, the "year of Africa," when more than a dozen African countries gained independence and proceeded to join the United Nations organization, where their representatives continued with the anti-imperialism crusade. Considering himself the African independence movement's "messiah," Nkrumah vowed not to rest until all imperialists were evicted from Africa.[61] This ambition, however, clashed with President Eisenhower's policy of maintaining the status quo in Africa.

After failing to make Nkrumah abandon his goals, the Eisenhower administration branded him a Communist. Nkrumah "was very definitely in the Communist camp," Secretary of State Christian Herter proclaimed in 1960. Soon the Western press joined the chorus against Nkrumah. But the outcry did not deter his nationalist crusade. Responding to his critics, Nkrumah stated: "This is not an idle dream. It is not impossible. I see it; I feel it; it is real; indeed I am living in it already."[62] Spurned by the West, Nkrumah turned to the

East, from which he received respect and assistance. Soon nationalist unrest spread to the Congo.

The Congo crisis began in 1960 shortly after that country gained independence from Belgium. The United States did not have a policy for Congo. In the wake of the unrest, the United States immediately styled Patrice Lumumba, the first prime minister of Congo, as another Communist "dupe." On August 18, 1960, Eisenhower is believed to have endorsed a CIA plan "for the assassination of the African leader [Lumumba]."[63] Kennedy had hoped to initiate a better policy to deal with Lumumba and other rebel groups in the Congo after Eisenhower left office, but it would be too late. Lumumba was beaten and killed by rebel troops on January 17, 1961. Kennedy agonized when, on February 13, he learned for the first time of the damage caused by American involvement in the assassination of the renowned African nationalist.

When Eisenhower left office, the United States policy in Africa was covert, narrow, and makeshift. Unwilling to follow his predecessor's approach, Kennedy sought to bring Nkrumah back to the Western fold. The new president realized that many African countries looked to Nkrumah for leadership, and Kennedy noted about Nkrumah that "It is worth a risk and could conceivably be a triumph." But the tone of Nkrumah's first correspondence showed how cold the relations between the two countries had become. Nkrumah wrote,

> What then are we to think when we find in the Congo the U.S. supporting a regime which is based on the denial of democracy and which only exists because international support, if not from the U.S. itself at least from countries closely allied to the U.S. such as Belgium, maintains a military dictatorship of a brutal and ineffectual type under which the Congolese Parliament is not permitted to meet. . . . If Mr. Lumumba were to be murdered by these stooges of Belgium colonialism or so ill-treated that he were to die, this would have a most serious effect upon the relations of the independent states with the U.S. and the other western powers.[64]

Risk taking is part of international diplomacy, and Kennedy was determined to regain the friendship of Nkrumah. In 1961, Kennedy committed the United States to finance the construction of the Volta Dam in Ghana. Also, Ghana became the first country

Shriver visited to try to sell the Peace Corps program. In late April, Shriver's team arrived in Accra, Ghana. Prepared but cautious, Shriver's team met with Nkrumah and listened to his views on the United States. Responding to the suggestion about the Peace Corps, Nkrumah said:

> Power radiation is going out from America to all the world, much of it harmful, some of it innocuous, some beneficial. Africans have to be careful and make the right distinctions, so as to refuse the bad rays and welcome the good. The CIA is a dangerous beam that should be resisted. From what you said, Mr. Shriver, the Peace Corps sounds good. We are ready to try it, and will invite a small number of teachers. We could use some plumbers and electricians, too. Can you get them here by August?[65]

Nkrumah, notwithstanding his suspicion of the United States, was persuaded by Shriver to accept the Peace Corps. The Peace Corps was a "splendid, bold idea," Nkrumah told Shriver.[66] Plans called for the first Peace Corps volunteers to arrive in Ghana on September 1, 1961. Kennedy now hoped that the financing of the Volta Dam and the Peace Corps would reverse Nkrumah's leftward trend. The road, however, remained rocky.

During the summer of 1961, Nkrumah made an extensive visit to the Eastern bloc nations. In speeches in the Communist countries, Nkrumah stressed that "the voice of Khrushchev is the voice of peace," and "the survival of the Soviet Union is an achievement we can emulate in Africa." Commenting on Nkrumah's popularity in the Soviet Union, Shriver remarked, "I think it is significant that a man who won the Lenin Prize wants [the] American Peace Corps in his schools."[67] Having received the Lenin Prize, Nkrumah promised to use Soviet help to destroy imperialism in Africa.

After these remarks were read in the United States, Robert Kennedy and many others requested that Kennedy reverse his position on the Volta Dam project. Nkrumah's decision to denounce the United States in the Soviet Union showed that he could not be America's trusted ally in Africa, Robert Kennedy believed. Furthermore, he declared that the Ghanaian leader was "playing footsies with the Soviet Union" and complained that giving American funds to Ghana was a dangerous precedent. Such assistance will encourage African countries to "play the Soviet Union off against the United States," Robert Kennedy added. Supporting his son, Joseph

Kennedy, Sr., intervened: "What the hell are you up to with that communist Nkrumah?" he asked the president.[68]

The heat was on the president. Senator Gore of Tennessee, chairman of the African Affairs subcommittee, called the loan to Ghana "most unfortunate." By giving loans to Nkrumah, "we support and strengthen a regime that is not only suppressing individual freedom but one which is oriented toward Communist Russia and Red China," Gore announced.[69]

Despite the intense pressure, President Kennedy made the pragmatic decision and approved the $37-million loan for the Volta Dam project. However, other assistance to Ghana was cut and restored only after Nkrumah was overthrown in 1966. The number of Peace Corps volunteers to that country was cut, but some still went. Whatever the problems in American-Ghanaian relations, the willingness of Nkrumah to receive the volunteers encouraged other African countries to accept them.

Like Nkrumah in Ghana, Sekou Touré, a self-educated and powerful leader, successfully moved Guinea to independence. In 1958, Touré renounced membership in the French community. Defending his decision, Touré stated that Guinea preferred "poverty in freedom" to "riches in slavery." Angered by Touré's actions, Charles de Gaulle ordered all French technicians to leave Guinea. In a classic case of childish revenge, Frenchmen raided the country, taking military uniforms off the bodies of soldiers, dishes, food, archival material, and everything that seemed remotely useful to the Guineans. Touré had become de Gaulle's prime enemy in Africa. Determined to punish Touré, de Gaulle asked Eisenhower to extend no help to the Guineans, a "crowd of malcontents."[70] Eisenhower heeded de Gaulle's advice, and no help was extended to Guinea. But America would later regret this decision.

Rejected by the West, Touré turned to the Eastern bloc. By 1961, there were more than 1,000 Soviet technicians in Guinea, and more than $110 million Eastern bloc credits had been extended to the country. As a result of this, the Eisenhower administration concluded that "Touré was a communist operative beyond hope of redemption." Quickly, Touré was labeled the Castro of Africa.[71]

But President Kennedy, who had lashed out at Eisenhower for losing momentum in Africa, was not satisfied with his predecessor's analysis. He was determined to alter the course of Guinea's history. Touré was too important a leader to be abandoned, Kennedy noted.

He ordered William Attwood, the new American ambassador to Guinea, to investigate the facts about that country and report directly to the White House. Attwood, a trained journalist, took his job seriously.

On May 5, 1961, he informed Kennedy of a preliminary conversation with Touré. "I suggested we . . . talk specifics such as establishing school administration training Guineans replace bloc personnel [*sic*]," Attwood wrote. Touré replied that he had been dissatisfied with Eisenhower's policy toward Guinea. Eisenhower did not respond to an invitation from Touré to visit Guinea, nor did he extend aid to that country. Guinea had no choice but to ask for Soviet help.[72]

Later, on May 12, Attwood provided a lengthy assessment of the Guinean situation. "The time is ripe for an American initiative . . . in Guinea," Attwood explained. He recommended that the United States step in and assist Guinea before the Russians engulfed the entire country. "A successful U.S. effort here would therefore have important international repercussions," Attwood continued.[73] That was what Kennedy wanted to hear.

To fulfill United States ambitions in Guinea, Kennedy turned again to Sargent Shriver. On June 9, Dean Rusk, the secretary of state, announced Shriver's scheduled visit to Guinea. The visit was successful. In addition to convincing Touré to accept the Peace Corps, Shriver also provided an assessment of Guinea. Shriver wrote:

> Guinea can be tested only over a period of let us say two years. During that time, we should be as concerned—if not more concerned—with the objective merits of aid proposals as Guinea's day-to-day reactions to these proposals indicate about her politics. At the end of this time we should have facts sufficient to enable us to make our overall judgment about the degree of Guinea's adherence to the principles acceptable to us. . . . Here we have an opportunity to move a country from an apparently clear Bloc orientation to a position of neutrality or even one of orientation to the West. This is the first such opportunity I know of in the underdeveloped world. The consequences of such in terms of our relations with countries like Mali or Ghana, or even Iraq or the UAR could be very good indeed.[74]

After Shriver's visit, Nkrumah's Ghana requested between fifty to seventy volunteers. Touré's Guinea asked for volunteers with technical skills. Shriver's diplomacy was successful. As the administration noted, "If we can successfully crack Ghana and Guinea, Mali may even turn to the West."[75]

In Guinea, the volunteers were to replace Soviet experts in that country. The presence of the volunteers contributed to the beginning of a new friendship between Washington and Conakry. In 1962, the benefits of such a bond paid off. Not only did Guinea expel Soviet experts, it also denied Russia landing rights during the Cuban missile crisis. The domino effect of this friendship was also clear. By improving relations with Washington, Guinea stopped supporting Communist guerrillas in neighboring countries, such as Cameroon.

Indeed, the Peace Corps activities in Ghana and Guinea were duplicated in other African countries. The newly independent African countries became major recipients of the Peace Corps volunteers. In 1962, Harris Wofford informed Kennedy about the importance of the Peace Corps in Africa, noting,

> this is a continent to win . . . for freedom. . . . What we do now while Africa is in flux will count for more than what we do two, four or ten years from now. Now we can play a central part in helping these new nations succeed. If we wait until they falter, it may be too late to prevent chaos or communism.[76]

The volunteers had to ensure that these countries did not "falter." By doing this, the volunteers repaired America's credibility and also made friends for the country.

3

Cameroon and Its Problems

"C'est la crise economie."[1] So say the poor, the rich, and Cameroonian officials today. First used in December 1986 by Paul Biya, the current president of the Cameroon Republic, to describe the economic plight of the country, *"la crise economie"* has become the sole explanation given by Cameroonians to the most urgent problems of the day—poverty, embezzlement, gross mismanagement, theft, and corruption. While some of these problems are of recent creation, others have been there since independence. In the beginning, the American Peace Corps volunteers worked in Cameroon helping to solve some of its problems.

Generally known as the "African continent in microcosm," Cameroon, with a size of approximately 183,000 square miles, is slightly larger than California (158,706 square miles). With the shape of an elongated triangle, Cameroon shares boundaries to the south with Equatorial Guinea, Gabon, and the People's Republic of Congo. To the east it is bound by Chad and the Central African Republic, and to the west by Nigeria. Sitting on the coast of West Africa, Cameroon's most conspicuous physical feature along the coastline is Mount Cameroon. With an elevation of 13,350 feet, Mount Cameroon is the highest mountain in West Africa.[2]

During the nightmare years of the trans-Atlantic slave trade, Cameroon served as a useful source for slaves. Generally labeled the "slave-trading middlemen," the Douala people of the Cameroon coast obtained slaves from the interior and sold them to Europeans. Until about 1850 the slave trade was the main economic activity of the Douala people. After the trans-Atlantic trade was abolished, the Doualas shifted their interest to the exportation of palm oil, palm kernels, and ivory.[3] Thus, before the nineteenth century the Cameroon coast was already a familiar area to European traders, missionaries, and explorers.

The desire to spread Christianity and to exploit the raw materials in Cameroon enabled Europeans to penetrate the interior of that territory in the nineteenth century. In 1845, Alfred Saker, a missionary

46

from England, established the Protestant Church in Douala. In order to recruit Cameroonians for his church, he translated the Bible into the Douala language. Thirteen years later, Saker and his English colleagues founded the city of Victoria. Following Saker were several English companies, including the John Holt Company and the Ambas Bay Trading Company, which were in Cameroon for business opportunities. Realizing the possibility of collaboration with English businessmen, the Douala people wrote and asked for Queen Victoria's protection.[4] But the request was turned down, as Britain saw little benefit in occupying the Cameroon coast at this time. Britain was to regret this decision as the scramble for Africa intensified in the latter part of the nineteenth century.

Previously uninterested in territorial conquest in Africa, Otto von Bismarck decided to join the race for territory in 1883. At the Berlin Conference (1884–85) European countries formally undertook the rape of Africa. Cameroon was handed over to Germany, and with the Berlin Conference over, German colonization in Cameroon began. German imperial rule in Cameroon lasted until 1914. As a defeated nation in World War I, Germany surrendered the country to the League of Nations. At the Versailles Conference in 1919, the victors divided the country into two zones. After division, both zones became mandates of the League. Britain and France, the greatest imperialist nations in contemporary history and the leaders of the League of Nations, became the new administrators of the two Cameroons. Thus, from 1922 to 1960, when Cameroon gained independence, it was colonized by these two European powers. The different colonization experiences of Cameroon by Germany, Britain, and France had a major impact on the Cameroonians.

German colonization in Cameroon lasted for almost thirty years. Through its various governors, the Germans imposed harsh and rigid rule in Cameroon. As a colonial power, Germany was determined to exploit the raw materials of its colony. But the path toward achieving this objective was rugged. In order to exploit the resources of the colony, the Germans had to penetrate the interior, establish roads between the coast and the rest of the territory, and subdue chiefs who were unwilling to compromise their autonomy. Germany used explorers, traders, missionaries, and the military to achieve these objectives. In 1886, the Swiss and German missionaries of the Basel Mission established themselves in Victoria. In the late 1880s the Germans used military means to suppress the people of the

Adamawa region. In the central and southern parts of the territory, the Germans exploited the tribal conflicts to establish their domination. Such large German companies as the Woermann Company, Gesellschaft Sud-Kamerun, and the Gesellschaft Nordwest-Kamerun entered into peaceful agreements with tribal leaders for trading purposes.[5]

German rule in Cameroon began in the midst of problems. In 1884 King Lock Priso of Hickory Town in the Douala region staged an uprising against German rule in the area. Though the Germans used their superior military advantage to suppress the revolt, uprisings against foreign domination continued in other parts of the territory. Several groups, including the Bulus, Keakas, Anyangs, Kpes, and Mbulus, revolted against German rule.[6] Though sporadic and isolated revolts were frequent against German colonization in Cameroon, they were generally short lived.

However, several tribes welcomed the Germans. Sultan Njoya of the powerful Bamum Kingdom welcomed the Germans and established excellent relations with the famous German explorer Eugen Zintgraff. The king of Bali not only shared a cordial relationship with the Germans, he also furnished the Germans with guides and encouraged them to visit other areas in the territory. Like the Bamum Kingdom, the Ewondos in Yaounde enjoyed a friendly relationship with the Germans.[7]

By 1910, almost the entire Cameroon was under German control. To exploit the resources of the territory, the Germans confiscated the land, instituted a rigid system of forced labor to exploit the resources, and extracted huge taxes from the colonized people. Those who could not afford the taxes paid with their labor. Such rigorous policies bred hatred among the colonized people.

Yet the German administration also made a positive contribution in the colony. During the administration of Governor Jesko von Puttkamer, large plantations were started in Cameroon. Established in 1895, the Victoria Plantation Company invested more than $2 million in the creation of plantations. A variety of crops, including bananas, rubber, tea, cocoa, palm oil, and coffee, was produced on these plantations. For a territory that relied on cash crops for its economic survival, von Puttkamer's policy to invest in plantations was timely, pragmatic, and valuable. These plantations served as the foundation of the Cameroon Development Corporation (CDC), the largest plantation in the country today. In the field of science, the Germans established the Botanical Garden at Victoria. This was a research facility used for the study of soil types and for the testing of a variety of crops to be produced in Cameroon. The production of palm oil, palm kernal, and cocoa was particularly encouraged. To fully exploit palm oil production, the Germans established a soap factory in Douala in 1908. Cocoa production was enhanced with the founding of the Kamerun Kakaogesellschaft Company to produce chocolate.[8] While the Germans, like other colonial powers, established these plantations and factories for their own interest, the Cameroonians who worked there acquired skills. These skills were used in later years to develop the territory. Equally important, the Germans contributed to the abolition of slavery in Cameroon, introduced the currency, waged a campaign against the brutal punishment inflicted on those people suspected of witchcraft, and discouraged human sacrifice.

During their thirty-year control of Cameroon, the Germans "laid a foundation for modern Cameroon's overhead capital (that is, basic transportation, communication, irrigation and power facilities)." In addition, the Germans assisted in the construction of the country's infrastructure. The building of harbors, railroads, bridges, roads, offices, and plantations was started by the Germans.[9] Though largely insignificant by today's standards, these projects were enormous for the time, as they paved the way for future development. And because Cameroonians did most of the work, they were able to learn additional skills.

Equally significant were the advances made in health care. The Germans initiated efforts to curtail the spread of disease—malaria, leprosy, smallpox, sleeping sickness, and yellow fever—in Cameroon. The Germans also encouraged and promoted both missionary and educational activity in the colony. Though the Germans insisted on the teaching of the German language in schools, it was a minute price to pay for all the progress they were implementing in Cameroon. Also, priority was given to the establishment of schools. By 1913, there existed four agricultural schools in Cameroon, located in Douala, Victoria, Yaounde, and Garoua. By this time the various religious groups had established 631 mission schools, with most of them owned by the Basel Mission.[10]

More important was that Cameroon stayed united under the Germans, thereby sparing the people the psychological pains that are legacies of division in other African countries. Another asset of German rule was that it established most of the present boundaries of Cameroon.[11]

Like every other colonial power, the Germans were in Cameroon to exploit the resources of that territory. Yet the Germans realized that in order to reap the harvest, they had to invest in and develop the territory. Despite the questionable methods, the economic and social advancements carried out in Cameroon by the Germans were enduring. As a result, revolts against German colonial rule in Cameroon were relatively few and generally short lived. Compared to later colonial powers in the territory, Cameroonians have continued to reserve their praises for the German administration. According to the Cameroonians, the Germans were "very strict, at times harsh, but always just."[12] All the development projects carried out in the territory by the German administration acted as curtain-raisers for future progress. The harsh but progressive policies allowed Cameroonians, in later years, to compare favorably the German colonial rule with other colonial administrations.

World War I inflicted a deadly blow on the advances carried out by the Germans in the colony. To meet the war effort, the Germans placed all development programs on hold. Allied victory in the war, coupled with the division of Cameroon, not only terminated German development in the colony but also led to the total evacuation of the German residents. France received a larger portion of Cameroon, and Britain took over two small areas bordering Nigeria. The British system of indirect rule in British Southern Cameroon and the rigid exploitation employed by the French rulers in East Cameroon sowed the seeds for future problems in the colony.

Cameroonians were quick to discover the shortcomings of the British and French administrations. These new masters were indifferent to the continuous development of the colony. Such indifference led to anger and hatred against Britain and France. A by-product of this ill will was an outburst of Cameroonian nationalism.

The mandate system failed to satisfy the ambitions of Cameroonians. After World War II, the United Nations replaced the defunct League of Nations, and in 1946 Southern Cameroon and East Cameroon, previously mandates of the League of Nations, became trust territories of the United Nations. Under the trusteeship system, Britain and France agreed under Article 76 of the United Nations charter to prepare the two Cameroons for "self-government or independence." Additionally, France and Britain were required by the charter "to promote the political, economic, social, and educational advancement of the inhabitants of the trust territories."[13] Despite a name change, the basic framework of the British and French administration remained unrevised. And Cameroonians remained unreconciled to the system.

The period after the formation of trust territories witnessed a renewed outburst of Cameroonian nationalism. Older political parties, which until now were mild in their demonstrations, combined with newly formed ones and began a vigorous demand for reunification and independence. The parties believed it was time to end imperialism. If the European administrators tried to keep their colonial empire, Cameroonians were ready for rebellion.

Several factors promoted independence movements in Cameroon. The beginnings of the Cold War and the United Nations appeal for the rapid abandonment of colonial possessions were important. But perhaps most decisive were the weaknesses of Britain and France exposed during and after the war; World War II turned these two European countries into second-rate powers and damaged their economies. Their immediate postwar concern was domestic economic rehabilitation. This urgent concern siphoned off funds that could be used to suppress rebel movements in the colonies. For the Cameroonians, the time was right now.

In the aftermath of World War II, Cameroonians became more determined to force Britain and France to honor their obligations to the territories as stated in the United Nations charter. Political activity in the two Cameroons had developed by the eve of World War II. Douala was the center stage of this emerging political awareness. Led by Paul Soppo Priso, a group of activists formed a political party, the Jeunesse Camerounaise Française (Jeucafra). Though the objectives of the party were ambivalent, its organizers advocated more French influence in Cameroon. The party's long-term objective, its leaders stated, was to secure full autonomy for East Cameroon. However, their timetable for achieving that goal was quite vague. During World War II, members of Jeucafra recruited Cameroonians to fight on France's side. One year after the formation of Jeucafra, Nigerian-based Cameroonians, including Emmanuel L. M. Endeley and Paul M. Kale, organized the Cameroons Youth League (CYL), a party dedicated to the interest of Southern Cameroon. Like Jeucafra, the aims of CYL were ambivalent. Its leaders were committed neither to the objective of securing more autonomy for English-speaking Cameroon nor to the development of the territory's economy. The party declined quickly.[14] Both Jeucafra and the CYL were among the early political parties formed in Cameroon. As a result, they suffered from built-in weaknesses. Though the two parties became comparable to toothless bulldogs, their existence paved the way for the emergence of other political parties.

The period between 1946 and 1952 saw a remarkable growth of political awareness in the two Cameroons. Increasingly these new parties realized that in order to be successful they must be truly representative of the territory by attracting support from the workers, the peasants, the middle class, and the tribal associations. More and more they focused their attention on securing autonomy and independence.

In 1946 Jeucafra, which had survived the war, was reorganized into the Union Camerounaise Française (Unicafra). The new party failed to satisfy the aspirations of Cameroonians, as it offered no agenda for Cameroon's political future. Impatient with the passivity of Unicafra, some of its members left and in 1947 established the more radical Rassemblement Camerounais (Racam). Unlike its predecessor, Racam's platform rejected France's policy of assimilation and Cameroon's membership in the French Union. Racam's objectives put the party on a collision course with French desires for the territory. As a result, Racam was short lived; it was banned the same year it was formed. Though Racam was declared illegal, it was succeeded by the Union des Populations du Cameroun (UPC).[15]

Established in 1948 by Reuben Um Nyobé, one of the cofounders of the defunct Racam, the UPC was determined "to group and unite the inhabitants of the territory in order to permit the most rapid evolution of the peoples and the raising of their standard of living." In short, the UPC stood for reunification of the two Cameroons and complete independence for Cameroon. "Everyone will recognize, speaking in Christian terms, that God created only one single Cameroon," Um Nyobé stated. Although the party was largely supported by workers and government employees, the UPC also established a firm alliance with other countries. Within Cameroon the UPC established firmer relations with the tribal political associations of the Ngondo and Kumsze in the Douala and Bamileke regions, respectively. Both traditional organizations were sympathetic to the UPC objective of reunification. To spread its message, the UPC published several newspapers, including *Voix du Peuple du Cameroun, L'Etoile, Lumière,* and *La Vérité.*[16]

Unable to curtail the activities of the UPC, the French blacklisted the party and its members. Leading members of the UPC called for an immediate end to French colonialism in Cameroon. France responded by branding the UPC "a party of radicals" and promised to suppress it. More threatening to France was that Dr. Roland Félix Moumié, one of the ideological forces behind the UPC, advocated the Communist tactics of Ho Chi Minh and Mao Tse-tung. He recommended similar methods for the UPC.

If the French were searching for an opportunity to outlaw the UPC, that moment came on May 20, 1955. On this day the UPC organized a revolt against French leadership in Cameroon. The uprising was a complete disaster, and the consequences were implemented harshly. In July the UPC was banned in East Cameroon.[17] This reversal began a new chapter in the life of the UPC.

Refusing to abide by the French victory, the UPC members began another phase in their struggle for Cameroon's independence. Vowing to continue with their objectives, the UPC, led by Um Nyobé and Theodore Mayi-Matip, went underground and resorted to terrorist methods. While some members traveled to Moscow, Khartoum, Accra, and Conakry in search of support, several members took refuge in Southern Cameroon, where French colonial laws were inapplicable. Wherever they went, they remained committed to their objectives. Their attacks, which included violent demonstrations at the United Nations, were most severe between 1955 and 1960.[18]

The center of political activity was not limited to East Cameroon. The actions of the UPC had spurred politicians in British Southern Cameroon to take the initiative in order to assume control of their territory. Increasingly, Southern Cameroon politicians rose and challenged British policy. They had grown impatient with a colonial policy that treated their territory as "a colony of a colony [Nigeria]."[19] These new actors on the political scene called for complete autonomy of British Southern Cameroon from Nigeria. According to them, autonomy for the territory "must" precede reunification and independence. As a result, they did not endorse the idea of reunification until the late 1940s.

In 1946, Endeley returned to Buea, his hometown in British Southern Cameroon, and joined the politics of the day. Three years later he combined several local organizations into the Cameroons

National Federation (CNF). Endeley's organization reluctantly endorsed reunification. A conglomerate of different organizations with
varied objectives, the CNF quickly ran into factional problems. Because the CNF was vague and ambivalent on the crucial issue of reunification, some of its original members abandoned the party and
became members of the Kamerun United National Congress
(KUNC). However, the life of KUNC was brief. Following a brief rec-
onciliation meeting, KUNC and CNF healed their wounds and
formed the Kamerun National Congress (KNC). The division, the re-
union, and the emergence of new parties was the order of the day in
British Southern Cameroon. Those were the days when political parties rose, split, and fell in rapid succession.

Exhausted from their dealings with the UPC, major politicians
in Southern Cameroon, including Endeley, Namaso Mbile, and
Paul Kale, disassociated themselves from UPC ideas. But their
decision did not discourage John Ngu Foncha, who believed that the
UPC deserved a chance. Foncha, who was later to become a major
force in Cameroon politics, continued to support the UPC. In March
1955, Foncha formed the Kamerun National Democratic Party
(KNDP). Foncha's party provided sanctuary to UPC members who
had fled persecution from East Cameroon to Southern Cameroon.
But soon problems developed in the relationship. Foncha had
hoped that the UPC would be sympathetic to his primary objective
of full autonomy for Southern Cameroon. The KNDP believed that
reunification and independence would come later. But the UPC
shelved Foncha's main objective and insisted on reunification and immediate independence. According to Foncha, the UPC was insensi-
tive to his aspirations. He had had enough. In 1957 Foncha withdrew
his support of the UPC and the party was banned in Southern
Cameroon. Declared illegal in the territory, the UPC members went
underground and swelled the ranks of the Maquisards, and Ndeh
Ntumazah formed One Kamerun, a party dedicated to the objectives
of the defunct UPC.

But by 1958, politics in Southern Cameroon was dominated by
Endeley and Foncha, two leaders who held opposite views regarding
the political future of Southern Cameroon. While Endeley continued
to flirt with the idea of "integration with Nigeria," Foncha vehe-
mently called for total separation from Nigeria. Both politicians took
that matter to the United Nations General Assembly where each presented his case.[20] They would resolve their differences in later years.

Meanwhile, however, the political drama on the nature of the future of Southern Cameroon continued, and the UPC intensified its guerrilla tactics.

The underground activities of the UPC showed France and Britain that the struggle for Cameroon's independence was an irreversible process. In 1958, under United Nations pressure, France gave in. Political problems in France, coupled with the uprisings in Algeria, helped accelerate the process of independence for Cameroon. Ahmadou Ahidjo was made premier of East Cameroon in preparation for full independence for Cameroon to be granted on January 1, 1960.

For French Cameroon it was only a matter of time, but for British Southern Cameroon the issue was more complicated. The major political leaders in the territory, Foncha and Endeley, disagreed on the nature of the future of British Southern Cameroon. By 1957 Endeley had made it clear that his party, the KNC, favored integration with Nigeria. Opposing the KNC was Foncha's KNDP, which advocated secession from Nigeria followed by reunification with East Cameroon. These issues would be decided in a plebiscite in the future.[21]

Regarding British Northern Cameroon, the political issues were less complicated. For almost forty-six years, that territory was ruled as an integral part of Nigeria; as a result, it was widely anticipated that British Northern Cameroon would vote to remain with Nigeria. On November 7, 1959, in a plebiscite to decide the future of their territory, voters in Northern Cameroon surprised most political observers of the area. In the plebiscite, "voters were asked whether they were in favor of postponing a decision of the territory's future until a later date, or remaining an integral part of Northern Nigeria after October, 1960." They voted 70,401 to 42,797 in favor of postponing a decision of the territory's future. Suspicious of fraud, the United Nations rejected the results of the plebiscite and rescheduled another plebiscite for February 11, 1961, this time to be held on the same day as the one in British Southern Cameroon.[22]

As French Cameroon prepared for its independence day celebration, there were feelings of fear and uncertainty. But there was another problem French Cameroon had to resolve, the terrorism of the UPC. On December 31, 1959, UPC terrorists launched a series of attacks in different parts of Cameroon. Several facilities in Douala were attacked, resulting in forty deaths. The UPC and its supporters requested Cameroonians to boycott the independence day celebration and promised more havoc on that day. Thus, the Cameroon Republic was born in problems. According to UPC leaders, Ahmadou Ahidjo, the first president, had sold out to France. And for Ahidjo the UPC had become a dagger in the heart. Despite the threats, the independence day celebration proceeded as planned. In his independence day speech, Ahidjo lashed out at the UPC as "antiquated romantics" and offered them an opportunity to "recognize their errors and join us today."[23] The UPC ignored Ahidjo's appeal and vowed to continue with their sabotage.

Following the independence day celebration, Ahidjo turned back to the problem of British Cameroon. Campaigning alongside John Ngu Foncha, leader of the Kamerun National Democratic Party, Ahidjo promised not to rest until the entire Cameroon was reunited. They had work to do. February 11, 1961, came fast. On this day British Southern Cameroon voted 233,571 to 97,741 in favor of reunification with the Cameroon Republic. Disappointingly, British Northern Cameroon voted 146,296 to 97,654 in favor of remaining with Nigeria. On October 1, British Southern Cameroon, now known as West Cameroon, became officially reunited with East Cameroon. Reunification terminated Britain's political domination of Southern Cameroon.

The constitution of 1961 turned the reunified Cameroon into a federation. This federation was composed of two parts, East and West Cameroon. Although the constitution was vague on the nature of the new federation, people in each state quickly assumed the responsibility for the betterment of their regions.[24] Ahmadou Ahidjo became the new president of the Federal Republic of Cameroon. John Ngu Foncha, an educator and a politician, was made prime minister of West Cameroon.

In 1961, West Cameroon had a size of roughly 16,581 square miles. With a tropical climate, West Cameroon receives heavy rainfall during the wet season. This climatic condition supports a vegetation of forestland in the southern part of the state and grassland in the northern portion. The major towns in West Cameroon at the time of independence included Kumba, Tiko, Victoria, Mamfe, Bamenda, and Buea. Under the constitution these towns were known as divisions and were headed by a government representative called the senior divisional officer (SDO, or prefect).

In contrast, East Cameroon, with 166,800 square miles, had a more varied climatic condition. The coastal region is characterized by tropical climatic conditions. Toward the north, the climate changes into semidesert. Among the numerous groups that existed in 1961 were fifty thousand pygmies in the eastern part of East Cameroon.[25] The main urban centers in East Cameroon at this time included Yaounde, Douala, and Nkongsamba.

Despite the attainment of independence and reunification, the UPC continued to sabotage Ahidjo's government. UPC activities presented the new republic with the first and most severe political problem. With continuous support from Sudan, the United Arab Republic, Ghana, Guinea, Russia, China, and many private groups located in Paris and London, the UPC deliberately disturbed the tranquility of the new republic. Compounding Ahidjo's early difficulties was his desire to obtain recognition for his government from other nations of the world, some of which supported the UPC.

Within Cameroon there existed several postindependence parties. Through patience and firm leadership, Ahidjo succeeded, in 1966, in uniting all these parties into the Cameroon National Union (CNU), the official party of the republic. The skill and ability used to achieve this objective showed "the restrained determination and perseverance which [were] the hallmarks of Ahidjo's *realpolitik*." After 1966, some UPC members and other opponents of the CNU were sent to jail; others either went into exile or were quickly eliminated.[26]

Cameroon now began facing the grim realities of independence. With a population of less than five million, Cameroon had more than 150 ethnic groups speaking more than 136 different languages. Tribal divisions and hatred were visible. It seemed the eviction of Britain and France had only given birth to civil conflict.

Moreover, the legacy of three colonial masters coupled with the new experience in federalism and bilingualism were early problems. The long period of separate administration left behind the most difficult legacy. Before 1961, the development policies of East and West Cameroon were totally different, and trade between the two zones was nonexistent.[27] While roads existed on the coast, access to the interior was almost impossible. Although the French constructed some minor railway tracks in East Cameroon, the British totally neglected this aspect of development. In fact, West Cameroon under British rule experienced major setbacks in development. Those were the years when everything linked to development came to a halt in West Cameroon.

Economically, the new republic was in a sorry state after independence. Industrialization was almost completely absent. The main source of revenue was from the sale of agricultural crops such as cocoa, coffee, bananas, palm oil, and rubber. Complicating the revenue problem was the fact that prices of these crops were dependent on world market conditions. Occasional fluctuation in prices often led to severe economic failures. Capital and manpower were in short supply. The poor roads made it difficult for cash crops to be transported to the main ports.

Other problems were more evident in West Cameroon. Reunification brought to an end West Cameroon's favored trade advantages with the Commonwealth countries. New policies designed to regularize the economy only helped to darken the economic picture in West Cameroon. The introduction of the Communauté Financière Africaine (CFA) franc as the region's currency in 1962 caused major inflation in West Cameroon. Prices of basic commodities skyrocketed.[28] With the limited revenue received from the sale of primary goods, many West Cameroonians quickly learned how to survive at subsistence level. Other attempts to reverse the British legacy included a law passed in 1962 requiring all vehicles to travel on the right-hand side of the road.

Additionally, West Cameroon was mostly rural. The few cities in the state were largely cut off from the rural areas, and some of the roads linking the cities were seasonal. For example, the Mamfe–Kumba road was almost impassable during the wet season. In this season only four-wheeled vehicles went to Mamfe. It was normal for vehicles to take ten hours to travel less than 200 miles.[29] Other areas experienced the same problem.

Equally depressing were the conditions in the rural areas. Typical of village conditions were those found in Bojongo. Peace Corps volunteers Andy and Kathy Edwards, stationed in Bojongo in 1962, recorded their observations of this community. Although located along the coast of West Cameroon,

> Bojongo is in the bush . . . its population is small and impoverished. Bojongo has been deteriorating for years but the deterioration has been accelerated by the recent failure in the banana crop. The educated youth move away as quickly as possible and return only to attend cry-dies [death celebrations]. The Bojongo area includes Bejorke, Bwana, Mukumba, Ekonde, Mponge, Lower Bojongo, Middle Bojongo and Upper Bojongo and other smaller villages, each with its chief and council. The story of each village is the same. The mission and the CDC

have taken the Bakweri land remaining for farming. . . . Cows, goats and pigs are kept as a kind of prestige article. They are a sign of wealth and are never eaten, never sold and their only possible economical use is as part of a bride price. The college is the only alive thing in Bojongo. Those that are employed are paid by the college: i.e. bricklayers, painters, carpenters, the washerman, and cooks. Outside of this very little money is found in Bojongo. Because of this the houses are of poor quality—very little zinc is used. The floors are mud, the roofs thatched and these are not kept in good repair.[30]

In the light of these problems, one estimate in 1960 indicated that West Cameroon would require at least $1.7 million per year to pay for its development. Despite this, West Cameroon realized that the problems that needed urgent solutions were road improvement and education. In the country's first five-year plan (1961–66), education was given the "second highest priority," following road improvement.[31] Education is a worthwhile investment, but in West Cameroon everything was lacking: teachers, books, teaching aids, classrooms, and other necessary facilities.

West Cameroon education was modeled after the British system. The school system imposed by the British imperialists consisted of primary or elementary, senior primary, and secondary schools, teacher training and technical colleges, and the college of arts, science, and technology. It was no easy task to progress from one stage to the next. Under the British administration the idea of a university was unthinkable in West Cameroon. (See Figure 1, which shows the stages and the shortest number of years a student had to spend in each stage. The chart shows the conventional flow of students through the education system.)

Though Britain dictated the system of education before 1961, the responsibility for establishing and running schools was largely in the hands of missionary groups. Most notable among these groups were the Roman Catholic Church, the Basel Mission, and the Cameroon Baptist Church. The Basel Mission, formed by German and Swiss missionaries, was established in Cameroon in 1886. Out of the 324 primary schools started in West Cameroon between 1945 and 1961, more than 300 were established by mission groups, with the Catholic Mission making the largest contribution.[32]

Perhaps the main shortcoming in this educational system was that most of the schools were located in the towns of Kumba, Limbe,

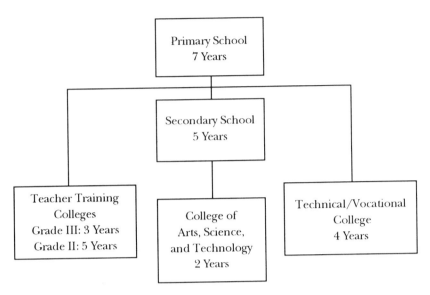

Figure 1. General structure of education system, West Cameroon. Source: Stanford Research Institute, *Education and Manpower*, 35.

Mamfe, and Bamenda divisions. As in other development projects, the villages were neglected. See table 1 for the distribution and ownership of primary schools between 1946 and 1960.

At reunification time there were 491 primary schools in West Cameroon, with a total enrollment of more than 80,000. Also in existence were three established secondary schools and six teacher training colleges. Enrollment in these schools was quite low. Of the 30 percent of the children who attended primary school, less than 1 percent of the group eventually graduated and enrolled in the three secondary schools in West Cameroon.[33]

The only technical school, the Government Trade Centre (GTC) at Ombe, had received a devastating blow after reunification. Its staff, mostly composed of British expatriates, chose to leave West Cameroon. Lacking a qualified staff to fill the vacuum, the school closed its doors. The trade center offered courses in vocational education, and students at the center studied such subjects as welding, carpentry, motor repairs, electronics, and construction.[34]

Primary school education in West Cameroon was severely handicapped. Based on the eight-year system devised by Britain, the

Table 1. Primary Schools, 1946–1960

Agency	Division						Total
	Victoria	Kumba	Mamfe	Bamenda	Wum	Nkambe	
Native authority	5	2	3	—	—	—	10
Basel Mission	7	19	24	50	9	6	115
Cameroon Baptist Mission	11	5	—	14	6	11	47
Roman Catholic Mission	11	25	23	51	21	11	142
Cameroon Development Corporation (CDC)	7	3	—	—	—	—	10
Total	41	54	50	115	36	28	324

Source: *Education and Manpower*, 18.

primary schools suffered from a "shortage of qualified teachers, textbooks, teaching aids and adequate classrooms." Teaching methods and syllabi were obsolete. The syllabus, in most cases, contained little information on Cameroonian affairs. In 1961, more than 60 percent of the primary school teachers were ill equipped, ill prepared, and uncertified, and a large number were hired to fill temporary positions. Several primary school classrooms were "poorly constructed and contain[ed] only the barest essentials—wooden desks, benches, and a single blackboard—which [were] often in short supply."[35]

Generally, secondary schools faced more acute problems. The absence of a national university in 1961 explains the shortage of a qualified teaching staff in these schools. Many of the school libraries, dependent upon books donated by charitable organizations, contained limited numbers of volumes, most of which were irrelevant to the courses taught in schools. Few schools had a science laboratory, and sanitary conditions and student housing were deplorable. But perhaps the biggest crime committed by Britain against secondary schools was the system of the London General Certificate of Education (GCE) examination established in West Cameroon. The syllabus for the examination was devised in London and contained no topics on Cameroonian affairs. Though Cameroonian teachers taught the students, the exams were made up and graded in London and the results sent back to Cameroon. Without a qualified teaching staff, the poor performance of the students on the GCE was not surprising.[36]

Of equal significance was the low enrollment in secondary schools. But for the bilingual secondary school, a government institution, all the other secondary schools were established and operated by mission groups. Many Cameroonian parents, living on a meager income, were unable to afford the tuition charged in these mission schools.[37] The net result was that most primary school graduates remained without secondary school education for a lack of money. The absence of graduates in the country made it almost impossible for the government to correct the situation. (The major postprimary institutions and their locations are indicated in table 2.)

Another important problem which confronted policymakers after reunification was the desire to restructure previous educational goals to meet national objectives. Among other things, mission schools emphasized the Scriptures. The main burden here was to search for "a compromise between the patterns inherited from the British in the West and from the French in the East."[38] More important, education became the responsibility of the federal government after independence. The government came up with a curriculum that was to serve the interest of the country and not just religious groups.

A chronic concern during these early years of the Cameroon Republic was the budgetary problem. Revenue obtained from the export of cash crops was insufficient to finance the country's budget. After reunification Britain extended a token gift of about 575,000 pounds to its former colony and withdrew the Commonwealth trade advantages of West Cameroon in September 1963. With an insolvent economy, West Cameroon incurred a deficit of 280,000 pounds in 1961. Thus, the parting gift London provided to West Cameroon was a drop in the bucket in resolving the territory's economic problems.

Table 2. Postprimary Institutions

School	Type	Location
Government Trade Centre	Vocational	Ombe
College of Science	Secondary	Bambui
St. Joseph's College	Secondary	Sasse
Queen of Holy Rosary College	Secondary	Okoyong (Mamfe)
Girls' Secondary School	Secondary	Victoria
Sacred Heart College	Secondary	Mankon
Baptist Teacher Training College	Secondary	Soppo (Buea)
R.C. Teacher Training College	Secondary	Soppo
R.C. Teacher Training Centre	Secondary	Bojongo
R.C. Teacher Training Centre	Secondary	Tatum
Basel Elementary Training Centre	Secondary	Batibo
Basel Women's Training Centre	Secondary	Azire (Bamenda)
Basel Preliminary Training Centre	Secondary	Bali
Baptist Preliminary Training Centre	Secondary	Bamunka

Source: Peace Corps Project Description (104), p. 5.

French financial assistance to East Cameroon was also meager. Of the $40 million given by France to East Cameroon in 1960–61, a considerable portion of it was used to finance salaries of "French technical counselors" and military experts in the country. Additionally, part of the money was allocated to finance the studies of Cameroonian students in France.[39] Not surprisingly, the bulk of the money ended up in France and not in Cameroon.

Realizing that it could not rely on the former colonial masters for help, the Cameroon government turned elsewhere. Following Cameroon's independence in 1960, the United States and Cameroon moved quickly to establish diplomatic relations. The United States sent economic assistance to Cameroon through the International Co-operation Administration (ICA). This cordial relationship quickly went sour when the United States failed "to support the position of Cameroonians on the results of a United Nations plebescite to determine the future of British Northern Cameroon." Following reunification in 1961, Cameroon reorganized its government and adopted a new constitution. As a result, Cameroon asked its ambassador to the United States, Aimé-Raymond N'Thepe, to present a new letter of credence to the president of the United States. When Kennedy hesitated to receive N'Thepe, the Cameroon government gave Leland Barrows, United States ambassador to that country, an ultimatum. "Unless Ambassador N'Thepe is allowed to see President Kennedy . . . the Cameroon government will no longer receive the American Ambassador," Barrows was informed. The ultimatum was unexpected, but it had results. L. D. Battle, executive secretary of the Department of State, after reviewing the circumstances, recommended urgent action from the president. Battle added that

> In the light of the special circumstances in this case, the Department considers it highly desirable that the Ambassador's call receive no publicity. We would hope, therefore, that this appointment could be omitted from the President's published schedule, and that the Ambassador's arrival and departure could be arranged to avoid contact with members of the press.[40]

The White House heeded Battle's suggestion. N'Thepe presented his letter of credence, and the crisis subsided. Meanwhile, Cameroon continued to receive assistance from the United States through Kennedy's new Agency for International Development (AID). Also, Ahmadou Ahidjo, Cameroon's president, was invited to Washington.

In an official visit to the United States in March 1962, Ahidjo informed President Kennedy of the continuous economic plight of Cameroon. Also, Ahidjo expressed to Kennedy his impatience with the British and French policies of persistent intervention in Cameroonian affairs. France, Ahidjo complained, had not reversed its traditional policy of economically exploiting its former colonies. Ahidjo emphasized to Kennedy the wreckage caused in Cameroon by the pro-Communist terrorist groups, the Maquisards.[41]

The news about the presence of the Maquisards made the need for economic aid urgent. Kennedy, who was committed to reversing the tide of communism "anywhere" and at "anytime," instructed the American ambassador in Cameroon, Leland Barrows, to ensure that Cameroon received the necessary assistance. Whether the terrorist groups were pro-Communist or not, it was certainly pragmatic politics by Ahidjo to emphasize the possible Communist threat in order to encourage immediate assistance from the New Frontier administration.

United States aid to Cameroon included road construction equipment, scholarships to students, and financial assistance. In 1963, there were fifteen Cameroonians studying engineering, agriculture, and cooperative and vocational education in American universities with American scholarship funds. Also in the same year, the United States extended a grant of 120 million francs CFA (about $400,000) to the Cameroon government for economic and social development. This grant was devoted to the reconstruction of those areas destroyed by the terrorists. To hasten the improvement of roads, the United States AID donated road equipment to Cameroon's Public Works Department (PWD), the agency charged with road development in the country.[42]

Assisting Cameroon's development was the organization called Operation Crossroads Africa (OCA). As a nonprofit organization, OCA helped "small communities to work together to meet common problems." In the early years of the Cameroon Republic, three units of OCA visited the country. Of these units, two groups served in East Cameroon, and the other unit assisted construction projects in Guzang and Batibo in West Cameroon.[43]

In September 1963, Ambassador Barrows presented a twin-engine DC-3 airplane to the Cameroon government as a gift from the United States.[44] In the absence of large airports and modern roads in Cameroon, this plane served to transport senior government officials from one part of the country to another.

Also in the same year the United States government extended a loan of $9.2 million to Cameroon. Road equipment donated to Cameroon in October included four Caterpillar tractors; two farm-size tractors; two front-end loaders; five motor graders; ten trucks; a rear-end dump; one low-boy trailer; one pneumatic roller; two air compressors and attachments; and one portable crushing and greening plant—all amounting to $464,170,000 (113,721,650,000 francs CFA).[45] To dramatize the new partnership, G. Mennen Williams, Kennedy's undersecretary for African affairs, visited Cameroon in 1963. Williams emphasized the wishes of the United States to contribute to the development of Cameroon. By today's standards, this aid was minute, but in the early 1960s it helped turn the tide for the development of Cameroon.

Simultaneously, Cameroon was concerned about the shortcomings in its educational development. To resolve these problems, the country turned once more to the United States. As early as August 19, 1961, in a note handed to the American ambassador by A. N. Jua, West Cameroon's minister of social services, the government of West Cameroon requested the services of the Peace Corps volunteers to assist in "teacher training, technical training, and secondary education beginning in January 1962." This request was further confirmed by John Ngu Foncha and A. N. Jua on August 25 in the American embassy. Later, in December, Ako D. Mengot, the director of education in West Cameroon, stressed the need for Peace Corps volunteers in a discussion with the American Peace Corps representative in Cameroon.[46]

Following the preliminary discussions, the government sent an official request to the Peace Corps in Washington, D.C. In January 1962, the Peace Corps representative informed the Cameroon government of the decision to send fifty-four graduates in fulfillment of the request. In his visit to Washington in March, Ahidjo reiterated to Kennedy the need for the Peace Corps to assist in the development of Cameroon.[47]

The summer of 1962 was a busy one for Peace Corps officials in Washington and Cameroon. Arrangements were made for the signing of the official papers concerning the request for Peace Corps volunteers. In May, Peace Corps-Washington informed the Cameroon government that it had allocated $50,000 for the construction of "modest" houses for the first set of volunteers to Cameroon. Of this amount, an initial sum of $25,000 was sent to Cameroon for the beginning of the job.[48] Washington promised to send the remainder of the money as soon as evidence was shown that the funds were used for the purpose intended.

On July 23, Peace Corps officials met in Yaounde, Cameroon, and signed the final agreement with the Cameroon government.[49] Despite all this paperwork, however, the most important tasks facing Peace Corps-Washington were the recruitment, selection, and training of the volunteers, the so-called ambassadors of democracy to Cameroon.

4

Recruitment, Training, and Selection

July 5, 1962, was a typical hot summer day in Athens, Ohio, when the new Peace Corps volunteers arrived at Ohio University to train for service in West Cameroon. The volunteers were young, ambitious, determined, and full of idealism. The group of twenty-one men and twenty-nine women came from twenty states of the United States, with less than 5 percent coming from the southern states. Their ages ranged from nineteen to thirty-six, with an average age of twenty-two.

Of the group, two volunteers were black, and more than 85 percent of the recruits, in their spare time, enjoyed such middle-class

First group of volunteers in training for service in Cameroon at Ohio University, August 1962, with Cameroonian officials in the front row. Courtesy of Roy P. Fairfield's Peace Corps collection.

hobbies as skiing, swimming, theater, and reading.[1] The trainees had joined the Peace Corps for various reasons. "Desire for adventure and an opportunity to try teaching," a volunteer gave as his reason for signing for Peace Corps services. Some became volunteers because of their "desire to travel and live in another culture"; others responded to "Kennedy's call to young Americans to volunteer overseas to help others." The agency provided young Americans with an opportunity to travel and see the world, several volunteers stated. For many young people, the Peace Corps Agency was the exciting place to be identified with in the early 1960s. Serving in the Peace Corps gave them a sense of purpose and belonging to the New Frontier administration. The mood of activism generated by the Kennedy administration encouraged many to volunteer. No wonder one volunteer explained his reason for joining the Peace Corps as "Impulse! Just couldn't stay away from the recruiting table."

Few of the trainees who arrived in Athens had ever heard of Cameroon, and an even smaller number knew the country's location on the world map. "Frankly, I had never heard of the place," a volunteer said of Cameroon before the training. "It was a country in Africa to be found in the atlas," another volunteer stated. Although more than 95 percent of the trainees knew absolutely "nothing" about the country, they were eager to begin their training.[2] They were determined and ready to go to work. Despite the enthusiasm, the volunteers nursed feelings of uncertainty and nervousness, as they were unsure of what was expected of them.

Originally fifty-six volunteers were to participate in the training, but by July 5, 1962, six had already dropped out. The fifty volunteers who came to Athens had met the rigorous Peace Corps recruitment standards. After completing a lengthy Peace Corps questionnaire, each volunteer wrote a six-hour exam. A returned volunteer described her experience and the nature of the exam when she wrote:

> more and more people kept pouring in—about 30 of us I guess. . . . That was fascinating. There were quite a few older people which surprised me. . . . There were some couples . . . and some with accents. The proctor wasn't too well organized and it took a full 45 minutes to get tests distributed and a few simple forms filled out. During this time I received my most startling impressions . . . the slowness of those adult middle aged ladies . . . they asked the dumbest questions . . . one wonders what motivates them and why . . . one lady had the wrong

test . . . she didn't listen and started her own. . . . Biology was quite hard and quite thorough, heavy on ecology and parasitology (which made me sick) . . . two hours for that . . . history . . . it wasn't too bad . . . the language aptitude was pure fun. . . . About half way through one lady started thumbing through her booklet, thoroughly exasperated, looked up to the proctor and said "I don't have any idea what's going on here. . . . " My bio friend and I got a sandwich together . . . back for the extra hour, . . . I for French . . . very hard. . . . Know I didn't make a good showing. Of the 30, only about 8 came back.

Also, the Peace Corps psychologist, who assumed enormous authority during the early years of the agency, put the volunteers through stiff testing. Of course, there were the routine checks of each volunteer by the Federal Bureau of Investigation (FBI). School officials in the volunteers' previous schools were questioned about their conduct, loyalty, and character. A volunteer noted this process when she wrote,

The civil service commission was around investigating me. How about that. . . . He talked to the housemother and then asked her for two kids who lived near me. She gave him the girl next door and the girl across the hall, both of whom I am fairly good friends with. . . . He asked them about my character, loyalty . . . if they had any reason to suspect me of anything, extracurricular activities, reputation. They really go into it pretty thoroughly. It gives you a kind of odd feeling—I'm glad I wasn't around at the time. . . . So that's over. Now if they'd only come through with another piece of paper or two, I'd be happy.

These elaborate and intensive procedures were designed to weed out as many applicants as possible. The screening ensured that those selected for the training were the "cream-of-the-crop, talented, fit, well-adjusted and devoted American men and women."[3]

Such tight selection was not limited to Peace Corps applicants. College campuses that hoped to host Peace Corps training sessions had to fulfill a number of requirements. Priority was given to campuses with experience in international development. To protect the agency's image, racially segregated universities were discouraged from applying for contracts. The Peace Corps did not segregate. Its rules stated that "the Peace Corps will not sign a training contract nor approve a training contract with any institution or organization which practices racial discrimination or segregation in the operation or maintenance of any of its facilities." Emphasizing the nonracist character of the Peace Corps Agency, Sargent Shriver told a Catholic Interracial Council in Chicago that

> I realize that the genius of the Peace Corps is its desire and ability to see people *as* people—to come to terms with human beings as persons apart from qualifying adjectives.
>> This is how we have gathered our staff. I wish you could visit our headquarters in Washington and meet the men and women who have stamped their images on the Peace Corps: the Jewish lawyer from Atlanta, the young Catholic teacher from Maryland, the Negro leader from California. They are there because we said: "We want people *who want to do a job for their country.*" The Peace Corps wants Negroes, and is seeking them. The Peace Corps wants people of all races and all religions, because we want qualified Americans.[4]

Ohio University applied for the training contract in the spring of 1962 and met little opposition.

Located in a small, remote, but dynamic town, Ohio University enjoyed the reputation of a progressive academic institution. The absence of negative metropolitan features in Athens and the hills that modify the summer temperatures made the town attractive for studies. The university already maintained the high standards of no discrimination in "race, color, religion, sex, age, national origin, or handicapped" before that policy became national more than a decade later. Further, the friendship and understanding shared by the town's inhabitants and the students were assets for the institution. Most important, the university, as early as 1958, had sponsored teacher training programs in Nigeria, West Africa.[5] The Nigerian work acquainted Ohio University professors with the educational problems of West Africa.

Ohio University operated an office of international programs with objectives similar to those of the Peace Corps. Therefore, the selection of the university from the numerous applicants was apt. It was time for the university to use its reservoir of professors with experience in international development. The contract to train the Peace Corps volunteers was signed in Washington by Ohio University President Vernon Alden in April 1962. A sum of $323,851.22 was allocated for the training, which lasted from July 5 to August 31, 1962.[6] To fulfill its objectives, Ohio University appointed Professor Roy P. Fairfield as project director.

Roy P. Fairfield standing to the right of Russell A. Milliken at a reception during the training session at Ohio University, July 1962. Courtesy of Roy P. Fairfield's Peace Corps collection.

Professor Fairfield had excellent credentials for the job. As a political scientist, he had acquired a wide range of experiences by 1962. Among other things, he had ten years of industrial experience and had served as professor of cultural and intellectual history. Once a Fulbright professor in Greece, Fairfield had traveled widely. He fully understood the American work ethic, that success and achievement were the by-products of hard work. And he was a committed believer of William James's philosophy that "the great use of life is to spend it for something that will outlast it."[7] Fairfield was in the right place at the right time.

Fairfield selected for his teaching staff some of the "best and the brightest" professors available from the different disciplines the volunteers were required to master before departing for Cameroon. Included in this group were Russell A. Milliken, William H. Cooper, John C. Donovan, Willard H. Elsbree, Carl G. Gustavson, Charlotte E. La Tourrette, Victor Theodore Le Vine, Robert Strausz-Hupé, David Levinson, Paul McStallworth, Mary A. McDonough, and Harry R. Rudin.[8] Professor Paul Gebauer, a Baptist missionary

Trainees Thomas and Evelyn Duston; Samuel Proctor, deputy director in charge of volunteers, Washington, D.C.; and Vernon R. Alden, president of Ohio University. Courtesy of Carl H. Denbow's Peace Corps collection.

who had spent thirty years in Cameroon, was brought in to provide practical experience on Cameroonian culture and realities. Also, Johnson Gabuin, Flavius Martin, and Daniel Muna, all Cameroonian students studying in the United States, were hired to participate in the program as "resource specialists." Their assigned role was to mingle, talk with, and assist the volunteers in clarifying the difference between myth and reality about Cameroon.

Peace Corps-Washington sent Joseph Zasloff, a political scientist, as its main training officer on campus. Other Peace Corps officials, among them a psychologist and a psychiatrist, often appeared at the training session unannounced. They were popularly called the "mysterious little men from Washington in black suits."[9] As could be expected, most volunteers remembered neither their names nor identification.

In addition to hosting the training, the university also appointed an Ohio University overseas representative. Though his primary function was to assist the official Peace Corps representative in Cameroon, he was assigned other tasks. His responsibilities included

The Reverend Professor Paul Gebauer points to the
location of Cameroon on a map of Africa, 1962. Courtesy of Roy P. Fairfield's Peace Corps collection.

seeing to the welfare of the volunteers, paying their minimal salaries
and vacation allowances, ensuring that the volunteers received
proper health care, and furnishing Ohio University with feedback
for future training programs. It was an important job. The success
of the volunteers in the field and future training programs was
largely dependent on the information the Ohio University overseas
representative channeled back to Athens. To effectively perform
these services, Ohio University appointed another scholar, Jack
Carmichael, as its overseas representative. A curriculum specialist,
Professor Carmichael understood the magic of living and toiling with
the volunteers.[10]

Fairfield's training session was elaborate and intensive. He used
the period between the signing of the contract and the beginning of
the training program to master the educational problems and needs
of West Cameroon. He understood that his job was interesting but

difficult, enriching and exhausting, and one that required total commitment. He had roughly twelve weeks to teach fifty young Americans to solve all the educational problems of West Cameroon. Early on he identified the specific needs of Cameroon (see table 3).

While the training was designed along the basic outlines provided by Peace Corps-Washington, Fairfield ensured that his program was tailored to meet the objectives set for West Cameroon. Time was no one's friend. Volunteers put in at least ten hours daily and were required to work "*eight* days a week."[11] The program was designed to be "rugged but . . . not impossible . . . tight, but not inhumane." Volunteers who complained of the demands of the schedule were reminded of the famous World War II slogan that "the difficult we do immediately, the impossible takes a little longer." This was a pioneer Peace Corps project for Ohio University, and to guarantee future Peace Corps projects, the university had to do a good job. According to Fairfield, failure was unthinkable. His energy, time, and skill were all committed.

The volunteers quickly realized that they had come to Athens for neither a honeymoon nor a summer vacation. Earlier, the trainees were introduced to the "poisonous" Peace Corps terms of "selected in" and "selected out." Volunteers were informed that attending the training session was not a guarantee for going overseas.[12] Those "selected out" during and after the training session were advised "to go try something else." The Peace Corps career of those "selected out" came to an abrupt end. While the Peace Corps training team avoided using the "selected-out" terminology, it became the magic term for the "little men" from Washington who occasionally visited the training site. To go overseas, the volunteers had to be noticed as good and hardworking men and women.

The curriculum of the session was all-encompassing. The volunteers were required to receive roughly 480 hours of lectures within a period of eight weeks. The instruction timetable covered eight areas of studies (see table 4).

In its application, West Cameroon requested teachers to fill the gap in the country's educational development. Yet the schedule shows that the course that was given more attention was American Studies and World Affairs. Such emphasis was necessary in order to attain the second and third objectives of the Peace Corps. The volunteers, while performing their services, were charged with the responsibility of rebuilding America's image and winning friends in Cameroon for the

Table 3. Areas for Volunteer Services and Skills Needed

School	Location	Number of Volunteers
Government Trade Centre	Ombe	7
College of Science	Bambui	9
St. Joseph's College	Sasse	5
Cameroon Protestant College	Bali	4
Queen of Rosary College	Okoyong (Mamfe)	4
Girls' Secondary School	Victoria	2
Sacred Heart College	Mankon	2
Baptist Teacher Training College	Soppo (Buea)	4
R.C. Teacher Training College	Soppo	2
R.C. Teacher Training Centre	Bojongo	2
R.C. Teacher Training Centre	Tatum	2
Basel Elementary Training Centre	Batibo	2
Basel Women's Training Centre	Azire (Bamenda)	2
Basel Preliminary Training Centre	Bali	1
Baptist Preliminary Training Centre	Bamunka	2

Skills Wanted

English literature	1	Librarian/bursar/admissions	1
English	8	Shorthand/typing	1
Mathematics	7	Librarian/registrar	1
History	1	Natural science	1
Geography	2	Education	4
General science	2	Botany	1
Biology	3	Chemistry	1
Physics	1	Zoology	1
Librarian/physical education	1	Physical education	2
Bursar	1	Laboratory technician	1

"Other Subjects" (Primary Teacher Education)

Shop, mathematics, and English	1	Masonry	1
Welding and sheetmetal	1	Machinist	1
Carpentry	1	Electricity	1
Auto and diesel mechanics	1		

Source: Fairfield, *Training Plan,* pp. 1–2, PCDRF.

Table 4. Instruction Schedule

Course	Hours
1. Area studies, to include the history and the political and cultural aspects of the host country and personal adaptation thereto.	95
2. Technical studies, to include the knowledge and skills required to perform the assigned job overseas.	110
3. Area studies and world affairs, to include contemporary international problems and the U.S. role in the world scene.	120
4. Health and medical training, to include first aid, personal hygiene, and preventive measures required in the assigned area.	30
5. Physical education and recreation, to include personal conditioning as well as practice in U.S. and host country games.	70
6. Language training, to include knowledge of language structure, basic vocabulary, conversational practice, and technical terms appropriate to the assignments.	20
7. Peace Corps orientation, to include aims and organization of the Peace Corps and the volunteer's role within it.	20
8. Instruction in the philosophy, strategy, tactics, and menace of communism.	15
Total	480

Source: Fairfield, *Training Plan*, p. 6, PCDRF.

United States. Despite this, some volunteers were impatient with the many hours devoted to American studies. Some denounced the "propaganda" that went with it and the "unnecessary emphasis" on communism as a major threat to world peace. A former volunteer described the courses on American studies as "a lot of academic garbage."[13] Other volunteers complained that the same number of hours spent on language training was devoted to the teaching of Peace Corps aims.

It was not uncommon to stress the East-West ideological conflict during the early 1960s. This emphasis was in line with some of the motives for the establishment of the Peace Corps Agency. Defending the position, the training team often informed the trainees that their training program was designed to go beyond the teaching responsibility by preparing them for unforeseen circumstances in Cameroon. In short, they had to become "whole persons." The volunteers, however, were cautioned that they must consider themselves as teachers and not as "ideological warrior[s], junior diplomat[s], or jungle adventurer[s]."[14]

Fairfield understood the difference between American and West Cameroonian educational systems. Utilizing his wit and copies of previous Peace Corps training programs from universities such as Harvard and Columbia, Fairfield skillfully crafted out the technical aspect of the program. Examinations in West Cameroon were based on the General Certificate of Education (GCE) administered by the University of London; and in East Cameroon exams were modeled after the French baccalaureate, though administered locally.

Understanding that most of the volunteers were totally unfamiliar with the British system, Fairfield obtained from Cameroonian education officials copies of the syllabi of the Grade III and Grade II teacher training colleges, the regulations and syllabi of the GCE, and the London City and Guilds syllabi and textbooks generally used in Cameroon to teach the various disciplines, including English, mathematics, history, geography, and economics. Secondary school students in Cameroon often had personal copies of syllabi which they considered to be their prized possessions. Because of the importance students attached to syllabi, they expected their teachers to organize their lectures based on what was stated in the syllabus. Teachers who failed to do so were labeled "poor teachers." In some cases students would not hesitate to inform such instructors that what they were teaching was not in the syllabus, and thus was uninteresting and irrelevant.

To emphasize the importance of the syllabus, the training officers cautioned the volunteers to "be sensitive to potential changes and developments" and were told that "their role was to assist rather than to determine" any changes. It was necessary for the training officers to stress the importance of using the syllabi, because in Cameroon "examinations and certificates" made "all the difference in the world between a mean and limited existence or a fortunate one."[15]

Struggling to understand the Cameroonian educational program, volunteers were also introduced to the methods of learning in Cameroon. Rote learning was still very popular in West Cameroon.

For this reason volunteers were informed that "much teaching is of the assign-study-recite-examine route, closely tied to the textbook." Additionally, they were taught that much emphasis was "placed upon keeping voluminous class notes and upon preparation primarily for examinations."[16]

Equally important was "the role of the teacher" in Cameroon. Though there existed "no guaranteed system for teaching non-teachers how to teach," Fairfield called on the volunteers to improvise and make do with the limited teaching resources in Cameroon. Teaching aids were almost completely absent. Without calculators, the trainees had to learn how to use such things as sticks and stones to teach simple addition, subtraction, and multiplication. Volunteers were encouraged to be innovative in creating teaching tools, such as "their own play equipment, using maps and charts and pictures instead of more refined audio-visual materials." In the final analysis, Fairfield informed the volunteers that as teachers in Cameroon their motto should be "adjustment, improvisation, creativeness, ingenuity." To avoid any ridicule of the system from the volunteers, Fairfield pointed to some of the inherent weaknesses of the American education system, by stating that "it is too concerned with degrees, with A's and B's, rather than with knowledge."[17] Each educational system had its flaws.

The volunteers in the training session came from varied backgrounds, and some were ill equipped for the job. But their determination was encouraging. More than 70 percent of the trainees had no teaching experience. Though all but four of the volunteers had at least a first degree (B.A. or B.S.), their knowledge of basic facts in world affairs was punctuated with myths.

Despite the high motivation the recruits showed, members of the training team nursed strong reservations about the trainees' ability to serve as America's "unofficial ambassadors." The real problem, the training officials wrote, was "how to develop sophistication in eight to ten weeks, especially among recent graduates who, for the most part, have been living in a world affairs vacuum." Fairfield, in an interview with journalist Robert C. Clapp, expressed his dissatisfaction with the trainees' knowledge. Following the interview, Clapp wrote, "With only eight weeks in which to train the volunteers, he [Fairfield] went on, it was discovered that they were amazingly ignorant of the very basic workings of our governmental system although they were about to teach others." Almost 50 percent of the volunteers were ignorant of the basic facts of American government and history. Few displayed skills and knowledge of the various disciplines before the training began. Also, the miscellaneous nature of the group presented the training officers with organizational problems, more especially as the training team wished to see the trainees go overseas.[18]

Compounding the early difficulties faced by Fairfield and his training team were the problems of discipline. Less than a week after the trainees arrived in Athens, several professors were "shocked by their [students'] naivete and lack of self-discipline." Both the students of Ohio University and the residents of Athens had "cause to wonder" at the "lack of discipline, in and out of class" among the volunteers. The cliques formed in the early part of the training only called for more criticism from the local people and the training officers. The cliques contributed to the organizational nightmares of the training officials. "Cliques among volunteers are detrimental to the whole," Gebauer wrote.[19]

Spending their first summer out of college in a tedious training program was not what these recent graduates had originally planned. The volunteers were frustrated by the tight schedule given to them. To ease their pain, they turned to humor. "Although Sargent Shriver is our leader, we are NOT S.S. men," they joked. Some even changed the name of the agency to "Peace Corpse." But the lack of discipline and the negative remarks were more than compensated for by the "good spirit and high motivation" of the volunteers.[20] In fact, all concerned enjoyed the bickering.

A volunteer's typical day began at 6:00 A.M. and continued until 10:00 P.M. The luxury of midday rest was never allowed. The daily routine was similar, and the entire week, with the exception of Sunday, followed a planned schedule (see table 5).

Such a tight schedule was necessary if the volunteers hoped to attain the objectives assigned to them in the Peace Corps Act. Priority was given to technical and English-language skills, after all the volunteers had to perform their teaching jobs in English.

Since the volunteers had received degrees from American universities, it was policy to emphasize the major differences between American English and that spoken in Cameroon. As a former colony of Britain, West Cameroonians had learned English from their British masters. Significant differences in spelling, sentence construction, and pronunciation existed. Volunteers were introduced to new spellings of familiar words—"centre" for *center*, "organisation" for

Table 5. Volunteers' Timetable

Time	Monday	Tuesday	Wednesday	Thursday	Friday	Saturday	Sunday
7–8:30	Physical	P.Ed.	P.Ed.	P.Ed.	P.Ed.	P.Ed.	
9–10	Area	Area	Area	Area	Area	Technical	
10–11	Area	Area	Area	Area	Area	Technical	
11–12	Technical	Technical	Technical	Technical	Technical	Technical	
Lunch							
1–2	World	Area	Study-Health	Area	World	Field	
2–3	World	Area	Study	Area	World	Field	
3–4	Technical	Technical	Study	World	Area	Field	
4–5	Technical	Technical	Study	Study	Area		
Dinner							
7:30–	Peace Corps orientation	Swimming	Panel	Study	Study	American folk and West African dance	

Source: Fairfield, *Training Plan*, p. 6.

organization, and so on. They were also taught different pronunciations of words such as "schedule" and "aluminum."[21] It was as though the volunteers were learning anew the basics of English grammar.

Complicating the language problem was Cameroon's new experience in bilingualism. It was becoming a tradition for some Cameroonians to use both French and English in one sentence, a language which was quickly nicknamed "franglais."[22] To ease the burden of the language lessons, Ohio University subscribed to two Cameroonian newspapers, the *Cameroon Times* and *La Presse du Cameroun,* which were used in the training session.

Also of importance was the emphasis on international studies, American government, and contemporary American problems. As "ambassadors of democracy" the volunteers were charged with the responsibility of spreading the good word on American government. Even some volunteers who had made A's and B's in American government and history courses were surprised to discover the major and minor gaps in their understanding of those subjects. As a result, the training team had to ensure that the volunteers mastered facts on American democracy.

Instruction also followed on the most urgent domestic problems in the United States. The volunteers were to be prepared to deal with questions on the "failures and the tensions in American life in the twentieth century," Fairfield wrote. And such problems were numerous. The problem of racism was given the highest priority. Concluding that American racism ran contrary to the widely publicized principles of democracy, the training officers prepared the volunteers for questions on this delicate subject. Topics such as "know your Little Rock facts," "integration: token or reality," "alternative theories of Negro behavior," and "significant achievements of the American Negro" became important study and discussion subjects. Trainees were informed that racism and discrimination ran contrary to the ideals of American democracy and that the government was committed to eliminating these twin evils from the society. To emphasize the magnitude of the problem, extracts from Cameroonian newspapers on the problem were distributed to the volunteers. In one of the assignments on "critical thinking," volunteers were given this extract from the *Cameroon Times:*

> Events in Alabama, U.S.A., where over 6000 defenseless
> Negroes have been arrested and thrown into jail, because they
> held demonstrations against segregation, have come as a surprise to only those who had erroneously regarded the United
> States as a free nation.
>
> The story of the American Negro is grim: In most of the
> Southern States, the Negro hasn't the franchise, he is barred
> from attending some of the State Universities, he is not allowed
> to worship God in the same church with the white man. . . .
>
> All this is happening in the United States. Yes, the United
> States. The country whose leader tells the world everyday that
> America is not only a democratic country but she is the leader
> of the so-called "free world." I am always amused when their
> statesmen trumpet this view.
>
> America, leader of the "free world" when twenty million
> Negroes are flagrantly denied their legitimate rights? This is
> not withstanding, the U.S. has taken the lead in criticizing the

governments of other countries for being undemocratic. . . . In Africa, when globe-trotting U.S. leaders are asked about the plight of the Negroes they usually tell us the Washington government is working relentlessly to improve the status of the negroes. . . . Far from dissuading the state government from depriving the Negroes of their rights, the federal government, by refusing to take action against those governments, is apparently lending moral support to the criminals.[23]

Such was the responsibility the volunteers had beyond their teaching assignments. Cameroonians were—and still are—curious and critical, likely to ask questions about the racial situation in the United States. Volunteers were to be equipped for interrogation.

Fearing the effect on the volunteers of not having access to the traditional American luxuries of cars, refrigerators, water system toilets, television, movies, telephones, and more, the Reverend Paul Gebauer was brought in to share his thirty-year experience in Cameroon. The Baptist minister understood the culture and the terrain of Cameroon. Utilizing his numerous slides, Gebauer informed the volunteers about some of the realities of life in Cameroon. They would have to do without some of what they considered necessities for the next two years, Gebauer said.

Initially the volunteers were shocked by the scenes of latrines, rugged roads, thatch houses, naked and barefooted children running around and by the absence of cars, television, and skyscrapers. However, the scenes in the slides were not too unfamiliar for some of the volunteers who had spent time in rural America, where they had read about and seen a similar life-style. But the slides renewed the spirit of determination in the volunteers.

The volunteers were also introduced to the various meals and eating habits in Cameroon. Food such as fufu, garri, cassava, cocoyams, and yams were served to them. The volunteers had to put fast food, such as hamburgers, on hold. The food, legends, scenes, and culture were new, but the volunteers were ready to adapt. Spirits were high.

The training session guaranteed that volunteers were in top physical condition before departing for Cameroon. They received vaccinations against such tropical diseases as malaria, dysentery, yellow fever, and typhoid fever, and they had an elaborate physical education program. This program included long hours of treks, hikes, and push-ups. Trekking was for many volunteers something they only read about in novels, but it was the daily fare in Cameroon. It was common for Cameroonians to trek at least eight miles daily to work and back. Because the volunteers were required to live with the people, they had to be prepared for these long treks.

Perhaps the most tedious aspect of the physical education was the Outward Bound training. In August 1962 the volunteers went on a ten-mile hike over the Buckeye Trail from Murray City to Burr Oak Lake in Hocking County, Ohio. The road was rugged and the hike most tiring. Surprisingly, no volunteer was hurt during the hike. The only casualty was Daniel Muna, a Cameroonian, who was bitten by mosquitoes.[24]

To give the volunteers practical experience, Ohio University arranged with the Zanesville High School officials for the trainees to teach there. This became the first teaching experience for most of the volunteers. Supervisors pointed out the strengths and weaknesses in the volunteers' teaching.

The serious effort of the volunteers was often marred by uncertainty. Each time the psychologist and the psychiatrist appeared on campus, the volunteers became nervous. They never knew if they would be "selected out" or "selected in," especially as the psychiatrist played a central role in the selection process.

The questions asked by the psychologist and psychiatrist were nerve racking. Ridiculous questions—"Have you ever talked to God?" "Do you think your private parts are beautiful?"—were common. More frightening was that the volunteers never understood why such questions were asked.[25] During such periods, the amount of cigarette smoking, tobacco chewing, and Coke and coffee drinking all doubled among the volunteers.

The psychiatrist had become one of Fairfield's biggest problems. "Those psychiatrists operated from the standpoint that the volunteers were sick to begin with," Fairfield said. He added:

> I would try to get the Peace Corps to cease and desist using on-site psychiatric approach to evaluating PCV emotional stability. Having two psychiatrists, plus psychologists, involved in evaluation certainly created an atmosphere which was paranoid to say the very least . . . the system in use at the time did create a heavy cloud over the general scene.[26]

According to Fairfield, the approach of the psychiatrists to the trainees was unfair and hope shattering. Philip S. Cook, Peace Corps training evaluation officer, was quick to notice the problem between Fairfield and one of the psychiatrists. Cook considered Fairfield's program excellent and added that "so far [Fairfield] has collided with no one except a psychiatrist imported from Cincinnati." More annoying to Fairfield was that the psychiatrist who came once a week to Ohio University requested that the entire training schedule be adjusted to "the timing of his one-day visits." This clash eventually spilled over to personalities as the project director began "telling the Trainees to ignore the doctor's comments and activities."[27]

Four weeks into the training program, the psychiatrist called one of his meetings. The outcome was the dismissal of four volunteers from the training program. Fairfield could do little to reverse the decision. His hands were tied. The psychiatrist was answerable to Peace Corps-Washington, not to the project director at Ohio University. Frustrated by this, Fairfield spent more time during the training period compiling notes to use against the psychiatrist in his final training report.[28] Considering the strong camaraderie that already existed among the volunteers before the decision, they felt cheated when their colleagues were selected out. Many were angry but chose to remain silent. They never knew who would be next.

Following the rejection of the four volunteers, a sense of frustration grew in the training site. The remaining volunteers had done everything asked of them, but their departure to Cameroon was still uncertain. During the final selection, six more volunteers were selected out. It was a sad experience for those denied the opportunity to pursue their Peace Corps career. Many volunteers who suffered a similar fate thought that the so-called period of training and final selection was really "deselection." Moritz Thomsen, though he did not participate in this session, reflected on his experience in another training program and concluded that

> the training [period] . . . was a period of structural tension, of subtle and purposive torture in which it was calculated that the individual trainee would be forced to reveal himself. The purpose of the training was not to change your character but to discover it, not to toughen you up or to implant proper motivations for Peace Corps service but to find out what your motivations were. Many potentially good volunteers have been eliminated from the program, a lot of them because they never figured out what it was trying to do.[29]

Thomsen's assessment seems comparable to those of all training programs. The Ohio University training team regretted the large number of volunteers selected out. During the one-week break given those selected to prepare for their departure to Cameroon, another volunteer changed his mind and did not continue with Peace Corps services. Of the fifty-six volunteers originally selected for training, only thirty-nine finally left for service in West Cameroon. Four of the volunteers heading for Cameroon were tagged as "high-risk"; the selection officers were convinced that these four could not be effective Peace Corps volunteers.[30]

The trainees launched a series of complaints against the selection methods. "Selection was clandestine, [and] . . . plot-ridden," a volunteer stated. Another volunteer found the Peace Corps guilty of violating its policy of "flexibility." According to volunteers, the training and selection allowed for no flexibility. Some volunteers drew a comparison between the Peace Corps and the military when they said, "In the Army, they break you down at the beginning of training, then ease up . . . in the Peace Corps they never stopped breaking you down." More disappointing to the trainees was the method used to inform those "selected out." Though several methods were used to achieve this purpose, the volunteers in Athens generally knew "they were on the way out if we were called to see a certain psychologist." Commenting on the same subject, one volunteer quipped, "notification . . . at the dinner table was faster, but brother, was it brutal!" As a result of these grievances several volunteers put certain training officers, including Fairfield, on their "blacklist."

The volunteers were not alone in their complaints against the selection process. Fairfield did not disguise his frustration with the selection process. At the end of the training, he complained to Peace Corps-Washington about its constant intervention. The constant watch exercised by Washington made it difficult for the university to plan and develop a thorough academic program for the session.[31] It appeared Washington was more interested in observing its ground rules than providing the volunteers with the adequate educational training they deserved.

Frequent intervention by Peace Corps-Washington not only created periods of tension during the training but also compromised the academic freedom traditionally associated with universities. Following the training program, Fairfield informed Peace Corps-Washington that "if the university is supposed to perform a job of general education, then, it would seem to me that *no* tentative commitments should be made at the outset of the program." A committed disciple of academic freedom, Fairfield used his experience as Peace Corps project director to make a general plea to all universities associated with Peace Corps training programs. He succinctly wrote:

If the university is to maintain those freedoms and prerogatives which maximize educational creativity on the campus, it must insist upon a relationship with the Peace Corps that might be summarized: Cooperation, yes! Control, no![32]

Fairfield also complained that, in the early phase of the program, the Peace Corps representative on campus committed a "strategic error." He failed to realize that some volunteers would not succeed with the training program, and he ignored the responsibility of the Cameroon government in the distribution and assignment of the volunteers.[33] This was a blunder of the first magnitude. Additionally, nothing was done to replace the trainees "selected out," though West Cameroon had been promised fifty-six Peace Corps volunteers.

Disappointed by the failure of Washington officials to respond to his complaints, Fairfield wrote:

In short, if the Project Director of a university project could make one call to headquarters rather than a dozen calls (often without satisfactory result), he might be relieved of frustration. Also, it might be less expensive and more efficient. During the past three months I've often remarked, "People in Washington are too busy telephoning to answer a letter!" I make this as a constructive and not a destructive suggestion, for I am extremely sensitive to the crash nature of the Peace Corps, also the extraordinary complexity of the program.[34]

Fairfield also denounced the role played by the psychiatrist. In a series of letters to Peace Corps-Washington, Fairfield complained about the enormous authority assigned to the psychiatrist during the selection process. In his letter to Rogers Finch, he said flatly, "A psychiatrist should not play so central a role."[35] A psychiatrist who spent little time with the volunteers was, it seemed obvious, not qualified to decide who had to leave the program. But Fairfield's complaints did not reverse Washington's policy, as the Peace Corps Agency continued to insist that the psychiatrist was there to determine the emotional stability of the trainees.

The role of the psychiatrist also contributed to the lack of self-discipline among the volunteers. Volunteers often protested against the selection process. Additionally, the rush employed in the selection process caused qualified volunteers to be selected out. Jack Carmichael expressed his disappointment over one particular case in a letter to Fairfield: "There was a girl . . . who I felt should have been looked at a little longer before we selected her out," Carmichael wrote.[36]

Another source of disagreement between Washington and the Ohio University training team was over financing. Washington surprised the training team when it sent Air Force personnel to audit the training program. Instead of considering the Ohio University–Peace Corps contract in "global" terms, the auditors "talked in line-item terms."[37] These actions were resented at Ohio University.

Time was a deciding factor in all aspects of the training program. Though Fairfield mildly complained about this problem, he was nevertheless the person who organized the more than ten-hours-a-day schedule for the volunteers. The tight schedule deprived the volunteers of the opportunity to mingle and test their ability to establish human relations with the people of Athens. The people of the community regretted that they were unable to discuss and visit more often with the volunteers.

The training officers, in their attempt to make better teachers out of the volunteers, neglected significant aspects of Cameroonian society. Little was done to educate volunteers on how to communicate with the people in Cameroon who could neither speak nor understand English. Despite the numerous dialects in Cameroon, the Pidgin English language (Wes Cos) was widely spoken.[38] Pidgin English cut through language barriers and had become the unofficial language of all Cameroonians. Yet these volunteers received almost no training in Pidgin English. The Peace Corps volunteers often found themselves unable to communicate with Cameroonians outside the classroom. This flaw affected the objectives of winning friends and teaching the local people about the United States.

Another omission was the neglect of Cameroonian bilingualism. No attempt was made to teach the volunteers French. West Cameroon, though predominantly English-speaking, was already experiencing the rapid encroachment of the French language in the region. Francophones were quickly taking up residence in West Cameroon. Yet it was almost impossible for the volunteers to communicate effectively with French-speaking Cameroonians because most of the volunteers neither spoke nor understood French.

There were other, more serious flaws in Fairfield's program. Although Fairfield understood that more than 95 percent of the schools in West Cameroon were owned and managed by mission groups, no attempt was made to educate the trainees on how to conduct themselves in mission schools. While such experts on Cameroonian affairs as Harry Rudin, Victor T. Le Vine, and David Gardinier participated in the training program, their role was limited to a few lectures on Cameroonian history. Despite the emphasis on Cameroonian problems, volunteers acquired little knowledge of how to resolve them. The numerous copies of syllabi from schools in West Cameroon were given little attention. Teaching methods were heavily weighted at the expense of the acquisition of substantial knowledge of the various subjects. Referring to this, one volunteer observed that "the atmosphere for training created a strong motivation to be selected to go to Cameroon, however, it didn't really give us much idea of what Cameroon would really be like." She added, "Though several people were weeded out, the Ohio U. education teachers . . . didn't give us much idea of how to cope with Cameroonian students."[39]

Equally significant was that the trainers neglected to effectively employ Cameroonians in the training program. Though Cameroonians such as Daniel Muna and Flavius Martin were recruited to assist as "resource specialists," they were obviously the wrong choices for such a project. A son of S. T. Muna, a senior cabinet member in Cameroon, Daniel Muna knew little about the problems of the masses or the down-and-out. Trained in Nigeria before proceeding to the United States for further studies, Muna was unaware of the critical educational problems and completely uninformed about the poverty-stricken areas in his country. Other Cameroonians who participated in the training came from similar backgrounds. Jack Carmichael reflected on this and correctly stated that "the limit of the [training] program was that it was conducted stateside and there was little or no teaching by people from the host country."[40]

The need to acquire experts in the various subjects in some cases produced a backlash. Certain professors brought in were unable to develop lectures for such a crash program. A professor, in an attempt to teach the impossibly broad topic of African art, "got lost in Nigeria with material she could not handle." Another professor charged with the teaching of English as a second language seems to have failed to perform adequately. Similar complaints were registered against several other professors.[41]

But these criticisms should not undermine the potential of Fairfield's program. A major innovation by the Ohio University training team was to give the volunteers an opportunity to continue with graduate studies while performing their services. Volunteers could earn as many as six credit hours through individual research. The process had the impact of encouraging volunteers to pursue further studies. To assist the volunteers, Fairfield and the other professors wrote countless letters of recommendation for them. Though most volunteers failed to use the graduate-study opportunity, it nevertheless showed the commitment of the team to help them during and after the Peace Corps service.[42]

The thirty-nine volunteers who left for Cameroon in September 1962 were not without flaws, some of their own making and others originating from the training session. Yet their courage, determination, and ability to overcome nervousness during the training outweighed these flaws. These were the real pioneers of New Frontier diplomacy to Cameroon. Never had West Cameroon seen a group of young, ambitious people abandon their luxurious environment to come help other, less-fortunate people.

The spirit of hard work and timeless effort shown by Fairfield and his staff paid off. Operating in a vacuum, with no previous experience in Cameroon, the training officers did a fine job. Perhaps the only people who did not forgive the training officers were the volunteers selected out. Fairfield and his colleagues look back at those months and consider them some of the most exciting and useful of their careers. Whatever the rights and wrongs of Fairfield's training program, it established a foundation and guidelines for future training programs for Peace Corps-Cameroon.

Following Fairfield's program were two other sessions held in 1963 and 1964 at Ohio University for volunteers proceeding to Cameroon. The Peace Corps officials in Washington had by this time concluded that the Peace Corps Agency had to establish a permanent training center at Ohio University for volunteers going to Cameroon.[43]

The training programs for the next two years were directed by Professor Carl Denbow, a mathematician at Ohio University. Denbow's major advantage was that he did not operate in a vacuum as his predecessor had to do; as a keen observer of the first training program, he had the advantage of learning from its mistakes. Feedback from the field and further research on Cameroon were additional

Carl H. Denbow, coordinator of the Peace Corps training program; His Excellency John Ngu Foncha, vice president of Cameroon; and Russell A. Milliken, director of the Center for International Programs of Ohio University, discuss the Peace Corps-Cameroon project at Ohio University, June 1964. Courtesy of Carl H. Denbow's Peace Corps collection.

assets to Denbow's program, yet he followed the guidelines established by Fairfield.[44] The tight schedule, the hikes and camp life, the long treks, and the use of scholars in the field were all inherent assets of the program.

Denbow was lucky that the volunteers who participated in his training programs were slightly older and more mature than the earlier ones. As a result, the problem of self-discipline was minimized. More important was that the teaching of Pidgin English became a requirement. To attain this objective, Denbow brought into the teaching staff Professor Gilbert Schneider, a linguist who had spent more than a decade in Cameroon. To ensure the effectiveness of the training in Pidgin English, trainees were assigned names in that language. Some of the names were Palaba, Was-net, Sofa, Moto-boy, and Panya.[45] Combining Schneider's knowledge with that of Paul Gebauer, Denbow was able to plan an elaborate but practical program.

After 1962, the Cameroon government also requested volunteers for community development projects. While the teaching objectives remained unchanged, the goal of community development was "to assist Cameroon communities to develop their resources of cooperative self-help and democratically sponsored and planned community betterment projects."[46] Such projects included the construction of bridges, roads, schools, houses, and hospitals; surveying; and improvements in sanitation and the digging of latrines. Agriculture extension workers were also needed to teach Cameroonian farmers new techniques. Therefore, the training of teachers and community development officers was quite demanding.

All this was accomplished with the introduction of new practical methods of learning. The program was occasionally "staggered" to ensure that experts available only at certain times were given the opportunity to lecture whenever they showed up. Specialists on Cameroon, such as Schneider, Gebauer, and students from Cameroon brought in for the training, spent long hours with the volunteers. During leisure and meal times, the volunteers bombarded these experts with all types of questions on Cameroon. It was routine that such discussions were carried out exclusively in Pidgin English.[47]

To ensure the practicality of the training, mock Cameroonian scenes were established. Scenes of Cameroonian markets were created (similar to American flea markets); they were more attuned to Cameroonian markets than any American store. Volunteers were required to sell and haggle in Pidgin English. Such Cameroonian foods as garri, yams, and cassava were sold, and the volunteers were taught how to prepare and eat food the Cameroonian way. While some used kerosene stoves, others prepared the food over burning wood and ate with their fingers. In fact, the training site was a miniature Cameroon in the United States, and Gilbert Schneider's simple exclamation summed it up: "It was exciting."[48]

Equally helpful to Carl Denbow's program was the feedback from volunteers already in Cameroon. Writing to Denbow, one volunteer suggested:

> Teacher training should comprise by far the major part of the program. The main problem is that you need people who are intimately familiar with Cameroonian educational problems. Ex-volunteers would be ideal. For example we were grievously misled in one important respect. Discipline is *very much* a factor

in teaching over here. We were given the mistaken notion that the students were models for good behavior, diligence and responsibility. . . . This is simply not true. If I had more space I could go into more detail on specific types of disciplinary problems, but that would take a small treatise.[49]

Denbow heeded this advice, and several professors were brought in to deliver a series of authoritative lectures on different types of discipline in a classroom. Also, the Ohio University team asked the volunteers already teaching in West Cameroon to evaluate a typical Cameroonian student. Responding to this request, one volunteer wrote:

In general I have found the Cameroonian student to be highly motivated and one of average or better ability. He is one who craves any kind of knowledge but lacks the experience and various cultural contacts which would enable him to fully understand new ideas. . . . A student would not think twice about questioning a tutor about the subject matter which is being taught and to even argue that something else is more important than what is being taught. . . . One of their favorite pastimes is trying to ask questions which seem to have no relevance to the lesson, but have the effect of putting the teacher on the spot. Once one becomes aware of this little trick—it is easily remedied.[50]

Such an assessment of the typical Cameroon student exposed in the most vivid manner the racism and the feelings of superiority imbedded in some of the volunteers. The typical Cameroonian student, according to some volunteers, is "one who craves any kind of knowledge but lacks the experience and various cultural contacts." This biased and shortsighted assessment glaringly reveals such bigotry. The irony of the matter was that volunteers whose knowledge of Cameroon was almost nil suddenly considered themselves well qualified to make judgments about that country's students and culture after living there for less than a year. However, such comments did not detract from the training sessions.

In the training sessions of 1964, letters written by Cameroon secondary students were brought to the volunteers. These letters, which emphasize the students' appreciation for volunteer services, boosted the morale of the trainees. Additionally, Denbow was able to convince John Ngu Foncha, Cameroon's vice president, to visit Ohio University during his official visit to the United States in 1964. Foncha's visit

Paul Gebauer; Douglas C. Kelly, Peace Corps volunteer leader; and Jack Carmichael, Ohio University's overseas coordinator for West Cameroon, converse with two Cameroonian officials, Stephen Tita and Daniel Ebongue. Courtesy of Carl H. Denbow's Peace Corps collection.

added flavor to the training. Another important Cameroonian official who visited and lectured in the training was A. D. Mengot, the director of education in West Cameroon. David Dwyer, William Kane, Douglas Lapp, and Terence and Alice Sidney, all returned Peace Corps volunteers from Cameroon, came and shared their "immediate experience" with the trainees.[51]

To resolve an earlier problem that Fairfield faced, Denbow invited people familiar to the Cameroonian educational system to participate in the training. Included in this group were J. C. Cairns, adviser of English teaching to the government of Eastern Nigeria; Father John Courtney, Sasse College, Cameroon; Father James Toba, Sacred Heart College, Mankon; and the Reverend and Mrs. Kermit Overton, Cameroon missionaries. Cameroonian students who were in the United States, such as Theresa Atang, Edwin Fondo, Susan Allo, Germanus Nchanji, and Simon Mpondo, were brought into the training as consultants. Lawrence Williams, Peace Corps representative in Cameroon, and his assistant, Lawrence O'Brien, visited Ohio University during the training and provided lectures on their firsthand experience in Cameroon.[52]

Trainees gave Denbow high scores for the training program. The presence of Gebauer, Schneider, the returned volunteers, and the talented Cameroonians encouraged the volunteers. These volunteers developed close friendships with one another and commended Denbow for creating an atmosphere in which such relationships were possible. Shortly before departing for Cameroon, Margo Tyrolt, "a confident, capable . . . [trainee who] could outrun most men and excelled in sports," expressed her satisfaction with the training in a letter to Denbow. She wrote:

> Meeting you and P.G. [Paul Gebauer] was the delicious, undeserved frosting for the . . . cake. P.G.'s capacity to love and to find life good is so refreshing in a world of cynical adults and you know what he means to a group. But I'm not sure you know how important you were to the Cam. III group. I've never had a "boss" or teacher that I respected or admired more. . . . I'm apprehensive—excited—a little frightened; but this summer has given me a new confidence I lacked before and I am hopeful about what I can do. Further I am optimistic about what Cam. III as a whole can do—but then how can we fail with your legacy of love.[53]

Tyrolt expressed the feelings of most of the volunteers who participated in Denbow's training program. Like several others, she was an exemplary trainee, Denbow wrote.

But the Peace Corps psychiatrist continued to uphold his reputation. Midway through the training programs, some volunteers were selected out; this process was repeated at the end of each session. Volunteers often reacted heatedly to this selection process. Occasionally they threatened to respond with strikes. Like Fairfield, Denbow launched a bitter complaint to Washington against the psychiatrist, but the Peace Corps Agency took no action.[54] The agency was convinced that the psychiatrist played an important role in the entire selection process.

Despite all its assets, Denbow's program was troubled by certain weaknesses. Like Fairfield's, Denbow's program continued to emphasize teaching methods at the expense of the assimilation of basic knowledge of the subjects the volunteers were expected to teach in Cameroon. Perhaps the biggest weakness was the training of volunteers to serve in community development projects. Volunteers were half-fed with development theories and were taken to such remote camps as Camp Harvida for the practical aspect of the training. Privately owned Camp Harvida was located about twenty-five miles east of Athens. At the camp the "volunteers were lost" and could not "handle situations away from classroom, away from academic exercises, away from organized care of the body." Such inadequacies were neglected by the training team, as little was done to sufficiently prepare the volunteers for the "great difficulties" in Cameroon after Camp Harvida. Also, the training team failed to utilize slides of current scenes in Cameroon in the training.[55] Perhaps these slides would have given the community development trainees a realistic picture of the type of jobs they had to perform in Cameroon.

Simultaneously, the training for volunteers going to East Cameroon was taking place at Oberlin College in 1963. Oberlin College was awarded the training contract because of "its excellent record in teaching French."[56] The college had a more elaborate program because it trained volunteers proceeding to French-speaking West African countries; volunteers going to Gabon and Ivory Coast also participated in the program. They received training to take up teaching and community development positions in those West African countries.

Like the Ohio University program, the scheduling was tight. Professor Donald R. Reich, the Oberlin project director, ensured that the trainees were kept busy most of the day. A typical day for these trainees began at seven in the morning and continued until ten at night. Occasionally, certain seminars lasted until midnight. While the basics in other subjects were taught, most of the attention was devoted to teaching French. Reich stressed that "failure to become proficient in French . . . will be the only one-shot flunk in the Oberlin training program." Volunteers were also given important facts about the sensitivity of Africans. The most notable example was "don't ever call Africans Negroes, they resent it."[57]

As expected, the Peace Corps psychiatrist was there as a significant official and continued to play a central role in the selection process. Expressing her feeling about the Washington people, Mikell Kloeters, a trainee for Cameroon, noted, "It is a scary thought to know you're being watched and observed all the time and being tested and analyzed. . . . The possibility of going to Africa seems kind of lost and vague at times—far off in some distant future."[58]

She spoke for the entire group. All the same, the constant scrutiny did not deter their efforts. The trainees continued to work hard. Responding to the tedious training, one volunteer observed that "it is going to be a long two years." A reporter who covered the session tacitly expressed his feeling at the end of the program that "it is a pleasure to be back to the old-fashioned eight-hour day."[59]

In later years the training sessions were transferred to Columbia and Boston universities. Peace Corps-Washington decided against establishing a permanent Peace Corps training home at Ohio University for volunteers going to Cameroon. Problems had developed between the trainers in Ohio University and Peace Corps-Washington. Ohio University officials had complained about the psychiatric examinations because they weeded out capable volunteers from the program. Also, these exams led to additional expenses for which Peace Corps-Washington refused to reimburse the university. Further complaints created a "suspicion within the minds of the people in Washington" that the Ohio University team was incapable of doing the job. By midway into the 1964 training session, Ohio University officials had had enough. When the university hired a contractor's overseas representative (COR) at a salary of $15,000, instead of the maximum of $14,000 allowed by the Peace Corps Agency, Washington stated that it could pay only $13,000. For Ohio University officials, Peace Corps-Washington had "screwed up." Because of Peace Corps bureaucracy and financial complications, Ohio University officials decided to tell Shriver and Peace Corps-Washington that "they wanted out of the damn Peace Corps business."[60] So ended the university's dream of hosting a permanent Peace Corps training program for Cameroon volunteers.

After 1966, the Peace Corps began training its volunteers in the host country, but the former trainers at Ohio University were long disappointed with the agency for giving the contracts of 1965 and 1966 to other universities. They could be proud, however, that the main guidelines for the training were those formulated at Ohio University.

Today, some Ohio University professors still believe that the program was taken away from the university because the Peace Corps had become too bureaucratic and cost minded. But most of all, they remember the excitement, the joy, and the ability to improvise and inject fresh ideas into a new program. Perhaps Carl Denbow spoke for all of them when he stated, "Those were the good old days."[61] Fairfield, Denbow, Carmichael, Gebauer, Schneider, Reich, and others are the forgotten members of the New Frontier administration. They trained, guided, and assisted the trainees, and it was time for the Peace Corps volunteers to utilize their acquired skills in Cameroon.

5

The Volunteers as Teachers

In the plane, as they departed for Cameroon on September 12, 1962, the Peace Corps volunteers rehearsed, recited, and chanted an anthem to the tune of "The Battle Hymn of the Republic":

> We started out in Athens just about eight weeks ago,
> To strengthen mind and body, and in teaching skills to grow.
> The more we've learned, the more we've seen how much
>   there is to know.
> Here we come, West Cameroon.
> (Chorus) PCVs will stand together,
>   PCVs will stand together,
>   PCVs will stand together,
>   Here we come, West Cameroon.
> We go to teach believing education will create
> A world without the fear of war and people without hate.
> When we begin to think and learn, then freedom cannot wait.
> Here we come, West Cameroon!

The flight was long and boring but occasionally flavored with last-minute gossip on Cameroon. The volunteers slept, woke, ate, and talked. Finally, on September 13, the plane descended and landed on a narrow strip cut out of the tropical vegetation. The pilot announced the long-awaited news: "Welcome to Douala! *Souyez la bienvenue à Douala.*" It was time for "Here We Come, West Cameroon," one more time.

Wasting little time in Douala, the volunteers boarded another plane for Tiko airport. The scene in Tiko reflected the season of the year. Thunder and pouring rain gave the volunteers their first taste of the tropical climate. Waiting for the volunteers were Chester Carter, American Peace Corps representative in Cameroon, and distinguished Cameroonian officials. They huddled together in their raincoats under multicolored umbrellas. From Tiko, the volunteers traveled in a motorcade to Buea, where they received the red carpet treatment from West Cameroonian officials.[1]

The original schedule required the volunteers to spend a week in Buea for in-country orientation before proceeding to their various stations. This plan was adjusted because the volunteers arrived in Cameroon at the time when schools were about to resume. Only two days were devoted to the in-country orientation.[2]

The orientation involved visiting with Cameroonian officials and educators. The volunteers toured parts of the Buea community and the neighboring towns such as Mutengene and Victoria. During this time the volunteers had their first taste of the real "kontri chop" (Cameroonian food). The early views of this town acted as a grim reminder of all the training slides and talks. Buea was the capital of West Cameroon and, with its glittering German-constructed buildings, was in many ways more modernized than most towns in the region. Yet the volunteers failed to disguise the initial shock at what they saw. One volunteer wrote:

> Three of us took off for the village, the native part of Buea and our first venture into the "real" traditional Africa. In spite of all you hear and read, the initial shock of the poor conditions is a little disconcerting—people urinating along the road, filth and dirt everywhere, mud floors and houses, food lying out in the open attracting insects, children naked and barefoot, crumbling homes, no screens or doors, chickens, goats, a pig. . . . But also there are signs of progress—schools and churches, a health center, numerous autos, colorful rubber sandals, brilliant multi-colored umbrellas, all sorts of .10 cent store goods in the little shops—boxes of TIDE soap. The women were clad in the loud, often unmatching clothes that seem so typical. . . . All the natives carry fantastically huge loads on their heads. . . . It is absolutely unbelievable the size of those loads at times. Even the kids do it. It is accompanied by a very curious swinging of hips side by side.[3]

Describing her first experience, Peace Corps volunteer Mary Asmundson Dunbar wrote:

> We were in a state of shock. We were exhausted from 22 hours in the plane, we were told to be dressed up so we went on a bus tour to the palm oil factory [CDC] in Victoria and elsewhere in high heeled shoes, etc. It was pouring rain and very muddy, so our clothes and shoes got drenched. The workers at the palm oil factory had nothing but shorts on and one was so raggedy that a cheek (buttock) showed through the back of his pants.

We felt miserable and out of place. Also, the houses looked like huts to us, and we were surprised at the poverty, at least I was.[4]

Other volunteers wrote similar letters back to the United States. These letters remained private, thereby avoiding the outcry which had occurred over a volunteer's description of Nigeria. The shanty scenes and way of life did not discourage the volunteers, but they realized that there was much work to be done. As one volunteer succinctly put it:

There is also something "soul-shaking" about all this. As you drive up the road from Ombe into Mutengene, you see the thatched roof houses, the people living their very simple existence. When you think back to the electronics course, you are teaching to the sons and brothers of those people [*sic*]. Here is the "leap" into the 20th century that the historians are talking about displayed in rather sharp relief.[5]

Following the orientation, the volunteers were moved to their various stations. Adjusting to the new environment and assignment was not easy. Even the means of transportation to the different stations was disheartening. The five Jeeps the Peace Corps Agency promised had not arrived in Cameroon. (When the Jeeps did arrive, they were of little service in heavy rainfall, and they earned the nickname of "green bathtubs.") Some volunteers had to rely on AID transportation to get to their stations. Those who did not have access to AID transportation used the Cameroonian Mami Wagon, which was the most popular means of transportation in the country.[6]

Besides transportation, there were other problems. Many volunteers discovered that they were assigned to teach subjects they neither took in college nor prepared for in training. One of the Peace Corps volunteers sent to Cameroon Protestant College in Bali was assigned to teach a course "which he had flunked in college." Another volunteer, assigned to Government School-Kumba, was asked to teach economics, a subject he never studied in college. A volunteer sent to Queen of the Holy Rosary School-Okoyong was given the impossible task of teaching French, a subject she was ill-equipped to teach, while another person, whose knowledge of European history "left much to be desired," was assigned to teach that subject. Other volunteers experienced the same problem. Local college officials defended these assignments by stating that they were never informed until very late "whom they were to get, either in terms of subject matter or sex of PCVs."[7] The volunteers were paying the price for administrative floundering.

Also of concern during these early weeks was the problem of housing. Though the Peace Corps Agency had supplied some funds for the construction of houses for the volunteers, most mission schools had undertaken this task without financial assistance. In the absence of any information from Washington and Ohio, mission schools constructed houses for one sex. Yet both sexes were sent to many of these schools. The problem was most evident in the Cameroon Protestant College (CPC) in Bali. CPC Bali had accommodations for either males or females, but not for both. The principal was surprised when two men and two women were sent to the school. The same problem surfaced in Great Soppo when three males and one female were sent to use the house constructed for four people of the same sex. Not surprisingly, the Baptist Mission refused to tolerate such a living arrangement. Some of the houses in communities such as Bojongo were still under construction. As a result, Andy and Kathy Edwards, assigned to Bojongo, had to spend several weeks with the missionaries. In December 1962, Fairfield visited the Edwardses in Bojongo and later wrote that "the Edwardses have been forced to live and eat in the same house with the fathers running the school. The physical conditions were shabby by almost any standard." The official concluded that they were living under "deplorable conditions."[8] Their house was not completed until January 1963.

Perhaps the most disgruntled people were the officials at the College of Science in Bambui, where Peace Corps volunteers were promised for the school.[9] After constructing excellent houses for them, officials learned that the Peace Corps had reversed its decision and no volunteers were coming to Bambui. Through administrative blundering, no one had informed the principal, Brother Ephrem in Bambui, that his school would receive no volunteers, an error that provoked anger among local officials against the Peace Corps.

Adding to the headaches was the acute shortage of household equipment. When the volunteers arrived, there was almost nothing in the new houses. Beds, mattresses, dishes, stoves, blinds, and other household equipment were unavailable. Washington failed in its responsibility to furnish the houses as promised. The volunteers found themselves in the embarrassing situation of borrowing dishes, stoves, and other household necessities simply "to stay afloat each day."[10] The young volunteers resented this situation.

Even the basic tools required for teaching were absent. Once in Cameroon, the volunteers discovered the serious shortage of books. West Cameroon had few bookstores, and most of the books available had little relevance to the subjects the volunteers were assigned to teach. A problem for all, the lack of textbooks was particularly severe for those volunteers who were expected to teach subjects they never took in college. Realizing this, the volunteers requested "emergency help." But the books did not arrive soon enough, as they were sent by ship.[11]

All these problems gave rise to impatience and antagonism, and these emotions were demonstrated in the Chester Carter affair. Though the first batch of volunteers was to serve exclusively in West Cameroon, Chester Carter, the American Peace Corps representative in the Cameroons, had an office in Yaounde, in East Cameroon, upon the insistence of the American ambassador. At a time when more than 95 percent of the volunteers were stationed in West Cameroon, the ambassador's decision was not pragmatic and hurt volunteer morale, as many of them were quick to point out that they were "leaderless." Others compared their situation to "a rudderless boat." Locating the Peace Corps office in Yaounde obviously gave the ambassador more authority over the daily operations of the agency, but this action had an adverse effect on the duties the volunteers were sent to Cameroon to perform. Complicating matters was the fact that the communication link between Yaounde and towns in West Cameroon was totally inadequate. This location made it difficult for Carter to fulfill his duties, which required constant visits to the respective schools of the volunteers. Not surprisingly, Carter failed to execute this function. Unaware that Carter had little to do with the decision to locate his office in Yaounde, the volunteers heaped all the blame on him. At a conference held in Buea on December 8, 1962, one volunteer commented, "Chester Carter, Chester Carter, let's see. . . . Wasn't he a man we met somewhere back in Ohio?" Carter's inability to fulfill his responsibilities hurt his image among the volunteers. Adding to Carter's problems was his wife's dislike of Cameroon. She could not adjust to local conditions. Jack Carmichael emphasized this problem when he wrote that

> much of Chet's difficulty . . . was due to the fact that his wife
> was unhappy and unable to adjust. . . . Although you are hiring

the man and not his wife, the lady of the house plays an important part in how the old man performs.[12]

The Peace Corps eventually transferred Carter out of Cameroon to
Tunisia in 1963 and replaced him with an attorney, Larry Williams.

The volunteers were also disappointed with the performance of
the Peace Corps doctor, who failed to familiarize himself with the
medical facilities in West Cameroon. At one time there were several
volunteers with health problems, including high fever, intestinal up-
sets, venereal disease, and aching bodies, but the doctor did not show
up to treat these cases. The doctor also refused to treat the servants of
the volunteers. Defending his position, he stated, "I'm not going out
of my way to build up a practice among expatriots [sic], nationals, missionaries or anybody." And as if his medical attitude were not enough
of a problem, his reckless driving had a negative impact on the Peace
Corps image in Cameroon as a whole.[13]

The volunteers also registered several complaints about the excessive drinking habit of the officer who "escorted" them to Cameroon,
which was unknown to the Peace Corps representative there. His
drinking problem made the volunteers skeptical of "the image of the
PC . . . if it persisted in using such a person for the function in question." The man's primary concern was alcohol and not the welfare of
the Peace Corps, the volunteers stated. One volunteer described him
as "the epitome of the Ugly American."[14]

These early problems resulted in a personality clash among Peace
Corps officials in Cameroon. Chester Carter's inaccessibility, the es-
cort's drinking problem, the doctor's possible neglect of the sick, and
Jack Carmichael's complaints against other Peace Corps officials in
Cameroon were issues that required immediate attention. As Peace
Corps representative, Carter, on December 9, 1962, called a meeting
to resolve the problems. At that meeting, the officials decided that
Carter had to move to Buea, and the doctor "should go." Eventually
the doctor was transferred out of Cameroon. Personality conflicts also
plagued the early efforts of the volunteers. These problems came to a
head at the Queen of the Holy Rosary Secondary School in Okoyong
where three women were teaching. The conflict among these volunteers was intense. The excessive religiosity of one of the volunteers
was resented by the other two. Tempers flared as arguments ranged
even so far as to the question of whether God himself had sent this
volunteer on the mission. Divine mandate or not, a volunteer at

Okoyong became one of the early volunteers to drop out of Peace Corps services in Cameroon.[15]

At the Cameroon Protestant College in Bali, four other Peace Corps volunteers got into "one another's hair." To resolve the problem, one was transferred to Sasse. The problematic cliques that volunteers had formed during training continued in Cameroon, though Carter intervened and told the volunteers either to straighten up or be dismissed from the Peace Corps.[16]

The early months of the Peace Corps service in Cameroon did not meet the standards expected by Washington. The reality of the country, the housing problem, the laissez-faire attitude of the Peace Corps representative, the poor transportation, and the shortage of household equipment and books constituted new challenges. But the volunteers remained committed to fulfilling their mission. By December 1962, they had settled in and adjusted to their new environment. After the first three months, the volunteers prepared to begin the second term with optimism. Even the tone of their letters to the United States changed. After their Christmas vacation, they eagerly awaited the beginning of the new term with new confidence. Morale was high. Ohio University continued its useful functions of encouraging the volunteers and sending them books.[17] Volunteers assigned to unfamiliar subjects became more confident. They were encouraged in their efforts by the increasing concern and appreciation Cameroonians showed for their services. The teacher problem in Cameroon was being solved.

Perhaps the most immediate and significant achievement of the Peace Corps educators was the reopening of the Government Trade Centre (GTC) in Ombe. GTC-Ombe had closed down when most of its teachers, British expatriates, left the country after reunification. But in 1962, the AID took over the administration of the school. Sheldon Cole, an AID worker, became the principal of GTC for the next four years. Cole arrived in West Cameroon in 1960 as an employee of the United States International Cooperation Administration (ICA). His first assignment in Cameroon was at the Government Teacher Training Centre (GTTC) in Kumba, where his achievements were impressive. Cole established the manual arts program at GTTC. When the ICA was reorganized under the Kennedy administration into the United States Agency for International Development (AID), Cole remained in Cameroon as an employee of AID. Because the

Peace Corps volunteer Daniel L. Teare and Cameroonian students in a mechanical drawing class at the Government Technical Centre, Ombe, 1964. Courtesy of the Media Center, Peace Corps Office, Washington, D.C.

reestablishment of GTC was top priority on the West Cameroon government's agenda and required the services of a talented and duty-conscious individual, E. D. Quan, acting permanent secretary of the West Cameroon Ministry of Education and Welfare, recommended Cole for the job. In recommending Cole for the principalship of Government Trade Centre, Quan wrote, "Mr. Cole will fit this post admirably well and it is hoped that he will assist as trades education adviser to the West Cameroon Ministry of Education. His service will be required as from September this year [1962]." Though disappointed that he received only four volunteers, instead of the seven requested, Cole was determined to turn GTC Ombe into an "Ivy League" among the secondary schools in Cameroon. He assigned the Peace Corps volunteers maximum work loads.[18]

While AID handled the administrative functions of the school, the Peace Corps volunteers filled an important gap in the teaching staff. The first set of volunteers assigned to the school included Edward Greene, Edward Douglass, Robert Christensen, and Michael Romaine. They taught electronics, welding, machine shop, english,

Peace Corps volunteer Willie M. Wilkerson, Jr., inspecting work done by his students in Ombe, 1964. Courtesy of the Media Center, Peace Corps Office, Washington, D.C.

woodworking, drafting, and sports.[19] Though AID took credit for reopening the institute, the real architects of academic revival in Ombe were the Peace Corps volunteers.

Because of the arrival of the Peace Corps volunteers GTC Ombe was expanded into a comprehensive technical college where students were trained in both technical and secondary school subjects. The volunteers assisted in the construction of the school hall. They put in extra hours to prepare for the "open house gala," scheduled for December 9, 1962, that marked the end of the first term. For that particular occasion, Ed Douglass and other Peace Corps volunteers developed a closed-circuit television setup. Many Cameroonian and American officials were delighted to know that the TV setup was the work of Peace Corps volunteers.[20]

While the volunteers upheld their reputation in Ombe, elsewhere other volunteers were also making a name for the Peace Corps Agency. At Sacred Heart College in Mankon, the Reverend Father Mulligan, the principal of the school, was impressed with the services of Peace Corps volunteers Bob Guthrie and Bill Murphy.

Peace Corps volunteer Ed Douglass helping to install an electrical lighting system at the campus of the Government Technical Centre, Ombe, 1962. Courtesy of the Media Center, Peace Corps Office, Washington, D.C.

Guthrie and Murphy taught mathematics, history, and French. Additionally, they assisted the creation of an athletic program, the construction of a school and bank, and the improvement of sanitation in the dormitories. When asked if his school needed more volunteers, Father Mulligan stated, "Send us more, but make sure they're like

Murphy and Guthrie."[21] That said it all for the Peace Corps' reputation in the school.

Many other volunteers were involved in extracurricular activities. They started such projects as music groups, philosophy clubs, and physical education programs. Some introduced baseball and softball to their schools.[22] Many engaged in lengthy discussions with their students and co-workers about the way of life in the United States. The volunteers were finally fulfilling the task assigned to them in the Peace Corps Act.

The arrival of the volunteers in Cameroon in 1962 marked the beginning of a new chapter in that country's educational development. The revival of the GTC and the replacement of British expatriates were new assets. The volunteers introduced bibliographies into the country and began the process of writing textbooks for Cameroonian schools. An important feature of these new educators was that all of them had at least a baccalaureate degree or its equivalent.[23] Gone were the days when British high school dropouts assumed important teaching positions in Cameroon.

For the next four years new Peace Corps volunteers were sent to Cameroon annually, so that by 1966 more than 150 Peace Corps volunteers had served in Cameroon. After 1962, Peace Corps services were extended to East Cameroon. The volunteers who served in East Cameroon had the primary function of improving the standards of English language instruction in their various schools.[24] As a tradition established by the first groups, volunteers also carried out continuous extracurricular activities. Their achievement in Cameroonian education was significant, and the impact was long lasting.

The volunteers began to eliminate rote learning in Cameroon. Concluding that rote learning was a major obstacle to progress in education, the volunteers waged a war against this educational technique. A typical Cameroonian student was serious, disciplined, determined, and hardworking.[25] Yet there were many inevitable "buts." The students were untrained in analytical thinking. They had instead been encouraged to memorize and reproduce information during exams. The old cliché that the teacher is always right was the rule, and teachers went unchallenged. This old educational system failed to encourage the students to develop their critical capabilities, to draw conclusions, and to apply generalizations to particular problems.

Commenting on the educational system established in Cameroon, a volunteer noted that it was frustrating because "it was principally geared towards note taking and exams." Supporting this assertion, another volunteer stated that in his class students often said, "Just give us notes to copy, please, Sir!" Perhaps the most glaring example of the focus on note taking by students occurred in a volunteer's chemistry class. In this instance the teacher wrote on the blackboard, "Observe and record what happens." Every student wrote down, "Observe and record what happens."[26]

Describing the strengths and weaknesses of the program at Queen of Rosary College, Okoyong, Peace Corps volunteer Linda Smith raised some of the problems with the educational system when she wrote:

> Although our school has a relatively large compound, there are less than 200 students so we get to know most of the girls pretty well. They are, for the most part, bright, interested (especially in America), curious and active students. It is difficult to realize how lacking their background is. Many times it is necessary to explain two or three related ideas before getting to the heart of the lesson. . . . Most of my time is spent teaching or on activities related to the school. It took a bit of adjusting to get used to the English system of Education and especially the Okoyong system of teaching arithmetic, algebra and geometry at the same time. The course is called "Maths" and uses three different books. During a recent Peace Corps conference many ideas for revision of the Math syllabus were discussed, but these must be approved by the Education Department of the government.[27]

Cameroonian students had memorized volumes of information on French and English history, but they could neither analyze nor discuss the significance of the information. At the same time, the colonial educational system had devoted no time to either Cameroonian or African studies. These fields were neglected by the British General Certificate of Education exam system.

The colonial educational system committed major crimes against African studies. Textbooks used in Cameroonian schools treated Africa as a continent with neither a history nor heroes. In such books, the voices of Africans were conspicuously quiet; they were reduced to invisible characters who were occasionally seen but not heard. Students learned about the Napoleons and the kings of France and

England but were taught little about the Shakas, Egyptian civilization, African medieval kingdoms, Africa's contribution to world
civilization, and African nationalism. Students even accepted and
promoted the colonial life-style. (For many of the students an expensive, less durable business suit tailored in France was preferable
to a less expensive, more durable suit made in Cameroon.) It was
common for students to know how long it took to grow and harvest corn in the West but not have the slightest idea of how long
it took to grow any crop in their backyard. The colonial educational system severely retarded the national consciousness of the
Cameroonian youth.

To challenge this system, the volunteers formulated a curriculum
and designed textbooks more attuned to the needs of Cameroonian
students. They also discussed and laid the foundation for the establishment of a Cameroonian exam board to replace the London GCE.
Though these early volunteers did not stay in Cameroon long enough
to see their ideas materialize, they began the process. In 1977,
Cameroon broke off from the London exam system and established
its own examination board.[28] Unfortunately, books on the history of
Cameroon have ignored the role the early Peace Corps volunteers
played in this process.

Additionally, the opening of new teacher training and secondary
schools in West Cameroon between 1962 and 1966 was made possible
by the volunteers. Teacher training institutes were significant in the
development of Cameroonian education. Not only were the students
in these schools free from the chains of the London GCE, but the
graduates of the school were charged with the responsibility of teaching in the primary schools.

New teacher training institutes were opened in 1962 and 1963.
Three more were opened in 1964. The three institutions opened in
1964 were St. John's at Nchang, the Basel Mission TTC at Nyssasso,
and the Baptist TTC at Ndu. The Government TTC at Kumba was
reopened.[29] Also, new "streams" of classes were added to those already in existence. The domino effect of these developments was
quickly felt as the number of primary schools and their enrollment
jumped. (For the increase in enrollment in teacher training and primary schools between 1962 and 1964, see tables 6 and 7.)

The underlying reason for the increase in enrollment was
the growth in teaching staff. The number of teachers in teacher
training institutions jumped from sixty in 1962 to ninety-six in 1964.

Table 6. Primary School Enrollment, 1961–1964

| | | Enrollment | | |
| | Number of | | | |
Year	Schools	Male	Female	Total
1961	590	62,748	23,509	86,257
1962	590	67,454	27,705	95,159
1963	646	73,206	32,863	106,069
1964	686	78,181	38,671	116,852

Source: *Education and Manpower,* 38.

Table 7. Teacher Training Enrollment, 1962–1964

Program	1962	1963	1964
Grade III	700	881	1,019
Grade II	175	275	355
Total	875	1,156	1,374

Source: *Education and Manpower,* 90.

Of this number, twenty-three were American Peace Corps volunteers, all degree holders. Therefore, the volunteers constituted the largest number of graduates on the staff. All in all, the volunteers made up roughly 85 percent of all the teachers with a post–high school degree.[30]

The volunteers saw the teacher training institutes as the best place to discourage rote learning. The graduates of these schools were sent to primary schools to teach. The volunteers concluded that once their student teachers refrained from rote learning, they would in turn discourage it among the primary school pupils assigned to them. To fulfill this objective, the volunteers devoted more time to discussions, during which they encouraged the students to think critically by asking challenging questions. They urged the students to always search for the significance of whichever topic they discussed in class. They also taught their students to question printed documents for their validity. These techniques of learning were new to the typical Cameroonian student.

The presence of volunteers also had an impact in secondary school education. Of the ninety-five secondary school teachers in West Cameroon in 1964, twenty-eight were Peace Corps volunteers. Though there were thirty-one Cameroonian teachers in the group, only one had a graduate degree. This Cameroonian graduate was employed by the Basel Mission in September 1964.[31] Again, the Peace Corps volunteers represented the largest number of graduates in West Cameroon's secondary schools.

Almost every aspect of secondary education experienced a positive change. As new secondary schools were opened, enrollment climbed. E. A. Ekiti, educational secretary of the Basel Mission, stated in 1964 that "the teacher problem" in Cameroon was solved with the "arrival of United States Peace Corps Volunteers." When the volunteers arrived in Cameroon in 1962, there were three established secondary schools with a total enrollment of 882 students. By 1965, there were fourteen secondary schools with a total enrollment of 2,250 students. Though most of the new schools were opened by missions groups, they were blunt and candid in conveying the message that such progress was made possible because of the availability of the volunteers.[32]

In East Cameroon, the volunteers continued to excel in their performance. Of the 105 volunteers in Cameroon in 1966, 76 served as teachers in West Cameroon while 16 taught English in schools in East Cameroon. The rest of the group was involved in other projects. The volunteers in East Cameroon carried a heavy workload. Many of them taught English to Cameroonian civil servants outside their regular school hours. Their extracurricular activities included teaching folk dances, games, sports, drama, ballet, and swimming.[33]

The Peace Corps volunteers came to West Cameroon during a critical moment of that region's history. At a time when Cameroon was struggling to institute its bilingualism, the volunteers ensured that the standards of English were maintained in West Cameroon. After the British left West Cameroon, English was on the verge of being eliminated in that region, but the timely arrival of the volunteers saved the situation.[34] Though the volunteers were caught at the crossroads of Cameroon's attempt to diminish the importance of English, they understood the desire of the West Cameroonians to maintain the English-speaking tradition of the region.

The desire of the volunteers to rescue English in West Cameroon did not go uncriticized by some federal officials. On November 2,

Peace Corps volunteer Adele Douglass helps students in her English class, 1963. Courtesy of the Media Center, Peace Corps Office, Washington, D.C.

1965, Bernard Fonlon, the deputy minister of foreign affairs, sent a letter to the U.S. ambassador in Yaounde. Fonlon, a man who spent most of his time in Yaounde and frequently boasted of being the first English-speaking Cameroonian to earn a doctoral degree, had blundered. Fonlon's note underrated the services performed by the Peace Corps volunteers in Cameroon. Fonlon wrote:

> Dans le cadre de l'Assistance Technique du Gouvernement Américain aux pays en voie de Développement, le Gouvernement Camerounais a bénéficié avec beaucoup de reconnaissance d'un contingent de volontaires du Corps de la Paix destiné à l'enseignement de l'Anglais dans les écoles Camerounaises. Or ces jeunes gens pleins de bonne volonté, possèdent malheureusement une connaissance très rudimentaire du français et peuvent de ce fait difficilement communiquer avec leur élèves. Malgré les nombreuses garanties qui ont été données sur ce point par les autorités américaines, aucune solution efficace n'a encore été apportée à ce problème.
>
> Par ailleurs la façon dont cet enseignement est dispensé montre une totale absence de toute méthode pédagogique valable. Il résulte de ces deux lacunes une grande inefficacité génératrice de découragement de la part des élèves.

Compte tenu des difficultés ci-dessus mentionnées, le Gouvernement de la République Fédérale du Cameroun désirerait qu'a l'avenir le travail des volontaires de la Paix au Cameroun soit plutôt orienté vers les activités d'éducation physique et sportive où s'avèrera certainement plus efficace.[35]

Briefly, Fonlon's note lashed out at the volunteers for having a "rudimentary knowledge of French," thereby being quite handicapped in communicating with the students. The volunteers were totally lacking in teaching methods, Fonlon added. As a result, Fonlon asked that the volunteer services be restricted to physical education and sports, where they excelled. The American embassy's response to Fonlon's letter was prompt. In a swift but polite response the embassy informed the Cameroon Foreign Ministry of its willingness to transfer the volunteers in Cameroon "as expeditiously as possible to assignments in other countries where volunteers with their qualifications are needed." But everything calmed down once Fonlon decided to listen to reason.

Fonlon's assessment was both biased and shortsighted. He failed to foresee the systematic attempts to undermine English, and he also ignored the remarkable services performed by the volunteers in the country. Like several others, Fonlon failed to consider the important role the volunteers played in the promotion of Cameroon's bilingualism. Fonlon was misinformed and had acted hastily.

Realizing his error, he later wrote, with specific reference to Cameroonian bilingualism, that "to allow one culture to oust the rest would be to mar an historic chance, to wreck the noble mission that Cameroon has been called upon to fulfill in the name of all of Africa." He added, "I will be satisfied if West Cameroon retains its cultural identity in Cameroon in much the same way that Wales kept its identity in the United Kingdom."[36] Fonlon's reversal suggests that he finally admitted the important role played by the Peace Corps in Cameroon. Though the spirit of bilingualism was more in speeches than in practice, the volunteers continued to assist the bilingual objective of the country.

Other government officials also criticized the teaching of the volunteers. Education officers in East Cameroon charged that the volunteers were ill equipped to teach English in French schools in East Cameroon. Encouraged by the French, some senior cabinet members continued to downgrade the services of the volunteers. Emphasizing this, a distinguished Cameroonian official in 1963 told Charles

Caldwell, a Peace Corps evaluator, to "be sure your young teachers are fully qualified when they come to us to teach English. I am under considerable political pressure from the French and cannot afford to misstep...."[37] Similar complaints were made by Frenchmen teaching in Cameroon. Again, the complaints were ill advised and biased. Some of the complaints resulted from the practice of attempting to undermine the English language. The volunteers did their assigned job; they were uninterested in the politics of bilingualism in Cameroon.

The French had a more pragmatic reason to criticize and sabotage the services of the volunteers. The French resented the popularity enjoyed by the volunteers among the Cameroonians. In addition, they unjustly assumed that the volunteers had taken away their jobs. French expatriates, in many cases unqualified, were well paid and occupied a bourgeois position in Cameroon. The use of volunteer services threatened the high salaries these Frenchmen enjoyed. The low salaries accepted by the volunteers made them more attractive than the men from France.

Also, the French resented the relatively simple life-style of the volunteers. Before the coming of the volunteers, Frenchmen had successfully indoctrinated the majority of the Cameroonians to believe that all white people belong to the upper class and are superior to Africans. The volunteers' habit of mingling and talking with the Cameroonian rank and file jeopardized this image. Increasingly, Cameroonians discovered that Americans were different from the French. Increasingly, Cameroonians established closer ties with their Peace Corps friends, who came into their homes, ate their food, talked, joked, and toiled with them.[38]

Similarly, the ordinary life-style of the volunteers endangered the firm grip the missionaries had over their Cameroonian subordinates in mission schools. All over Cameroon the entire caste system was about to be dismantled. The problems with the missionaries were forthcoming, especially as the volunteers received little instruction on the atmosphere in mission schools during training. Though 95 percent of the schools in Cameroon were started by missionaries, they also established a system of racial superiority in these institutions. The volunteers were determined to see the system reversed. Peace Corps volunteers were not alone in this effort, as Ako D. Mengot, Director of Education and cultural delegate in Buea, West Cameroon, already had lashed out at missionary practices when he wrote:

Effective Camerooniasation of the Mission Colleges calls
for a change of attitude on the part of some missionaries. A
Cameroonian need not wear the pastor's collar or the priest's
cassock in order to become the Vice-Principal, or Principal of a
college. And if there are still missionaries who still think that
the African must change his colour, or his cultural beliefs, before he can be considered for a responsible post, such missionaries must realize that Cameroonians have arrived and they
must be made to assume positions of responsibility in the educational institutions of their country.[39]

In their attempt to reverse the practices in mission schools, the
Peace Corps volunteers were assisting Cameroonians in a longtime
crusade against missionary domination. Because the Cameroonian
teachers had been made to accept the status quo in mission schools,
Peace Corps volunteers concluded that in order to challenge the system, they must take the initiative. Volunteers denounced the use of
books at Saker Baptist Secondary School with references such as " . . .
and the Black Hand of Rome reached over Africa."[40] According to the
volunteers, the missionaries had continuously used any means available to adhere to their old beliefs, which in several cases were racist.

In another instance at the Baptist Teacher Training College
(BTTC) in Great Soppo, a Peace Corps volunteer told the principal
that he would neither conduct chapel nor teach religion. The volunteer added, "I had made up my mind that I would offer to conduct
chapel once in a while, figuring I could talk about the Golden Rule
and things like that. But when they ordered me to do it, I just decided
that was no way to operate."[41] The school's principal was astonished,
but there was little he could do.

The BTTC missionaries were quite notorious in their treatment
of volunteers. Explaining his relationship with the principal there,
Peace Corps volunteer Freeman Pollard wrote, "The North American
Baptist Director . . . hated my guts because I would not attend church
services; and because I represented some kind of threat to the law and
order because of my good relationship with students and African
instructors."[42] In another instance the missionaries at the Baptist
mission rejected a volunteer because she was Catholic, but they had to
reverse the decision because of threats from the Cameroon
government.

One after the other, the volunteers told the missionaries "where
to get off." In 1964, the volunteers launched a bitter assault against

the housing policies that assigned Cameroonian teachers in mission schools to terrible accommodations. "These tutors are supposed to be the best African tutors in the country, and look at their housing," a volunteer anguished. After threats of a strike, the missionaries gave in and began assigning better accommodations to Cameroonian teachers.[43]

Through such actions the volunteers encouraged their Cameroonian co-workers to participate in the administration of the institutions. By doing this, they also fulfilled the second and third objectives of the Peace Corps. They convinced the Cameroonian teachers of their own equality in their own schools. The European missionaries feared that the collapse of their "exclusive club" was inevitable with the spread of such ideas.[44] This was perhaps one of the greatest achievements of the volunteers in mission schools. Their efforts toward creating a more balanced and equal environment were highly significant. For the first time, Cameroonian teachers were able to challenge the status quo.

Equally important was that the changes requested by the Peace Corps volunteers exposed the dilemma faced by the missionaries. On the one hand, they needed the volunteers to teach, and on the other, they could not tolerate the volunteers' attempts to reverse existing colonial beliefs. Thus while Cameroonians, with the assistance of the volunteers, were determined "to leap into the twentieth century," the missionaries were unprepared for such a move. To salvage their reputation, the missionaries set up an extensive propaganda machine that charged that the volunteers were "uncommitted to Christian beliefs and ideals."[45]

The marked development resulting from the presence of the volunteers led to a verbal feud among certain mission groups. In 1963, the Baptist Mission accused the Catholic Mission of exploiting the Peace Corps volunteers.[46] According to the Baptist Mission, the Catholic Mission had opened new schools without the availability of a staff. Thus the mission relied entirely on the Peace Corps for staffing. Such charges were groundless. The government asked mission groups about the need for the Peace Corps volunteers before requesting them from the United States. Equally fictitious was the allegation that the use of volunteers by the Catholic Mission blurred the lines provided in the constitutional amendment calling for the separation of state and church.

The grievances registered against the volunteers involved questions not directly related to the development of Cameroon. As a result, these grievances were given little attention at the highest level. Whatever the charges, the volunteers between 1962 and 1966 went beyond their assigned responsibilities in the Peace Corps Act. Perhaps their achievement and contributions were best expressed by John Ngu Foncha when he stated:

The Peace Corps teachers have become an educational influence of great importance in our country. Through them, American culture is being introduced in the Federal Republic of Cameroon. We have seen and appreciated American educational methods and now we have the opportunity to emulate these. Americans are practical in their education system. A young country like ours needs practical education.

Especially significant was that the presence of volunteers in Cameroon led to the establishment of an Educational Testing Center in Buea.[47] Though it was originally created to help volunteers interested in pursuing graduate studies after their service, the center also welcomed Cameroonians who intended to pursue similar objectives in the United States.

Despite the achievement of the volunteers, some inevitable flaws continued. Attempts to discuss some of these weaknesses in organized workshops and conferences produced little in the way of correction. Highest on the list of problems was the teaching method employed by the volunteers.

Lacking experience with the Cameroonian educational system as a whole, the volunteers often made certain errors in their service between 1962 and 1966. Many volunteers, though enthusiastic, lacked a commitment to their teaching jobs. The Peace Corps attracted the volunteers for various reasons, and many were uninterested in teaching after they arrived in Cameroon. It was common for volunteers to inform their students and co-workers that "I'm teaching for this tour only. I'm not a teacher. I never intend to teach again." Other such remarks included, "Frankly I couldn't care less about the G.C.E. . . . Most of our teaching problems stem from poor primary schooling. I'm determined to visit a primary school before my tour is up." Some volunteers openly challenged the school administration in front of the students by stating that "this school could go far if it had the proper leadership."[48] Such remarks, or the thinking that underlay them, adversely affected the volunteers' performance and discouraged the Cameroonian students who viewed educational achievement as the only road to paradise.

The failure to commit themselves to their teaching gave rise to other problems. The most frequent criticism school principals made against the volunteers was that of inadequate class preparation. Volunteers often went to class without knowing the subject to teach for the day. Their lectures often lacked coordination, organization, and a sense of direction. Some found themselves in the uncomfortable situation of being unable to answer simple questions asked in class. One Peace Corps official in Cameroon observed that "most PCV teachers in Cameroon are distinct amateurs in the field of education (by stateside standards) and probably could not retain a teaching position in any reputable educational system in the United States." The official added, "In general, the performance of approximately one half of the West Cameroon Peace Corps volunteers is marginal, or worse; the remaining half satisfactory or better." Though the Peace Corps representative spoke to the volunteers in conferences and individually about this, the problem persisted. In some cases the performance of some of the volunteers was totally inadequate. Referring to one in particular, Jack Carmichael wrote:

> We have a much more serious problem facing us at the moment in the person of. . . . He is most ineffective in the classroom, is causing much discontent and argument among the PCVs (can't get along with any of them and is very defensive). There is quite a bit of reaction to him among Cameroonians, particularly in the Buea area, our problem is what will sending him home do to him. There is some feeling that it could completely shatter him. I suspect that he will be the next one going home, but we'll wait and see.[49]

School administrators were disappointed with the poor discipline in the classes taught by volunteers. In their effort to establish cordial relationships with the Cameroonian secondary school students, the volunteers failed to realize that these teenaged students, given the opportunity, could become very undisciplined. The classes were generally "too lax," and the volunteers were lenient and passed too many students in examinations.[50] This did not silence their critics.

Although most students enjoyed the company and classes of the volunteers, they did not hesitate to criticize the Peace Corps for failing to understand the format of the GCE examinations. Volunteers did not understand that the goal of the secondary student was to pass the GCE ordinary level or advanced level exams. As a result, students taught by the volunteers often performed poorly on the GCE exam. By 1965, students in their final years in college preferred to be taught by British teachers, who understood the British GCE system. This problem was brought officially to the attention of the West Cameroon prime minister in 1965, when the students of Cameroon Protestant College in Bali told him that "they wanted only British teachers for English."[51] On the GCE exam of the previous year only seven of thirty-five students passed English in the ordinary level exams. Not surprisingly, the students blamed their failures on their Peace Corps teachers.

In the same vein, the students of Baptist Academy went on strike denouncing the teaching performance of the volunteers. Their most pronounced grievance was that "we follow the American system. . . . We don't want it." Students of the Baptist Academy also presented complaints against the high tuition and the school's administrators. But the charges against the volunteers received more press coverage because other schools had presented similar complaints. Expressing his opinion on the crisis in Baptist Academy, a newspaper editor wrote that though the students complained about the absence of teachers, the school had three Peace Corps volunteers on its staff.[52] Such comments only increased the criticism against volunteer services.

Many of the academic problems of the volunteers originated from an error made shortly after they arrived in Cameroon in 1962. Not only did volunteers fail to understand the Cameroonian educational system, but many found themselves teaching courses they had neither taken in college nor prepared for in training. Volunteers such as Barbara Psarakis and Dick Weber, who knew very little about Cameroon, found themselves teaching Cameroon history. There were several examples. A survey taken in 1966 showed that more than 60 percent of the volunteers were teaching subjects with which they were unfamiliar.[53]

In 1964, 85 percent of the volunteers taught music, a course most of them did not take in college. The following year students at the College of Arts and Science protested against their biology teacher, a volunteer. She knew as much about biology as the students, yet she had to prepare them for the GCE advanced level exams. Criticizing the performance of some volunteers, a former student stated that "in science subjects the volunteers were lacking." Another ex-student endorsed this comment when he added, "the volunteers were theoretically sound but weak in lab work."[54]

All over the country volunteers who were art majors taught calculus and other scientific subjects. The students' inability to understand the American accent was an added problem. As one volunteer put it, "the biggest hindrance to our effective teaching overseas is . . . this American accent of ours. I guess the only solution is time and contact."[55] These problems were complicated by the absence of textbooks and other teaching aids.

While the volunteers were determined to eliminate rote learning in Cameroon, they failed to understand the origins and reasons for rote learning. Further, they were unsure what to replace it with. Some of the volunteers blamed rote learning on the British system of education. In explaining why the Cameroonian student believed in memorization, Mongo Beti, the noted Cameroonian novelist, wrote that the

> tiny tots would turn up from backwood villages thirty or forty miles up-country. . . . They formed a miserable floating population, these kids; lodged with distant relatives who happened to live near the school, underfed, scrawny, bullied all day by ignorant monitors. The books in front of them presented a universe which had nothing in common with the one they knew; they battled endlessly with the unknown, astonished and desperate and terrified.

Memorization provided the Cameroonian student with a feeling of being knowledgeable. Once the information was memorized, the student was guaranteed of doing well on the exams.[56] But the volunteers sought to change this system without providing the students with an equally important substitute that would ensure success on exams. The volunteers did not realize that rote learning was an integral part of the colonial educational system. Thus, the Cameroonian students resisted all the attempts to change rote learning, and the volunteers failed in their goal.

Other problems that persisted concerned the relationship between the volunteers in mission schools and their missionary administrators. Peace Corps regulations stated that volunteers were not obligated to abide by any religious rules. Yet in Cameroon, some principals required the volunteers either to teach religion or join the students in daily prayers, something some volunteers flatly refused to do. This problem, which was never completely resolved, continued to detract from the performance of the volunteers.

Socially, the missionaries maintained a constant watch over the volunteers. The missionaries rejected the idea of female volunteers visiting with male volunteers. In one instance the principal of the Baptist Missionary Secondary School told Stanley Meisler, the Peace Corps evaluator, "I do think the Peace Corps should have a policy prohibiting the male volunteers from shacking up with the female volunteers."[57] The volunteers refused to adhere to such doctrinal rules. Putting their social life on hold was not a Peace Corps requirement.

In a similar vein the missionaries denounced "all-night drinking parties" among the volunteers. Certain volunteers occasionally drank to excess, but this did not affect their job performance. The missionaries believed the volunteers had to adhere to prohibition. They also criticized the volunteers for staying out late. In one case the principal of the Baptist Teacher Training College "closed the gates to volunteers who stayed out late at night."[58] Peace never existed between the volunteers and the missionary administrators in mission schools.

Whatever the complaints and bickering, and whatever the weaknesses of the volunteers, it remains true that their services were essential. At a time when illiteracy was a serious social problem in West Cameroon, the volunteers stepped in and contributed enormously in educating the Cameroonians. The volunteers accepted the challenges of preparing and teaching four or more subjects. Because of the shortage of teachers, some volunteers agreed to teach courses they had not prepared for in college, thereby exposing themselves to criticism. They never gave up. They made a difficult job look easy. Despite the complaints about their conduct in mission schools and their teaching style, there was never a time when school administrators hinted that the volunteers should leave West Cameroon. Rather, the principals continuously requested more volunteers.

Given the difficult task they faced, the volunteers did very well. They planned school timetables, started many libraries and social clubs in schools, encouraged a variety of athletic programs, and laid a foundation for the creation of a curriculum more attuned to Cameroonian needs. They rescued English in that country at a critical time. And their presence created an urgency about opening new schools, something that would never have taken place without them.

Their ambition, courage, and friendliness were important qualities emulated by Cameroonian students. They gave Cameroonians a whole new understanding of education by demonstrating that it did not mean separation from the common man, as suggested by the Europeans who created an elitist and exclusive way of life in Cameroon. Their attempt to dismantle racist practices in mission schools encouraged Cameroonian co-workers to employ the same tactics and take charge of their institutions in later years.

Perhaps the main weakness of the volunteers was that they were young, human, and therefore vulnerable in certain circumstances. Quite naturally, some drank and organized parties. Another fault, which was not of their making, was that the two-year contract signed by each volunteer was too short and thereby led to occasional discontinuity in long-term projects. No wonder Cameroonian students always lamented each time a group of volunteers returned to the United States after serving the two years.[59] They regretted the departure of their new friends.

6

Volunteers in Community Development

Because of the importance of community development, the Peace Corps volunteers were assigned the responsibility of promoting rural development in Cameroon. Rural development is defined as "improving living standards of the mass of the low-income population residing in rural areas and making the process of development self-sustaining." An effective rural development officer had to mobilize the resources, design and implement projects beneficial to the community, and have the capability to encourage community residents to participate in the implementation of the projects. A rural development officer could acquire his skills either through formal education or during a long period of experience at work, which results in "learning by doing." Cameroon in the early 1960s was the right site for rural development programs. In this country, the "rural poor . . . [had] little access to services, facilities, and resources that . . . improve[d] their living standards and increase[d] their incomes and many lack[ed] . . . shelter, health care, and adequate nutrition."[1]

The Peace Corps volunteers were expected to be agents of modernization. Their duties included road and bridge construction, agricultural development, organization of cooperatives, digging of latrines, reform of health services, resettlement projects, and the improvement of sanitation. Total commitment was required if the volunteers were to fulfill the responsibilities assigned to them. The training officers encouraged the volunteers to participate in community development services even when they also had a teaching assignment. But there were volunteers specifically sent to Cameroon for rural development. By 1966, there were more than sixteen Peace Corps volunteers doing community development work.[2]

Though thirteen volunteers were specifically assigned to community development projects in 1963, Peace Corps volunteers who arrived in Cameroon the previous year were already involved in such projects. In the spring and summer of 1963, Doug Dorr and Dave

Biesemeyer trekked for seventeen days to Akwaya. Generally known as Mamfe Overside, Akwaya, with its several villages and population of 50,000, was virtually cut off from the rest of Cameroon. The only access between Akwaya and Mamfe was a narrow footpath. Because of this, several Cameroonians identified Akwaya as "bush place." Door and Biesemeyer trekked the entire journey to Akwaya. During their trip they "mapped out possible road sites, made economic and social surveys of twenty-five villages," and this information was then turned over to the Department of Community Development for future work in the region.[3] The data collected by the volunteers was vital, as the Cameroon government had ignored any development projects for Akwaya because of inadequate information on the area.

Other volunteers were involved in similar projects. Doug Lapp organized the local people to work on the Bailey Bridge project in Widikum. Bob Guthrie, Bill Murphy, Ginny Lundstrom, and Anabel Leinbach visited and made surveys in the Wum area. Jerry and Darlene Larson visited and collected important data on the Bamenda region. Several volunteers worked at the Shishong Maternity Center and Orphanage. Marge Brickman devoted her ten-week summer vacation to working with the Women's Organization of the Department of Community Development in the Banso area. Jim Kellenberger and Bill Kane spent their vacation serving on projects assigned to them by the Department of Community Development. Kris Westfall and Rosalie Stanley worked in Bifang, a small village off the road from Widikum. The volunteers devoted their first summer to community development projects.[4]

By performing such jobs in the villages and towns, the volunteers left in the areas an admirable impression of Americans. They identified with the hardships of the local people. As the first white people ever to visit some of the villages, the volunteers frequently heard children chant to each other the welcoming lines of "come see white man dey dig road." As the children entertained the volunteers, so did their parents. Each time the volunteers departed from a village, they left behind people feeling good about the United States. Perhaps the most significant community development project undertaken in 1963 by volunteers was the work done in Bojongo by Katherine and Andy Edwards. They were sent to Bojongo as teachers but used their spare time in community development work.[5]

Bojongo was a rural community with a subsistence economy. The main residents of the area were the Bakwerians. A notable feature of life in this community was the prevalence of domestic animals—pigs, sheep, goats, and cows were allowed to roam freely in the community. There were no fences for these animals. It was common practice for animals to wander into the homes of the rural people. Such hospitality to animals in living rooms and bedrooms was unhealthy for the inhabitants, for the pigs and goats left different diseases in these homes. The most common infections from the animals came from chiggers, lice, and ticks. Disturbed at such living conditions, Kathy and George Edwards started the ambitious project of constructing pens for the animals. This project was bound to provoke opposition, as it involved reversing a way of life for the Bojongo people. The Edwardses understood the problem but were determined to effect a change, if not for the local residents, at least to make Bojongo a better place for the future volunteers sent there.[6]

Once the idea was born, the Edwardses discussed their plans with Cameroonian co-workers on the staff in the Teacher Training College in Bojongo. The Cameroonians showed enthusiasm for the project. The Edwardses and their Cameroonian co-workers approached the local chiefs with their project. On the day of the first meeting, the Edwardses took along with them palm wine to give to the chiefs. They had also practiced and improved their Pidgin English before the meeting. Initially, there was opposition, but patience, complemented by careful calculation, finally won over the chiefs. In a series of meetings the chiefs convinced the Bojongo populace to accept the plan. Having completed the preliminary stages, everyone was invited to participate in the construction of the fence. Division of labor became the rule. While some brought sticks from the dense forest, others dug holes and built the fence. The women supplied food. The job was tedious and at times hazardous, but even the pouring rainfall did not stop the work.[7]

The ability to encourage mass participation produced far-reaching results. Bojongo must be made a better place to live, the Edwardses said to their Peace Corps colleagues. Finally, the job was completed. A new way of life was born for the animals and the people in the community. The children were freed from growing up with chiggers, lice, and ticks. It was a remarkable achievement. The Bojongo fence soon attracted attention all over Cameroon. The neighboring Bakwerians copied the Bojongo example and erected fences. When the project began, few foresaw the long-term advantages of it. Other Peace Corps volunteers rushed to Bojongo and contributed their services. A volunteer who participated in the project described his experience:

> They have completed the work on the fencing and now they are laying pipes to transport water about three miles to the fenced area, so we all went down that awful road to Bojongo, donned our oldest clothes, and trekked out into the bush to work with the villagers to carry 20-feet lengths of pipe and fastened it together with wrenches and spanners. I don't think I ever worked so much in my life. At points it was very tough and worse than that 10-mile hike (at O.U. in 1962) and I thought that was the worst thing I ever had to do. But we all thoroughly enjoyed helping George and Kitty and the villagers . . . and they were most grateful for our assistance in the project.[8]

The completed fence represented the success of voluntary services. At the official opening of the fence, John Ngu Foncha eloquently stated that "with the effort of this fence and with the continued interest of the natives in agricultural products, there is every evidence that a new day will dawn for Bojongo." Dedicating the fence, the Honorable J. N. Lafon, West Cameroon secretary of state for local government, enthusiastically announced:

> This, in my opinion, could prove to be a truly historic occasion. All over our country, domestic animals—cows, goats and pigs— are allowed a freedom of movement which turns them into a millstone round the people's necks. Where human hands have sown, these animals reap. The volume of crops they destroy or consume each year is a national calamity. The weary journeys they force our womenfolk to make each day, seeking farms beyond the range of the animals' predatory hooves, is a national disgrace. These creatures, which should contribute to the national wealth, conspire to keep our people poor. From being our servants they have become our masters. Here, in Bojongo, the first stand against their domination has been made. . . . The Bojongo cow fence, born in the mind of our good friend, Andy Edwards of the Peace Corps, nurtured by his constant care, industry, and determination and brought to fruition by the sweat and toil of the people of this town, is an example of intelligent

self-help which, in my own opinion, should be blazoned throughout the country.[9]

The fence was hailed all over Cameroon, but this was only one part of the Edwardses' development plan for Bojongo. Through the assistance of the United States Department of Agriculture and Michigan State University, the Edwardses studied Bojongo soil in order to introduce the cultivation of new crops in the region. The Edwardses hoped "to have cash crops planted . . . and . . . harvested,"[10] but time was not on their side. Their Peace Corps contract now came to an end. Nevertheless, their fence project established a worthwhile precedent. This was the type of pioneer project Cameroon needed in the early 1960s.

In the other parts of Cameroon, the volunteers organized cooperatives and corn mill societies. In the preindependence years in Cameroon, the cooperatives that existed were forums for political agitation against the domination of the country by colonial masters. But those started by the volunteers were designed to enable the rural people to control their markets and also to involve them in the development of Cameroon at large. Additionally, the cooperatives ensured the supply of basic needs to members. Volunteers assumed that the cooperatives would significantly raise the standard of living of the people. In 1964, the Bamenda Handwork Cooperative was established by Peace Corps volunteers. The main objective of this cooperative was to assist its members in selling their goods, thereby encouraging them to increase their production. Immediate progress was noticed after its formation. Its membership climbed to 425 by November 1964, and the cooperative accumulated 650,000 francs CFA in sales.[11]

By 1966, the cooperative had 1,200 members, and they expanded their efforts to include the production of chairs, tables, such weapons as bows and arrows, and other artifacts. Additionally, they produced clothing, bags, wallets, and shoes. The organization took the decisive step to expand its market when it exported goods to the United States for sale. At the peak of its operation, the cooperative received a service vehicle from the Agency for International Development.[12]

A significant feature of the Bamenda Handwork Cooperative was that it cut through tribal lines. This was a remarkable achievement because the members of the numerous tribes in Cameroon had a long history of distrust for one another. Now they were able to join the same

cooperative to achieve identical goals. Cameroonians hailed the inter-
tribal cooperative, but a lack of government support slowed the continuous growth of the cooperative: the Cameroon government failed
to provide much needed financial assistance.[13] Other cooperatives
formed in Cameroon by the volunteers faced the same problems.

The formation of corn mill societies was not new in Cameroon,
but the devotion of the Peace Corps volunteers to them promoted and
enhanced the emergence of more societies. The volunteers noticed
that all over Cameroon "women worked from dawn to dark in the
fields and had to come home and grind corn with two stones for
evening chop [food]." In 1963, Peace Corps volunteers Betty Ann
Hughes and Edith Pana accompanied Mrs. Lindsay, the Cameroonian
responsible for creating women's corn mill societies in the villages of
Kumba Division, to the Bakossi heartland. This was the first time
Hughes and Pana had gone to a Cameroonian village since they had
arrived in that country. For the volunteers this was a rare opportunity
to see the village inhabitants at work and to understand their life-
style. The people lived in "small round huts made of bamboo, mud,
and thatch, with conical thatched roofs, no windows, and a wooden
door about four feet high." The volunteers were surprised at the com-
fort in these huts and the simple life-style of the women. Because the
volunteers understood the importance of accepting food when offered in Cameroonian culture, they were pleased to be treated to
"bean pudding" by one of the Bakossi women. One volunteer did not
forget that experience:

> In one hut the woman was making . . . a kind of bean
> pudding. . . . To make it, she put raw white beans into a wide
> wooden bowl and then mashed and beat them into a paste,
> adding water from a gourd cup on the floor, and pepper. Now
> this is no ordinary pepper, and no ordinary dose of pepper ei-
> ther. It is so hot that it will burn the teeth out of the poor un-
> initiated white man who eats it unaware. . . . The bean paste
> looks harmless . . . but when I dipped the very tip of my little
> finger into it and licked off about one-third of that, I thought
> my tongue would never be the same again, and my whole
> mouth burned terribly. But there I was with nowhere to wipe
> my finger off, being stared at by the grinning women around
> the fire, so I had to summon all my courage and lick my finger
> clean. Is this what it means to be a Peace Corps volunteer?[14]

Though such experiences were worthwhile, the volunteers understood that they had come to the Bakossi land on a multipurpose mission and had to get to work. They had to convince the Bakossi people to join corn mill societies and participate in the daily operation of their activities. The corn mill societies promoted the growing of corn, vegetables, fruits, and other crops. New foodstuffs were needed if the Bakossi people were to diversify their diet instead of just growing and eating cocoyams, a starchy food. Each corn mill society bought a grinding machine to facilitate the work of the women.

But the responsibilities of the corn mill societies went beyond the routine grinding of corn. Education was also part of each society's responsibility. The society organized classes for its members and taught health care, sanitation, nutrition, new farming techniques, and cookery.[15] The volunteers encouraged the Bakossi women to continue with their meetings even in the absence of a government official. Equally important was that the presence of Peace Corps volunteers in the area rejuvenated the awareness of community development projects in the region. Although the Cameroon government gave the corn mill societies minimum support, morale remained high.

Following their visit to the Bakossi region, Eddie Pana and Betty Ann Hughes made several trips to the Banso region. Because some of the communities in the region had no motor roads, the two volunteers trekked most of the journey. The communities Pana and Hughes visited included Takui, Ndzeru, Sangfir, Tatum, Oku, Njikijem, Fubi, Mbam-Oku, Ngertang, Mbim, Bun, Njottin, Mbiame, and Meluf. In each of the communities, the volunteers held meetings in which they encouraged the women to hold regular sessions of the corn mill societies. During such meetings, the local women informed the volunteers of some of their most urgent problems. In all the communities the residents complained about the absence of roads, bridges, clean water, and nearby clinics.[16]

Eddie Pana and Betty Ann Hughes taught the Banso women sanitation and domestic science and advised the tribal people to hold literacy classes. The volunteers were impressed with the enthusiasm shown by the Banso villagers in the corn mill societies. Meeting attendance was regular. Suggestions offered by the Banso women revealed their enthusiasm for the societies.

Returning from their field trip, the Peace Corps volunteers furnished to the Department of Economic Development a list of recommendations for improvement in the areas they visited. Perhaps the most significant suggestion made was

> to counteract the unrealistic promises of the politicians, which have given the people the idea that the government can do everything for them, there is no need for a campaign to educate the people in the purposes and functions of government, the Native Authority, the Community Development department, as well as in what they should be expected to do for themselves. They need to realize how much of what they complain about can be remedied by working together within each village to solve their problems, as well as working and planning among different villages and tribes.[17]

The treks under the broiling sun, coupled with the determination and zeal to conquer the journey through winding and stony footpaths, gave the volunteers a taste of the struggles of the local people. Whether in Akwaya, Banso region, Bakossi area, or any other village, the conditions were similar. Commenting on some of the scenes in the villages, a volunteer stated that "we were told during training that conditions were gonna be bad but we were never told to expect frightful conditions." But the ability of the volunteers to relieve these conditions was greatly appreciated by the rural people. Never had many of them seen a "white man" trek several miles to visit and work in their village.[18] Whether or not the local people heeded the advice of the volunteers, they happily responded when summoned for a meeting organized by them.

Despite these efforts of the volunteers, however, many problems persisted. Like most people, society members preferred continuity to change. They were used to the traditional ways of doing things; consequently, they rejected any attempts designed to alter that life-style. The Bakossi people were unwilling to reverse their established way of life. Other problems included the cost of bridges, roads, fences, and school buildings. There was a shortage of money. Also, too few volunteers were available to work with corn mill societies. Thus, those who were working with them were unable to make constant visits to the societies in the various parts of the country.[19] As was the case in many other rural development projects, the government did not contribute to the survival of these societies. All through the 1960s the societies struggled for survival.

Construction was another major function of the volunteers in Cameroon. The volunteers were expected to engage in surveying, mapping, and bridge and road construction. Those charged with these responsibilities were placed under the direction of the Ministry of Community Development. Despite the noticeable absence of surveyors and engineers in Cameroon, road construction was given the highest priority in the country's first five-year development plan. Volunteers surveyed and mapped possible road sites in various parts of Cameroon. While doing this, they collected important data about the location and population of some of the villages they visited. This was significant because the government ministries did not have information on some of the villages. Some of the material collected provided the government with valuable data to be used for the planning of future development projects.[20]

The involvement of the volunteers in this type of service enhanced contact with the Cameroonians. Working side by side with the local people, the volunteers were able to learn the way of life and the culture of the country as the Cameroonians simultaneously "acquired a greater understanding of America and its people." Therefore, community development services provided a direct means for the fulfillment of the second and third objectives in the Peace Corps Act. One volunteer who participated in a corn mill project in Banso stated:

> The women in these villages have never heard of America. Even Africa means nothing to them. They are not even curious about the people over the next hill. But they love us and appreciate us and we keep trying to explain who we are and how we got here.[21]

In performing their services, the volunteers in certain cases worked alongside AID workers. Some of the volunteers taught the Cameroonians how to operate the heavy machinery AID donated to the Public Works Department. With the help of AID and the volunteers, the Cameroon government was able to undertake road maintenance projects.[22] Moreover, Cameroonians who worked with the volunteers acquired skills that were utilized in other parts of the country.

Working alongside the AID officers was never easy for the volunteers. The volunteers believed there was a clash between their objectives and those of AID, and they resented the idea of associating with that agency. The volunteers considered their help to Cameroon as genuine, but they saw AID assistance tied up with "political strings." The policy of the Agency for International Development, to engage in "showmanship" and to make public its aid, was scorned by the Peace Corps volunteers. A volunteer remarked of the agency that "the only sign of AID is a beer truck with the clasped hands insignia."[23]

A typical instance of uneasy cooperation was in the construction of the Cameroon College of Arts and Science. Although the United States was not the sole sponsor of the project, AID put up a huge sign that read:

THE

COLLEGE OF ARTS, SCIENCE AND TECHNOLOGY

A DEVELOPMENT PROJECT

OF THE

GOVERNMENT OF THE FEDERAL REPUBLIC

OF CAMEROON

WITH

FINANCIAL AND TECHNICAL ASSISTANCE

OF THE

GOVERNMENT OF THE UNITED STATES

OF

AMERICA

This sign was viewed negatively by Peace Corps volunteers working on the project. "The students are infuriated at the sign. . . . Nobody wants to be reminded of their debt," the volunteers insisted. Abetted by the anger of students, the volunteers informed Stanley Meisler, the Peace Corps evaluator, that "no Peace Corps volunteer joined the Peace Corps to put the American flag abroad."[24] The volunteers might have had genuine concern about the nature of AID functions, but their indignation revealed either their naïveté or lack of understanding of the three objectives of the Peace Corps Agency. As President Truman had described the Truman Doctrine and the Marshall Plan in the 1940s as "two halves of the same walnut," the sign and the services were both sides of the same coin.

Other problems were involved in the clash in personalities between AID workers and Peace Corps volunteers. While the AID workers resembled the snobbish characters described in *The Ugly American,* the volunteers saw themselves as "new breeds and fresh ideas" in American diplomacy. According to the volunteers, the AID workers were "old . . . men enjoying colonial life" in Cameroon. One volunteer in the College of Science noted with regret that "the wife of the science adviser [AID worker] beat her own child for giving a Cameroonian worker water from the refrigerator instead of from the tap." Repeatedly, the volunteers lamented that the AID workers took credit for volunteer services. Expressing his disappointment about this situation, one volunteer noted:

> I'm rather resentful . . . that you got us at cheap prices to do AID's work. You should have given us four times as much money plus 22 percent hardship pay. It's a pretty smart move on the part of the U.S. government.

Such grievances inevitably affected the performance of the volunteers. One group of volunteers summarized the relationship in their completion of service conference: "PC/AID cooperation is practically nonexistent."[25]

Compounding the difficulties were the problems that the American embassy had with the volunteers, some of which existed purely on grounds of principles. Embassy officials erroneously believed that the popularity of the volunteers had become a threat to their domineering influence, more especially as the volunteers would not take orders from the embassy. The embassy asked a volunteer to report on "the number of heads she saw in the market . . . heads of bandits decapitated by government soldiers." When she refused, the embassy's dislike for the volunteers increased. Other volunteers were sent letters asking for information about their stations. They did not respond to such requests. The volunteers would not do the embassy's dirty work. In another instance a dispute erupted when some volunteers accused embassy officials of buying all the Skippy Peanut Butter available in West Cameroon, thereby leaving none for the volunteers. Following a review of the charges, Leland Barrows, the U.S. ambassador to Cameroon, dismissed them as reckless rumors perpetrated by young people who could not get their own way. Barrows questioned the motives of the volunteers for spreading such stories and defended embassy officials by stating that if they bought peanut butter, then their actions were legal. Barrows challenged the volunteers to make their own peanut butter: "If your volunteers want peanut butter so badly, why don't they go out and make it? They're Peace Corps volunteers. I can give them a recipe," Barrows said. There were other minor incidents, all of which pointed to the uneasy relationship that existed between the volunteers and U.S. officials attached to other departments in Cameroon. According to the volunteers, Barrows had "little love for the Peace Corps." It is not surprising that in outlining his achievements in Cameroon during his six years there, he made no reference to the Peace Corps.[26] Peace Corps volunteers did not forgive him for such an omission.

Despite the achievements made in Bojongo and the corn mill societies, the overall Peace Corps community development work in Cameroon was a failure. Born in uncertainty, Peace Corps community development projects in Cameroon remained problematic. Since relatively few volunteers were assigned to rural development, the major achievements were accomplished by those whose primary responsibility was in the teaching field. During the twelve-week training program volunteers took voluminous notes on development theories. Also, they were taught techniques in surveying and construction. But once in the field, they discovered that they were ill equipped and ill prepared for the task. They never fully understood the terrain and village conditions in Cameroon.[27] They were neither trained surveyors nor draftsmen nor architects. The volunteers were B.A. generalists without any experience in community development, and in such work, they found themselves in limbo.

Realizing their shortcomings, the volunteers resorted to the role of advisers. This did not solve the problem, as the new assignment exposed their weaknesses to the Cameroonians. More importantly, the volunteers were in the wrong place; they were trained to be doers, not advisers. Cameroon already had too many advisers from France, Britain, and AID offices. Some of the volunteers had problems reading measurements, yet they found themselves in the position of advising qualified Cameroonian road builders. Others took credit for designs and survey work done by Cameroonians.[28] The volunteers were sometimes guilty of the charges they levied against AID workers in the College of Science. All in all the training of these volunteers as surveyors and road builders was flawed and completely inadequate. They were in the wrong place with the wrong education.

Agriculture in Cameroon presented a more thorny problem for the volunteers. In 1965, the Peace Corps Agency extended its services in Cameroon to agricultural development, and twelve volunteers were assigned to the project. The volunteers assigned to the Department of Agriculture were to serve as extension workers. They had to study soil types in order to introduce new crops and teach new farming methods, and they were charged with the organization of poultry farms and rural youth clubs.[29]

Lacking the basic knowledge of Cameroonian agricultural patterns and the ability to encourage the peasants to accept changes through mass participation, the volunteers found themselves operating in a total vacuum. The volunteers neither included the farmers in their planning nor lectured them on the advantages of new farming techniques. Their knowledge about the types of diseases that infected crops was nil. The volunteers never took up accommodation in the villages; they lived in luxurious houses outside the rural community. They appeared in the villages in the late morning and left in the afternoon.[30] Such a schedule denied them the opportunity to spend more time with the rural people, something that was necessary if the farmers were to accept any change. For these reasons, instead of considering the volunteers as people who wanted to improve the lives of the residents of the community, the farmers viewed them with suspicion.

As extension workers, the volunteers performed poorly. Untrained in agricultural extension services, the volunteers operated with uncertainty. They failed to provide "concrete expertise" to the rural population. Compounding this difficulty was the inability of the volunteers to work alongside Cameroonian extension workers. The volunteers, who neither understood the reasoning of the rural people nor spoke their language, felt uncomfortable in their attempts to perform the job. They were "ill-financed, ill-trained, ill-equipped with a technical package, and consequently very poor in quality." This was the problem of all non-African extension workers. Finally, the volunteers gave the rural people advice on a "take it or leave it" basis. Of course, they left it.[31]

Yet the volunteers did not cause all the problems in agricultural development. The Cameroon government shared part of the blame. The government rejected all appeals to fund agricultural development in the rural areas. Lacking means of transportation, new seeds, and other necessary capital, the volunteers attempted to perform an already difficult job under terrible conditions. The result was not surprising. Everything failed. In 1967, Peggy Anderson, the Peace Corps evaluator, suggested that the agency not replace the volunteers in agricultural development after their contract ran out. The agriculture program was "ill-conceived, badly planned and for all practical purposes unsupported. . . . It is a lesson in nightmares," Anderson wrote.[32]

Another project urged by the Cameroon government and started by the volunteers was that of resettlement. In 1963, the volunteers undertook the ambitious project of resettling the island people of Bota Island and Victoria. The aim was to relocate these people in areas which were easily accessible to modernization, to better housing, adequate health care, water supply, latrines, roads, and educational facilities. The volunteers were alarmed by the high rate of infant mortality on the islands. They were determined to resettle the people. But the entire project was handicapped for lack of money.[33] Financial estimates were ignored by the Cameroon government, and the project never went beyond its initial stage. This failure demonstrated a familiar volunteer error. They neither adequately studied the project nor thoroughly examined its feasibility before jumping into it.

Peace Corps volunteers were also assigned to teach Cameroonians the craft of public administration, and several volunteers worked in different departments in West Cameroon.[34] Here again the volunteers floundered. Untrained in bureaucratic management, the B.A. generalists turned into "sit-arounders" in offices. The entire public administration project raises serious questions, as Peace Corps-Washington itself did not believe in the theories of organizational management as propounded by public administration experts.

Because of the acute shortage of medical doctors and public health officers in Cameroon, Peace Corps-Washington tried to provide services in this field. The ten volunteers assigned to work in Zones de Demonstration d'Action de Santé Publique were expected to teach sanitation, health care, nutrition, prenatal care, and child care. Stationed in the Haut Nkam and Nyong et Kele regions, the volunteers faced major problems. Untrained in the local languages and in French, the volunteers could not communicate effectively with the local people. And though the volunteers assisted in digging latrines, the local people questioned the value of the service, since the volunteers did not use latrines, instead using the water system toilet in their reserved residential areas.[35]

An example of the shortcomings of volunteer services in this project was in their attempt to teach pregnant women the essentials of eating nourishing food in order to guarantee the health of the unborn child. In one of the lectures, a pregnant lady who challenged the idea of changing her diet to include more protein told her volunteer teacher that she preferred a small baby because "delivery will be easier for me."[36] Lacking the proper education to challenge such beliefs, the volunteer failed to respond adequately. There were several such cases. The volunteers assigned to public health were given a difficult task. They were not trained medical officers. During their four and one-half months of training, they were told what problems to expect, but not how to resolve them. It is no surprise that Peace Corps-Washington did not drastically expand the public health project in later years. It was flawed from the beginning.

The failure of the volunteers in community development points to a larger dilemma faced by developmentalists in the Less Developed Countries (LDC) during the early 1960s. During the training, the volunteers studied abstract theories of development devised from the experience of Western industrial nations. Once in Cameroon, they discovered that these theories were inapplicable. Thus, the Peace Corps failure in the early 1960s was also a failure of development studies.[37]

The limited attention paid to community development by the Cameroon government further thwarted the undertakings of the volunteers. The government neither supplied the finances nor the vehicles for the projects. Community development was not a top priority in Cameroon's first five-year development plan. Even some of the cooperatives started by the volunteers disintegrated for the lack of financial support from the government. Some Cameroonian surveyors refused to cooperate with the Peace Corps on the assumption that their "white bosses" preferred the volunteers to them. To these Cameroonians, the volunteers were a "bone in their throat."[38]

But all was not a total disaster. The volunteers' ability to penetrate rural areas with their politeness gave the peasants an everlasting impression of Americans. Americans were polite, friendly, and more thoughtful than the Europeans, the peasants observed. This was a remarkable impression left in the villages, and it fulfilled the second and third objectives of the Peace Corps Act.

All in all, the achievements of the Peace Corps volunteers in community development, though limited, resulted from their own on-the-spot initiative rather than bureaucratic planning. Once in Cameroon, the volunteers went beyond their call of duty and gave assistance wherever possible. Many devoted their summers to community development work, some spent long hours after school working in school gardens, and others donated their services where needed. Occasionally they failed to make substantial gains, but they never gave up. Robert Kennedy once said, "Few will have the greatness to bend history itself; but each of us can work to change a small portion of events, and in the total of all those acts will be written the history of this generation."[39] The limited success of the volunteers in community development made a difference.

On a practical level, the best that could be said about volunteer services in community development is that, like those responding to President Kennedy's inaugural urging, they had only begun. Like Kennedy, the volunteers in community development never reached their meridian. In later years, Cameroonians saw more Peace Corps volunteers in community development. Their services improved, along with the impression of the United States in that country. But the volunteers who served in the country between 1962 and 1966 left portraits and pictures of John F. Kennedy hanging in the houses of Cameroonians alongside those of important family members.[40]

7

Living in Cameroon

The time the Peace Corps volunteers spent in Cameroon was full of joy and pain, happiness and sadness, isolation and togetherness, experience and adventure. More than 90 percent of the volunteers lived, adjusted, and adapted to Cameroonian life. For the first time most of the volunteers lived in a society in which they were the minority. In certain locations the volunteers were the first foreigners and whites to visit and live there. Yet the treatment of this minority contrasted with that given to similar groups in the United States.[1] A totally new experience, the food, roads, environment, houses, and way of life were all different. Everything was exciting.

For each new volunteer, life in Cameroon began with uncertainty, fear, and nervousness. Unsure of the new environment and its people, the volunteers clustered together during the early days. Volunteers spent 40 percent of their time outside their job, with many putting in twenty-five hours or less each week on their job. Several volunteers had a fourteen-hour teaching load each week in their respective schools, leaving them much free time to experience life in Cameroon. In West Cameroon, where there were at least three volunteers in each town, they continued to live, talk, and dine together. The situation was different in East Cameroon, where the shortage of volunteers made it impossible for more than one volunteer to be sent to certain towns.[2]

The hazardous events in Cameroon in the early 1960s somewhat pushed the volunteers together. The sabotage caused by pro-UPC people and the continuous killings carried out by the Maquisards caused each foreigner in Cameroon some apprehension. In 1963 two Americans were shot at in Cameroon as a result of political upheavals.[3]

Adding to this tension was the natural suspicion of foreigners by Cameroonians. With a recent memory of imperialism, Cameroonians were distrustful of the incoming volunteers. Without any previous knowledge and experience of Americans, most Cameroonians had no reason to expect that the new Western visitors would be different. Those who bore the brunt of this skepticism were in the first group of volunteers. Cameroonians used their experience with the first group of volunteers to reexamine (or to form) their impressions of Americans.

Writing to her parents back in the United States, Mikell Kloeters described her group's first contact with the East Cameroonian populace. She wrote, "Everyone really stared at us and no one waved or smiled as they did in West Cameroon but there was no hostility or impoliteness."[4] But this mistrust and suspicion did not last long.

The volunteers had certain assets that other foreigners lacked. During the training, the "grand old veteran," the Reverend Paul Gebauer, gave the volunteers a series of lectures which he called "Cameroon Cautions or, Advice of an Old Hand to Youth." These lectures focused on the "do's and don'ts" in Cameroon. Gebauer told the volunteers:

> Watch your language, as a people they [Cameroonians] weigh words and especially curses. . . . Relegate to the privacy of your home the affections of married love. . . . Let local etiquettes guide your dates with nationals. . . . Let nothing, except P.C. regulations, hinder you in your endeavors of identification with nationals and national hopes. BEWARE of local politics. . . . You will grow weary at times. Doubts will come to you in the presence of opposition and failure. The tropics and your Cameroonians will test all that your [*sic*] are and all that you have. In your strange environment, far from home you may ask, like the Hebrews of old in Babylon: "How shall we sing the Lord's song in a strange land."[5]

Though they went to Cameroon to assist in the development of that country, many of them were interested in the experience of living in another culture. Despite the repeated warnings given to them during training that they were not to consider themselves "jungle adventurers," the volunteers did just that.[6] The initial logistic problems did not slow their ambition as they quickly settled in. Also, feelings of uncertainty and fear rapidly evaporated. During the training sessions, the volunteers were cautioned to treat the host people as their equals and avoid negative remarks about the culture of the Cameroonians. They adhered to this advice, and their tact became an asset.

Cameroonians are strongly nationalistic. Family and communal life are emphasized. The volunteers joined the chorus in admiring the communal life-style. It was in marked contrast to what one volunteer called the "individualistic and money-grabbing" life in the United States. The volunteers noticed the ability of the Cameroonians to share and sympathize with the problems of their neighbors. Unannounced visits to neighbors were part of the Cameroonian life-style. The volunteers were encouraged by the host country people to walk in and out of their houses at any time of the day.

As Peace Corps volunteers quickly adjusted to this life-style, so did the Cameroonians quickly accept them. Dinner invitations to the volunteers came from both poor and rich Cameroonians. The people rightly assumed that by dining with the volunteers, they would have the opportunity to learn about them and also to learn about American ways. In whichever house the volunteers visited for dinner, an abundance of food was set on the table. In fact, Cameroonians overate, according to U.S. standards. Describing her experience at dinner in a Cameroonian home, one volunteer wrote:

> My first invitation from an African—dinner at Mofiro's. Other people were invited too—all Africans. Never have I seen so much food put on the table for one meal. We started with fried potatoes and omelette. Then some seasoned liver and noodles. In between huge chunks of bread. I was already quite full when she brought out the main course—couscous. . . . I couldn't even try everything. But the rest of the people just ate and ate. . . . After all that—salad and fruit. Spirits were high . . . a really great evening.

Eric Swenson, a returned Peace Corps volunteer from Yabassi in Douala, sounded the same theme to his parents. Swenson wrote:

> We were invited for lunch. I have never seen such a feast in my life. Soup, beef and potatoes, chicken and rice, beef and plantains, fish and spinach, some other course, and pineapples for dessert. One is actually expected to eat a good size portion of each of these courses. I made the mistake of taking two helpings of one course without knowing that it was just the beginning.[7]

This experience destroyed the myth of universal starving in Africa that volunteers were told during training and by some of their college professors. "The food here is good and plentiful," Swenson wrote. From Buea, Mary-Ann Tirone Smith and her colleagues echoed the familiar theme of food in Cameroon.[8] Everything was one long party after another. The volunteers were happy and felt welcome. They could not disguise their appreciation of the Cameroonians. Never had they seen people give so much to people they knew so little. Eating alongside the Cameroonians, the volunteers learned and adjusted to a key commandment in these homes: Cameroonians expect guests to eat the food offered them. It is a sign of friendship and good luck.

Dining together only marked the beginning of a new friendship. The domino effect of each visit to a Cameroonian home by any volunteer was almost immediate. As the volunteers came and went, the good word was spread about them in town, something that resulted in more invitations from Cameroonians. The volunteers had "expected the worst" when the Cameroonians stared at them shortly after they arrived in Douala. Now the tide had changed in their favor. They were having the "best of times." The volunteers became the heroes and the "new kids in town." All over Cameroon their friendly and polite reputation preceded them. Comments such as "she [he] goes out walking with Africans and talks to them, this is an American," became familiar descriptions of these youths.[9] They were making a name for themselves. They were adored.

To live up to their reputation, the volunteers became regulars at the market. Market days in the various parts of Cameroon were considered special. Everyone showed up. The market was not only a place where people came to buy and sell goods but where other important functions were carried out. In the process of serving traditional market functions, the market in Cameroon is a "social center where news and gossip . . . spread, friends are met, new people are introduced, legal disputes are settled, and respects are paid to chiefs and elders." Additionally, the market serves as a place of "entertainment where dances, work parties, christening and wedding parties all eventually congregate."[10]

The volunteers usually accompanied their Cameroonian friends to these markets, something the French and British expatriates never did. By this time the volunteers realized that their smiles and politeness were the magic of attraction. In the markets the volunteers glittered and sparkled. Responding to this, Cameroonians clustered around them. The volunteers became the center of attraction. The French disliked them, but not the Cameroonians.[11]

Peace Corps volunteers Alton Scarborough, Jr., and Linda A. Smith wandering in the local market in Cameroon, 1964. Courtesy of the Media Center, Peace Corps Office, Washington, D.C.

The habit of participating in Cameroon life was extended to the festivities of that country. While holidays such as Thanksgiving, Columbus Day, and the Fourth of July meant nothing to the Cameroonians, the volunteers celebrated these days with their Cameroonian friends. They also wholeheartedly participated in the celebrations of important days in Cameroon. During such occasions both the Americans and the Cameroonians explained the historical significance of the days, and the meals prepared for the celebrations were a mixture of Cameroonian and American food. Pizza, hamburgers, plantains, doughnuts, couscous, peanut butter soup, stew, salad, koki, Cameroonian beer, and whisky were regulars on the menu.[12] Such occasions became unofficial cultural exchange programs.

Expecting to find familiar celebrations of days such as Christmas and New Year's, the volunteers were surprised by the differences in common holidays. As in many Christian countries, Christmas celebrations were given the highest priority in many Cameroonian homes, yet celebrated differently. No one dreamed of a white Christmas in Cameroon; rather, they expected some of the highest temperatures of the year. Referring to this, a Peace Corps volunteer remarked, "Can you imagine walking in shirt sleeves to Christmas midnight services?" There were no Christmas trees surrounded by colorful wrapped packages, and no Santa Claus. It was a different Christmas in Cameroon. Describing his observation of Christmas Day, one volunteer wrote:

> Our Christmas in Cameroon is not the commercialized display you experience at home, but rather a time for the family to come together and to travel from place to place greeting friends with "Happy Christmas" and enjoying a feast of fufu-corn, garri and possibly a roasted goat or pig. It is a time to wear new clothes and a time for fellowship together in the local church, whether it is in the bush or in one of the local villages. The smaller children will travel from place to place in their "juju" outfits and will put on dancing displays for anyone inter-ested in watching; and the little girls will carry flowers and "dash" them to strangers on the road as their token of Christmas greetings.[13]

On social occasions the volunteers adopted the typical Cameroon-ian drinking habit. Among the most lucrative business enterprises in Cameroon were the on-license and off-license stores that sold li-quor. The official difference between the two was that whereas the off-license was smaller and was supposed to close at 8:00 P.M., the on-license store could stay open until midnight. But in the absence of strict law enforcement, most stores stayed open all day and night. Other drinking spots included bars and nightclubs. Whichever place the volunteers went to, they drank as the Cameroonians drank. All-night drinking was encouraged by their Cameroonian company, who normally had a large appetite for alcohol. Several volunteers agreed that "the status you develop in the community has a direct relation with your drinking habits and . . . it would be difficult for a non-drinker to make his way," and "friendships were made over a mimbo [palm wine] or beer at the local bar," the volunteer added.[14] The drinks were cheap, and this was all part of living in Cameroon.

The volunteers also discovered in Cameroon a new relationship with the opposite sex. The volunteers were young and most of them unmarried; and coming from the United States in the 1960s, where sex had become "America's last frontier," the volunteers had not taken a vow of celibacy.[15] Some volunteers married their Peace Corps colleagues, and others dated other Peace Corps volunteers. A large number, however, preferred to establish relationships with Cameroonians.

Changes in male-female relationships in Cameroon in the 1960s were not as rapid as those taking place in the United States. The man was still the dominant figure, and the role of married women in the society was still quite restricted. The Cameroonian home was similar to what Betty Freidan described as "the comfortable concentration camp." But this secondary position assigned to women did not maintain the moral fabric of the society. Describing the nature of relationships in Cameroon, a volunteer wrote,

> As far as African sex life goes I would say it is uninhibited. Other than the few families who follow a Western religious doctrine and closely guard their daughters until marriage, there is no stigma of shame, sin or illegality to free love. In fact, one who does not partake of women will be considered "very serious" . . . partake has only one meaning for the African—fornication . . . all women have a one track mind and think only of fornication when a man is the subject of conversation. . . . Although it is considered very bad to take one woman here and another there, there are few people including married couples who are faithful to one another. In fact a mutually exclusive relationship is unexpected on the man's side anyway.[16]

This volunteer, by stating that those who adhered to the "western religious doctrine" were the only well-behaved people in the society, had failed to capture a vivid picture of the social relationships in the country. Like many societies at the time, Cameroon stood at the crossroad of a social revolution, though such changes were not as rapid as those taking place in the United States.

Shortly after the volunteers arrived in the country, they adjusted to this life-style. Missing the sexual revolution taking place in the United States, the male volunteers dated Cameroonian females, especially as the volunteers were told during training to "let local etiquettes guide your dates with nationals." The volunteers heeded this advice. In principle, the volunteers denounced the moral breakdown and "promiscuity" identified with the society, but in practice the men acted like the typical Cameroonian male. They were part of the masculine mystique on the move in the society. The ambivalence of Peace Corps-Washington on the issue of social relationships in the host country encouraged such actions.[17]

In the midst of this, the female volunteers pondered as to how to react to the situation, especially since the training sessions did not address such problems. Those who were unmarried, and did not date their Peace Corps colleagues, refused to be subjected to the kind of role assigned to the Cameroonian woman. Initially they played the role of night watchmen—folded their arms, waited, and saw how events unfolded themselves. Repeatedly they complained that Peace Corps training had not prepared them for this situation. They felt "susceptible to the young Africans." A female volunteer wrote that Cameroonian men were "fine looking," but

> they promise the moon and promise all sorts of devotion. It's a combination of African and French cultures. I've seen upsetting problems. The African male is physically attractive. Girls are swept off their feet and then let down. This was not covered much in training. It should be discussed from the woman's point of view. . . . Any single white girl is the object of many amorous men here. But you can tell them no, and they take it. That's it. You're still friends. Africans are pretty thick-skinned, and you have to be pretty thick-skinned. People are very direct with their propositions and can be answered directly.[18]

Such a description points to the frustration and dilemma the female volunteers faced. On the one hand they hoped to have a relationship, and on the other they labeled the host country's men as "pretty thick-skinned." Because of the paternalistic attitude which was very much a part of Western culture at the time, some of the female volunteers failed to realize that men who do not take "no" for an answer were not unique to Cameroonian society. However, most female volunteers were reluctant to date, and several remained unreconciled to the dating habits in Cameroon. In the beginning they also complained that "they were not visited often enough by the male volunteers." A female volunteer expressed her frustration when she stated that one Cameroonian *"petit functionnariries* [sic] (the 'pointed-shoe' set) . . . came knocking at her door one evening 'to get the lay of the land.' " Another volunteer resented the constant visits when she pronounced that "my only problem is making it perfectly clear . . . that I am not here to keep the male population of Africa happy. International relations can go just so far."[19]

According to the volunteers, African men proposed faster than sailors swore. There was hardly a single female volunteer who was not proposed to at least once. In a specific incident at a dinner table in

Foumban, one man proposed that Mikell Kloeters become his sixth wife. Though he promised her all the finest things in life, she laughed it off as a joke.[20]

Struggling to adjust to this situation, the volunteers wrote numerous letters to Peace Corps-Washington requesting advice. Washington did not respond. Even the suggestions to include "dating in the host country" on the training program ended in the dustbin. The silence of Washington indicated that the Peace Corps Agency would not tell the volunteers "when, whom, and where to date." The bureaucrats in Washington were more concerned with the attainment of the Peace Corps objectives than with the social life of the volunteers.[21]

More upsetting to some female volunteers was that some of their secondary school students asked them for dates. It was a difficult situation. Some volunteers solved their dating problem by traveling long distances out of Cameroon to date volunteers serving in other countries.[22] Many, however, established relationships with Cameroonians.

These problems were never completely resolved. Because of the exceptional position the volunteers occupied, whatever they did and wherever they went became of interest and was news to the neighboring people. It was an awkward situation for them, but perhaps a price they paid for being popular in their various towns. Some of the relationships established were worthwhile, and in certain cases marriage was seriously discussed.[23]

Some female volunteers hoped that having Cameroonian boyfriends would spare them the numerous proposals and personal questions the host country people continuously asked, as Cameroon culture was suspicious of single women in their twenties and thirties. According to legend, unmarried women at that age were either "barren, spoiled, or not serious enough." Female volunteers were frequently scrutinized with questions: "Why are you not married?" "Can't you have children?" "Did your parents reject you?" Describing this to her parents, one volunteer wrote, "an African opinion . . . [is that] we American girls aren't serious enough, just school and work!!!" Another volunteer commented that "Cameroonians . . . wanted to know what made me tick," and they asked questions such as "why aren't you married? Can't your father find you a husband?"[24] Tired of explaining her goals to the Cameroonian women, Mary-Ann Tirone Smith tells in her book, as others have done in informal accounts, how she decided to respond to such questions by telling her interrogators what they wanted to hear.

The curiosity of the Cameroonians went beyond the marital status of the female volunteers. The host country people were concerned about the racial problems in the United States and hoped that the volunteers would explain to them the rationale for continuing American racism. Racial uprisings in towns such as Birmingham, Albany (Georgia), and Selma held the front pages of world newspapers. The volunteers had to deal with the problem Dean Rusk pointed out in 1961, that "the biggest single burden that we carry on our backs in our foreign relations in the 1960s is the problem of racial discrimination at home. There is no question about it."[25]

More surprising to Cameroonians was that African officials visiting the United States were not served in some restaurants.[26] Cameroonians wanted to know why white Americans would discriminate against blacks in the United States but agree to serve and live in a black country. The volunteers were prepared during training to confront such questions. Yet with the mounting racial crisis in the United States the volunteers found themselves in the embarrassing situation of being unable to explain American racism. In most cases they shifted the blame for the race riots to the politicians. Reluctantly their Cameroonian friends accepted this answer. They were more interested in maintaining the established friendship than wrecking it because of crises taking place thousands of miles away from their country.

Perhaps the most frustrating racial questions were directed to the black Peace Corps volunteers. One of the volunteers was asked, "How did you escape from Birmingham?" "Do you have white friends in the United States?" "How is life in the ghetto?" Echoing a similar theme, another volunteer stated, "I do remember being surprised at the students' reaction at me as a Black American."[27]

Though less than 4 percent of the volunteers were black, some volunteers were convinced that the poor treatment of blacks in the United States had serious repercussions on their service and social relations in Cameroon. Cameroonians seemed to believe the stereotypes of black Americans. This was demonstrated in their attempts to undermine the qualifications of black volunteers and to doubt the honesty of some of their responses to questions during discussions. "They [the Cameroonian students] didn't seem to think it was proper for a Negro to be teaching Africans," a black volunteer stated.[28] Part of the explanation for the doubts displayed over black volunteers, however, probably originated from the legacy of imperialism. All through Cameroon's history, the European imperialists had given that country's people the impression that blacks were ignorant.

However, responding to questions dealing with racial issues did not take up all the free time of the volunteers. As Peace Corps volunteers, the Americans were entitled to forty-five days of vacation each year. These days were used for traveling to other parts of Cameroon and Africa. Describing the travels and activities of volunteers in Cameroon, Fairfield wrote:

> Others [volunteers] write to relate "wild" experiences travelling across country in a Land Rover, frequenting "the little house in the back" with its "very active spiders," exercising restraint in the urge to introduce Kola blight or blow up the beer plant because of the frightful taste of each, recounting the story of a five-day jaunt across the Ndop Plain with a public official . . . struggling with stove set into a fireplace with no airtight connection with the chimney, experiencing awe at the magnificent scenery on the Ring Road with its "extraordinary vistas," . . . struggling to reconcile American democratic ideals with the views currently encountered in the novels of James Baldwin (which they are reading) . . . expressing excitement and feeling of challenge in setting up a new household in a strange country with strange artifacts, and, and, and.[29]

Many volunteers traveled to African cities such as Abidjan, Casablanca, Lagos, Accra, and Port Harcourt. Though Peace Corps policy restricted the volunteers from vacationing outside their continent of service, some volunteers did travel to Europe and the Middle East. Peace Corps service provided most of the volunteers with their first opportunity to see the world, and the volunteers hoped to make the best use of an opportunity that might never come again. In 1963, Jack Carmichael wrote about the travels of some of the volunteers:

> The following people have been or are still in Nigeria: Tom Donnelan, Betty Ann Hughes, Mary Cavas, Al Bridgewater, Murphy, Herring, Kinney, Martin, Pollard, Weber, Carey, Nesler, Smith, Cambron, Haugh, Lundstrom. . . . Dave Biesmeyer went to Ivory Coast and Nigeria. Twelve fellows went to Fernando Po for a week: Herschbach, Teare, Schumann, Wilkerson, Roy, Christensen, Kramer, Swanson, Scarborough, Tubbs, Demb and Haywood . . . Doug Lapp went

to the Congo and Gabon to see Schweitzer; so did Brickman and Greene; Pana and Romaine took a boat trip to Gabon. Anabel Leinbach went to Kenya with her mother and the Edwardses are spending three weeks in the Canary Islands. So you can see that people have been traveling . . . Larsons and Douglasses have gone North around the Ring Road and to Foumban; Gladys Bannister spent three or four days in Yaounde.[30]

The visits to other countries gave the volunteers a wider perspective on Africa. As they traveled, they broadened their understanding of the different cultures in Africa. The journeys contributed toward the Peace Corps objective that the volunteers return and share their experience in Africa with people in the United States. The Peace Corps Agency was confident that this understanding would contribute to a better formulation of American foreign policy toward these countries in later years.

Later on in their careers, some volunteers, such as Mary-Ann Tirone Smith and David Dwyer, wrote books about their experiences in Africa. Others went out of their way to learn some native languages. This was necessary in order to talk with Africans who did not understand English, French, or Pidgin English. Today many ex-volunteers still have vivid memories of those travels, and all say that those were some of the best moments of their lives.

Yet everything in the volunteer life in Cameroon was not exciting. There were aspects of Cameroonian culture that the volunteers never really accepted. They resented the Cameroonians' "lack of a sense of time and responsibility." Like many in other parts of the world, Cameroonians did not adhere to the rule of promptness. The volunteers realized with dismay that what a Cameroonian calls two o'clock is really four or five o'clock. They quickly learned what "African time" meant. Many believed they could not rely on an appointment with a Cameroonian. One volunteer noted that if a Cameroonian told you that he was stopping by for a visit, you should "not wait because often he doesn't show up." Cameroonians always honored the last appointment of the day; therefore they forgot those given in the early part of the day. The volunteers observed that this was extended to the job. Describing the Cameroonian work ethic, one volunteer wrote that Cameroonians were generally "laid back (as we used to say in the 60's), conscientious, but didn't let time schedules get in their way." Though the volunteers described Cameroonians as hardworking people, they also noted that they seldom arrived to work on time.[31] Of course, when people had to trek for miles to their job site, it was certainly easy to be late.

Also upsetting for the volunteers was the habit of people popping into their houses unannounced. Volunteers had many friends, and these people often dropped by to visit. Occasionally the volunteers resented this practice, yet they did nothing to discourage it. In a country where few telephones existed, there was no way the friends could have warned the volunteers of their arrival or visit. The volunteers themselves indulged in this practice. It was the way of life.

Isolation was a more serious problem for the volunteers. Granted, they had many friends in Cameroon, but there were moments when the volunteers felt lonely and depressed. Those were the occasions when they missed their families in the United States. Also, their loneliness revived the culture shock that had almost disappeared during their stay in the country. Attempts to reverse their depression through rereading pamphlets on "Adjusting Overseas" were usually unsuccessful. To relieve the pain of loneliness, some volunteers owned pets.[32] These down times, however, did not often last long, as many Cameroonians took upon themselves the responsibility of cheering up their American friends.

Another aspect of life that the volunteers disliked (though this was not Cameroonian) was the constant ingesting of pills and other medications. Located in the tropics, Cameroon played host to diseases such as filaria, malaria, dysentery, and typhoid fever. To protect the volunteers from these diseases, the Peace Corps made it policy to constantly provide them with large numbers of pills. The old saying that an ounce of prevention is better than a pound of cure was the rule. Peace Corps doctors preferred to prevent the disease than treat it after it had already attacked the volunteers. This was something the volunteers never got used to. But volunteers who did not take the medication occasionally suffered from malaria attacks.

In certain instances, some volunteers were hospitalized. This was a nightmare. They neither liked the hospital conditions nor the meals brought to them. Until recently, patients admitted to hospitals in Cameroon were expected to arrange for their own food, and volunteers denounced the hospital policy of not feeding its patients. Also disappointing was that the country did not have enough doctors to provide adequate watch over the patients. In truth, the volunteers expected too much. It was all these inadequacies that made the Peace

Corps experience necessary and worthwhile. Looking back on those days, many volunteers appreciate the struggles of people in developing countries. As one volunteer put it in a questionnaire response, "No one really knows what is meant by post-independent problems until he experiences them." The volunteers experienced some of the hazards—and a few of the daily troubles—of what is for many the real world.

Despite the positive features of the volunteers' experience in Cameroon, there were disturbing aspects about their life-style in this country. Money, housing, friends, food—everything came too easily. The volunteers came to Cameroon to live among the local people, but they occupied large luxurious buildings in the different towns. They lived in quarters reserved exclusively for expatriates. "They [Peace Corps volunteers] are living much like the expatriates they replaced and differ only in the fact that they have a better relationship with their students," an observer stated. Whether in mission schools or not, the volunteers lived in areas reserved for whites. One black volunteer remarked that "it's the first time I've ever lived in an all-white community."[33] Certain volunteers commented that their residence in Cameroon was better than their lodgings in the United States. Because it was almost an official policy for the Cameroonians to stay out of those quarters, the volunteers did little to change this. As a result, the volunteers were not different from the "organizational bourgeoisie" who took charge of African countries in the postindependence era.

The "scandalous allowance" of $145 ($155 to volunteers in East Cameroon) given to each volunteer per month only encouraged an ostentatious life-style.[34] At a time when the average Cameroonian civil servant earned less than $90 a month, the volunteers found themselves among the "filthy rich" in the country. American Peace Corps volunteers earned more money than volunteers from other countries. Each volunteer had a servant who cleaned the house and cooked. In 1962 Peace Corps evaluator Wilson McCarthy visited some of the volunteers and later wrote: "The volunteers are living a very good life in the Cameroons, as they say, 'better than we live back home.' I found all of the housing exceptionally good. Every volunteer employs servants and in one case five volunteers have three servants, a cook, a houseboy, and a small boy. Their allowance is more than adequate." While some volunteers bought luxurious French Citröen cars, others acquired expensive motorcycles.[35] Even when complaints forced the Peace Corps Agency to reduce the allowance to $105 per month, little changed in life-style. The volunteers continued with their affluent life-style and enjoyed the "big man" reputation in Cameroon.

Peace Corps volunteers spent much of their time in exclusive clubs such as the Buea Mountain Club. Reserved for Cameroon's upper class, the Buea Mountain Club was designed and built by German architects, but the Cameroonians who established the club modeled it after the typical conservative English tradition. Members often popped into the club in the morning for tea, in the afternoon for drinks and lunch, and in the evening for more drinks and the day's gossip. Nonmembers were not served.[36]

Spending their money lavishly on expensive goods and vacations because they paid neither for housing nor other utilities, the volunteers failed to destroy the ugly expatriate image traditionally associated with expatriates in Cameroon. The attempt to mitigate this lifestyle with visits to Cameroonian homes was not sufficient to change the reality. Perhaps this experience calls for a broad critical examination of what the Peace Corps Agency meant by the volunteers' "living a simple life."

Despite the emphasis on treating Cameroonians as equals, with respect and dignity, certain volunteers continued to underrate the host country people. "To hell with the natives," a volunteer responded when asked to spend more time working in the villages.[37] Such a statement shows that though the volunteers were expected to dismantle the superiority image indoctrinated into Cameroonians by expatriates from European countries, some volunteers actually enjoyed the feeling of the white man's superiority in that country.

Some of the problems the volunteers had with American embassy officials and AID workers originated from the latter's complaints about the volunteers' life-styles. Admittedly, embassy officials had an exclusive life-style, but they understood that Peace Corps policy required the volunteers to spend most of their time within the community learning about the people and also teaching them about life in the United States. Instead of doing this, some volunteers spent their vacations in expensive holiday resorts in Casablanca, Abidjan, Lagos, and other such places. Though the volunteers were free to travel anywhere in Africa during their vacations, they overdid it. Describing the experience of a vacation to the island of Fernando Po, a volunteer wrote:

Now picture this: a full moon sending streams of light on the ocean, silhouetting the African fishermen in their dugout canoes; ships anchored at sea with their lights twinkling like distant jewels; Spanish music being played in the distance; waves softly rolling into the shore; warm, balmy breezes bending the palm trees . . . it was a perfect vacation . . . shopping, eating (four or five course lunches and dinners. . . .), swimming, sleeping, reading. Never ever did I expect to have such a luxurious vacation while in the Peace Corps.[38]

It was a life-style resented by the embassy officials. Peace Corps volunteers were introduced to certain luxuries of life that would have been unavailable to them had they not signed up for volunteer services. Such luxuries the Cameroonians saw only because they worked so hard to provide them.

Whatever the luxuries, or the problems, they experienced in Cameroon, some volunteers preferred to stay there in order to avoid the draft for the Vietnam War. As this war escalated, so did the difficulties of the volunteers in explaining the reasons for U.S. involvement in Vietnam. Cameroonians grew increasingly critical and suspicious of American foreign policy. Questions concerning Vietnam became the volunteers' Achilles' heel in Cameroon. Frequent questions asked of volunteers at this time included: "Why is your country fighting in Vietnam?" "What is America doing in Vietnam?" The *Cameroon Times* and *La Presse du Cameroun* carried stories and photographs of casualties resulting from American imperialism in Vietnam. Peace Corps volunteers were unable to provide adequate answers to questions dealing with the subject. Former volunteers have written that to resolve their problem they developed techniques to avoid discussions of the Vietnam War each time the topic came up.

All in all, living in Cameroon was an enriching experience for the volunteers. The Peace Corps provided the volunteers with a "psychosocial moratorium"; they were afforded an "opportunity to withdraw temporarily from the lives they had been living, an opportunity to experience new and adventurous kinds of stimulation which allowed them to reevaluate their lives." They lived and experienced life in another culture. Additionally, living in Cameroon enabled the volunteers to "either reinforce their old ideas and patterns of behaviour or establish new ones."[39]

Serving in Cameroon "taught me the experience of adjusting to, dealing with and living in an 'alien' culture which caused me to mature and develop a much greater sense of self-reliance," a volunteer wrote. Another stated that in Cameroon he learned tolerance and patience: "No one can change the world—one can only make it a little better." Others learned a "great deal about cross cultural education and a lot about the dynamics of a country becoming independent after many years of colonial rule and domination."[40]

The Peace Corps experience helped the volunteers mature, develop, and plan their future careers. When they joined the Peace Corps, they were highly provincial. Even their knowledge of Africa was clouded with myths of jungle-forest, famine, people living in crumbling houses, children suffering from Kwashiorkor, cannibalism, and other barbarisms—all picked up from casual reading and films. After living in Cameroon, they knew better. They learned to dismiss stereotypes and clichés used to describe any country in the immense land mass once known as the "dark continent." Most volunteers also changed their opinions of the United States after living in Cameroon. Emphasizing this aspect of her Peace Corps experience, Mary Asmundson Dunbar wrote that "we volunteers did provide teaching and other skills, but we mostly learned a lot about ourselves, our country and Cameroonian culture." Her impressions and beliefs were similarly expressed by several other returned volunteers.[41]

Perhaps the most important lesson the experience taught them was that people all over the world are the same in many ways. They understood that other people are as committed to their culture as Americans are to theirs. For the volunteers, life would never be the same again. There would be changes and adjustments for the better. No one summarizes "living in Cameroon" better than Freeman T. Pollard and David J. Dwyer, both returned Peace Corps volunteers from Cameroon, who wrote:

> My service in the Peace Corps made a tremendous differen[ce] in my life. The entire direction of my professional life has been influenced by Peace Corps service, and I hope my personal life and outlook reflect the diversity I learned to appreciate as a volunteer.
>
> As far as service to the country [Cameroon] is concerned, it is clear to me that I gained far more than I [thought I] could possibly gain, for Cameroonians taught me things that I could not easily find in my own culture, namely that what is important in life is not high energy technology, but the importance of human relations, family, friends and so forth. When I went to

Cameroon, I was a citizen of the United States, when I returned I possessed no feeling of nationalism. Since that time I have found myself working with peace and justice oriented groups in my own community.[42]

8

Cameroonians Evaluate Volunteer Services

In July 1964, the first batch of Peace Corps volunteers departed Cameroon for the United States. Since then this process has been repeated each succeeding year. The volunteers who returned took along with them memories, gifts, and an ocean of experience. They left behind loved ones, friends, gifts, hope, and a way of life. They left behind Cameroonians thinking of the "great paradise" in the United States. Each year when July arrives, both the departing volunteers and their Cameroonian friends lament the time to say good-bye.

Through the volunteers, Cameroonians learned of America and came to understand Americans and their way of life. Thanks to the efforts of the young Peace Corps volunteers, Americans were seen as

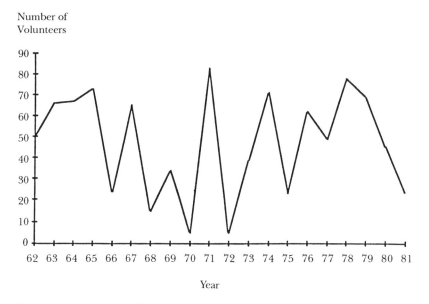

Figure 2. Volunteers who served in Cameroon between 1962 and 1981.

polite, hardworking, friendly, and understanding. As Harry Truman had used a stroke of the pen to proclaim the goals of American foreign policy in 1947 for the rest of the century, the early Peace Corps volunteers had succeeded in giving an entire generation of Cameroonians a lasting favorable opinion of the United States.[1]

The volunteers participated effectively in the educational development of Cameroon. Their presence made possible the opening of new academic institutions. In the field of community development, Cameroonians were satisfied with the work of the volunteers. They showed Cameroonians that people from the West were equal to other people in the world. Though disliked by the French, the volunteers established strong ties with the Cameroonian rank and file. In the villages the volunteers often heard the people say "we di glad plenti for forseka you done come for help we [we appreciate your help in our country]." "Mami" Angela Tanyi, a lady currently in her late sixties, expressed her satisfaction with the behavior of the volunteers when she stated, "dat people bin chop kontri chop, dey be like my picken dem plenti, they be be my picken them friend, my picken dey like that white man them [Those volunteers ate Cameroonian food and were very friendly to my children. My children very much appreciated the volunteers]."[2]

Because of the friendly attitude of Peace Corps volunteers, Cameroonians moved quickly to compare their behavior with that of the French expatriates. For the first time, Cameroonians met, conversed, and dined with whites who neither felt superior nor were snobs. Unlike the French, the volunteers treated Cameroonians as equals and recognized that everyone belongs to the same human race. A former student of the volunteers who later received a master's degree from an American university was frank in his description of volunteer performance and behavior, saying:

> At that time there was so much underdevelopment in the country. Those who say today that Cameroon is "underdevelop" need to find a different word to describe Cameroon in the early 1960s before the volunteers came to help. . . . The Peace Corps is the biggest thing America has done for Cameroon. . . . These young Americans had their weaknesses but just the fact that these Kennedy boys came to struggle with us, I think, is the most important thing. . . . You say you hail from Kumba, tell me if you are old enough to remember, how many white men used to visit Cameroonians before Kennedy's Peace Corps came.

Peace Corps volunteer Mary-Ann Tirone Smith (third from left) and Barbara Eason (second from left) enjoy a drink with two of their Cameroonian friends, Elizabeth Kibot (left) and Grace Tarkang, Buea, 1967. Courtesy of Mary-Ann Tirone Smith's Peace Corps collection.

The Peace Corps people were friendly. I can remember us playing ball with them. They did not know how to play football [soccer]. . . . It's so long ago, I cannot remember everything. . . . They ate the food your big mami [grandmother] cooked. Tell me . . . could a Frenchman who felt so much better than us have done that? I think these volunteers made Cameroonians proud of their country . . . they put on Cameroonian clothes and not the French suits which I see a lot of young people wearing today. The people made us proud of our culture. Just

Peace Corps volunteer Ben Hoskins enjoys an afternoon with his neighbors in the outskirts of Buea, 1968. Courtesy of the Media Center, Peace Corps Office, Washington, D.C.

because they did work we considered degrading made us proud to do the same work.[3]

Several Cameroonians agreed with this assertion. Whether in Foumban, Buea, or Mankon, the volunteers received praises from Cameroonians for the work they did. During their visit to the Bakossi region, Edith Pana and Betty Ann Hughes felt very honored when Mrs. Lindsay, the Cameroonian who went with them, told the Bakossi women: "Look at these young women; they have university educations and yet they have come to Africa, left their homes and families, to come to help you and teach you. But we cannot find one Cameroonian who is willing to give his knowledge and his service to you, without pay as these people are." It was a high point in Pana's and Hughes's Peace Corps careers. The Bakossi women appreciated their service.[4]

When John F. Kennedy described the problems of the Third World as "towering and unprecedented," he also requested a "towering and unprecedented response."[5] He never foresaw how far the vol-

Table 8. Advancement in Cameroon Education Enrollment in Various Schools

Year	Preschool	Primary	Secondary	Technical	Teacher Training
1959	5,668	435,479	9,305	4,553	1,417
1961	—	467,970	—	—	—
1964	—	693,268	23,356	6,814	1,474
1965	20,160	713,603	28,529	10,275	—
1967	22,958	819,189	32,300	11,058	2,151

Source: United Nations *Statistical Year Book*, 1963, p. 625; 1966, p. 728; 1967, p. 736; 1969, p. 178.

unteers would go to attain these objectives. Cameroonians agreed that the volunteers waged a war on their country's problems. Appreciating the services of the volunteers, Cameroonians showered them with gifts, traditional dances, and honest friendship. The volunteers disproved the old African proverb to "never trust a white man."

In education the volunteers performed a tremendous service at a critical juncture in Cameroon history. At a time when the few educated Cameroonians in the country abandoned teaching to take up more lucrative public service positions, the volunteers stepped in and replaced them.[6] Notice the advancement in Cameroonian education as shown in table 8. Though the entire credit for these advancements cannot be attributed solely to the volunteers, their contribution was significant.

Recalling the remarkable contribution made by the volunteers in the early 1960s, Solomon Tandeng Muna, former president of the Cameroon National Assembly, said:

> When we obtained our independence, there was an exodus of Europeans, technicians, and teachers. Among those who came to help us were the Peace Corps volunteers. This was important to West Cameroon, because it is an English-speaking area, so we had volunteers in our schools. I was prime minister of West Cameroon then, and always in touch with the Peace Corps leaders and with the volunteers when I made my tours. Right in my village there is the fish farm which is being run by a Peace

Corps volunteers. Not only that, I have a personal fish pond which is a demonstration project. Apart from these activities, they took part in cooperative societies, getting people to work together. Sometimes we would see a single lady in a village, in a small house, spending her time with people. Or a young man on a motorbike going through very rugged roads. I think they have done a great deal to contribute to our development, particularly among the peasant families.[7]

Sounding a similar message was Sadou Daoudou, Cameroon's former minister of public service. Daoudou stated in reference to the Peace Corps service,

I would like to cite a Chinese proverb to highlight the meaning of the Peace Corps. There is a Chinese proverb which says that instead of giving a hungry man a fish, it's better to teach him how to fish. Because, in my opinion, and this is rather important, because the assistance offered us through cooperative programs—whether it be the Peace Corps or a technical assistance program or the volunteers for progress—is extremely important and perhaps even more important than the financial aid provided by friendly governments because, for example, when the Peace Corps volunteers teach our farmers how to up the volume and the quality of their production—how to better produce their products—this is a lesson which can never be taken away once it is learned, while financial aid is subject to cancellation at any time. This latter form of aid can be cut off from one day to the next, while the lessons taught by technical assistance experts or the Peace Corps will be passed down to future generations.[8]

Perhaps no politician provided a better assessment of Peace Corps services in Cameroon than John Ngu Foncha.

I cannot recount the benefits we have derived by the presence of the Peace Corps in West Cameroon. After independence we had nearly closed all our higher educational institutions but this was avoided by the timely arrival of the Peace Corps without whom it would have been almost impossible to have continued these institutions. The progress of education is important and we are certain that by your coming we will be able to pursue our educational programmes in a surer way. We hope . . . we will be able to send more of our boys and girls abroad so that in a few years we can have them back as qualified tutors.

There are other things which the Peace Corps volunteers have done apart from their normal duties. Within the year they have assisted in various activities—planning and surveying of new roads and helping in community development efforts, rural water supplies etc.—jobs which did not concern them but which they found themselves and spent their holidays doing.

We have had the good fortune of getting you here as men and women who have had practical education. I am taking the opportunity to ask Cameroonians to learn this form of education from you. I hope that during your stay here you will find the opportunity to instil in the minds of Cameroonians the necessity for this practical work, because education by itself, knowledge by itself is of no use until put into practical effect.[9]

Muna, Daoudou, and Foncha spoke for a whole generation of Cameroonian politicians—Emmanuel T. Egbe, Ahmadou Ahidjo, and others. All expressed the same theme. They were among the people who signed the birth certificate of the Cameroon nation. And as the earliest politicians of the republic, they understood more than any one else the magnitude of the problems the nation faced. The exodus of the expatriates and the elimination of illiteracy, poverty, poor roads, economic dislocation, and wreckage caused by the Maquisards were all staggering problems. The motives behind the Peace Corps volunteers, diplomatic or humanitarian, were of little interest to these politicians. They wanted to see the problems of Cameroon solved. And the timely arrival of the volunteers was hailed by these pioneer politicians. Without the volunteers, Cameroon's educational system alone would have been dealt a shattering blow.

According to these leaders, the volunteers performed services beyond their assigned tasks. Not only did they excel in their jobs, they introduced Cameroonians to practical education. Education in itself was worthless unless put to use. When Foncha welcomed the second batch of volunteers to Cameroon, he honored the day as "the greatest day in the history of the Cameroonian Nation." After evaluating the numerous services performed by the first group of volunteers, Foncha concluded that these Americans were a "must" in Cameroon if the country hoped to hasten its educational advancement. Additionally, Mengot, director of education in West Cameroon, echoed Foncha's message when he told the volunteers that "your presence is appreciated not only by the Cameroon Government but by all lovers of progress of civilization and of human rights." Writing to Sargent

Shriver in 1964, Jacques Kuoh Moukouri, Cameroon's ambassador to the United States, informed Shriver of the positive contribution of the Peace Corps volunteers in Cameroon. Moukouri wrote, *"Je sais cette occasion pour vous faire part de la satisfaction qu'éprouve mon Gouvernement au vus des résultats positifs que l'oeuvre du 'Peace Corps' est en voie d'obtenir au Cameroun."*[10]

Because the volunteers played a significant role in Cameroon's development, Cameroonians moved quickly to respond to anything that threatened the continuation of the program. For the volunteers to serve in any country, the Peace Corps Agency had to be guaranteed political stability. Though Cameroon was stable, the *New York Times* in 1964 carried an inaccurate story about a civil war in the country.[11] Mengot assailed the story and assured the volunteers in training at Ohio University of the sound political climate in Cameroon. To assure Washington of the safety of the volunteers, Cameroonian officials informed the Peace Corps office that the activities of the UPC and the Maquisards did not extend to non-Cameroonians.

Simultaneously, when a biased article appeared in *Christianity Today* blaming the volunteers for causing havoc among sectarian groups in Cameroon, the Peace Corps Agency, the Cameroon Baptist Mission, and other denominations in the country refuted the charges. The article, titled "Religion and the Peace Corps," charged that the volunteers had preached "counter-Christian influence in mission schools" and that such a "diluting effect" was "resented by African Christians as much as by the missionary task force." Supporting its story, the paper quoted a volunteer who told his Cameroonian students that he believed in neither Christ nor the Resurrection. The volunteer had come to Cameroon "only for kicks," the paper added. Additionally, the article accused the Peace Corps Agency of "dumping unwanted Peace Corps volunteers on Cameroonian mission schools."[12]

The article touched a raw nerve. Peace Corps-Washington and mission groups in Cameroon viewed the article as insulting and described it as one loaded with half-truths and lies written by a journalist determined to use any means to advance his career. With a gifted stroke of the pen, Sargent Shriver reminded the editors of *Christianity Today* of the objectives of the Peace Corps. Volunteers were in Cameroon at the request of that country's government and had done nothing wrong, Shriver wrote. He dismissed the "counter-religious" charges by stating that it was Peace Corps policy for volunteers to disengage from "rcligious prosclytizing." Furthermore, the director of the Peace Corps pointed out that the volunteers were not obliged "to participate in religious observances contrary to their own faiths." Shriver added, "We respect the freedom of the Peace Corps volunteers to hold [their] religious convictions . . . we insist, however, that the volunteers behave in a manner which will not violate the standards of the institutions to which they are assigned."[13] In sum, Shriver informed the newspaper that the article had done a disservice by providing a distorted image of volunteer services. Perhaps the only crime the volunteers committed was to encourage Cameroonians to take the initiative on issues concerning their schools.

The Baptist missions in Cameroon considered the article vicious and sensational, designed to perpetuate sectarian conflicts in the country. George Lang, acting field secretary of the Baptist Mission in Cameroon, was blunt in his response to the charges in *Christianity Today.* He wrote:

> I wish to make the following points clear about the article, the periodical, and the writer. The writer of the article and editor of the periodical, Mr. Carl F. Henry, is *not* affiliated in any way with the Cameroon Baptist Mission nor with the North American Baptist Denomination, which is our supporting organization in the United States. Mr. Henry may be a Baptist, but there are many different Baptist groups in the United States, and the Baptist group with which he is connected is different from our own Baptist organization. . . . Since receiving the article, I have shown it to a number of our missionaries here in Cameroon. They have indicated to me their displeasure about the article . . . we feel that Mr. Henry's article is . . . an attack on us as Cameroon Baptists and on our work in Cameroon, and we are not happy about it.[14]

Commending the work of the Peace Corps volunteers, George Lang added, "without the help received from the Peace Corps," the Baptist Mission would be unable to execute its "responsibility for helping the youth of Cameroon." Flavius Martin, a Cameroonian and an ordained minister, praised the services of the volunteers in Cameroon: "The Peace Corps members attend our churches regularly, their services in our schools are as selfless as those of others, they make friends easily and live among the people, demonstrating the spirit of friendship." Equally he commended Peace Corps character when he added that "they have done well: they were well selected . . . I may say with deep humility, that this is a triumph for Dr. Paul Gebauer and the Athens, Ohio, Group." Supporting Martin's assertion, Foncha pronounced, "I do know . . . that the Baptist Mission is grateful for . . . the Peace Corps volunteers."[15]

Cameroonian politicians and elders were not the only people heaping praises on the volunteers. A series of letters written by secondary school students expressed gratitude to volunteers for being in Cameroon at a critical point in that country's history. All over Cameroon, students were "crazy" about the volunteers. Not often did they have people who served as their teachers and friends. British and French teachers distanced themselves from the students. The volunteers reversed this colonial practice. They mingled, talked, dined, and played different games with their students.[16] It was a real treat for the students, who spread the good word about the volunteers to their parents.

No one provided a better summary of the effectiveness of the volunteers and the lament over their departure than Alfred Mimba, head prefect of Baptist Teachers Training College. Mimba stated:

> Within your two years' stay here you have played a very significant role in the progress and stabilization of our country's economy. Not only have you helped our government in saving money, but your teaching has been of the inspiring type. The zeal and enthusiasm you have shown in your work has given those who have come under you the impetus to work harder. There are things we have learnt which would have been unknown to us without your being here. We have learnt much about American culture and their system of education. Coupled [compared] with the English system of education we have been previously used to, we now stand in a position to weigh these two cultures and systems together and be able to strike at a medium.
>
> You have not only been good classroom teachers but you have participated in all our games, and have introduced new games to us. You have not only taken part in the games connected with the college but you have been able to introduce games such as volleyball, basketball to villages around the vicinity of the college. You've been able to conduct classes with private individuals in the villages around Buea. We have enjoyed your attitudes towards students in general although the diversity of our culture has sometimes disagreed as a result of lack of

Peace Corps volunteer Mary-Ann Tirone Smith in the library that she helped establish in Buea, 1966. Courtesy of Mary-Ann Tirone Smith's Peace Corps collection.

understanding for each other. Even though all these occurred, it still gave rise to learning.

As S. T. Muna spoke for Cameroonian politicians, Alfred Mimba spoke for a whole generation of Cameroonian students. A secondary school student at the time, Mimba experienced the problems and was part of the unfolding process of educational progress made in Cameroon by the volunteers and those with whom they worked. Like many of his colleagues, he used books, sports equipment, and teaching aids provided by the Peace Corps.[17]

Through the organizational efforts of the volunteers, books and other school equipment were donated by American agencies to various secondary schools in Cameroon. The books were important, as most of the school libraries were lacking in material on various subjects. Volunteers who organized libraries—Mary-Ann Tirone Smith

Peace Corps volunteer Mikell Kloeters and some Cameroonian friends during a trip to the suburbs of Foumban, 1964. Courtesy of Mikell Kloeters's Peace Corps collection.

was one—furnished them with books donated by American agencies. The donated athletic equipment advanced sporting activities in the schools. While much of the sporting equipment donations have been discontinued, the Peace Corps has not stopped its policy of assisting with providing books whenever possible. Books marked "Donated by the Peace Corps" are still available in many of these college libraries.[18] For the Cameroonian student, the arrival of the volunteers in Cameroon was a literary and scholarly bonanza.

Outside education, Cameroonians showed their appreciation to volunteers in several other ways. Because of the affection the people of Foumban developed for Mikell Kloeters, one man promised to marry her just to make sure she did not return to the United States. In Buea, when Mary-Ann Tirone Smith requested Cameroonians to construct a cupboard for a card catalogue for the library she established, the response was immediate. "They came up with a card catalogue that was more magnificent than any piece of furniture I'd ever seen," Smith wrote. When the Edwardses asked for help with their fence project in Bojongo, the Bojongo people happily answered that call. In attending soccer games, young Cameroonians often assisted the volunteers in purchasing their tickets, thereby protecting them from the struggle often involved.[19] Cameroonians would not have responded to a call from Frenchmen.

The attitude of the volunteers encouraged some Cameroonians to visit the United States. In 1964, Seidou Njoya Njimouluh, the sultan of Foumban, was so moved by the performance of volunteer Mikell Kloeters among his people that he visited the United States. To show appreciation for her work—Kloeters was the only volunteer in his town at the time—the sultan and Queen Ramatou visited her parents in Dayton, Ohio.[20] Returning from the United States, the sultan sounded more and more like the volunteers; he preached the good word about the United States.

Because of the strong camaraderie among the volunteers and the host country people, Cameroonians felt comfortable discussing a variety of issues with their American friends. Though cautioned during training to stay away from political discussions, the volunteers became full participants in such conversations with their friends. And Cameroonians enjoyed it. Writing to the United States, a volunteer in Cameroon stated:

> I suppose you've heard some of the news from here. On New Year's Day war broke out between the Bakossi and the Bamileke at Tombel and I think about 300 people were killed.
>
> The Mayor of Bafang told Al Miller, who in turn told us, that a coup was planned against Ahidjo . . . around the first of December. They planned to shoot him at the Douala airport but the plot was discovered in time and the ring-leader, Finance Minister Kamga was tossed in jail and demoted to Minister of Tourism and the whole thing was shut up under the pretext that Kamga had written some controversial pamphlets.[21]

Equally important was that Cameroonians also saw the volunteers trustworthy enough to share gossip with. The gossip ranged from trivia to national issues. In some cases volunteers received their clues from reading the *Cameroon Times*, a newspaper that carried sensational stories such as "Jailed for Stealing Fowl," and to investigate such stories, volunteers always turned to their Cameroonian friends. A volunteer narrated one of these stories to his friend in the United States. He wrote:

> Here is some information which I doubt will interest you. But it is really bad though. You must have heard that one Sec. of

State, Mr. Nganje resigned. He copulated with a sick nurse in the Buea hospital. When the nurse for the night knocked at the door, nobody spoke. The nurse in charge was then afraid . . . so she phoned the police. . . . The door was broken and they were found in bed. So he was asked either to resign for personal reasons or be dismissed and the reason told. He took the former. Niba Fabs of Radio Buea did same in the office. And when somebody met him, he beat and sent the man away. The man invited the police and he was dismissed. This guy is the son of S. T. Muna. The S.D.O. of Victoria, Mr. Ngwa, did same, forcing the lady. . . . You may doubt how I know all this. Christopher Fundoh's aunt is a very high ranking mid-wife in the Buea hospital. She was called in for most of the examinations and so she told Fundoh who told me.[22]

All over Cameroon, Cameroonians established closer ties with the volunteers, shared their thoughts with them, and taught them how to dance "high-life." Peace Corps volunteer Roger Schneier, who had a weekly broadcast of jazz music for almost six months over Radio Buea, a reputable radio station in the country, helped Cameroonians acquire a better taste for that kind of music. A retired radio man in Cameroon regretted that those radio shows came to an end. "Jazz is refined music," he said.[23]

Cameroonian students found another option for further studies. Before the advent of the volunteers, Britain, France, and Germany were the only three countries Cameroonians visited for advanced studies. Discovering from the volunteers the importance of practical education, young Cameroonians added the United States to the list of the countries they preferred for further studies. The Cameroon government began awarding scholarships to students to study in the United States. Some returned volunteers encouraged their Cameroonian friends to come to the United States for studies. Many established long-lasting pen-friendships with Americans. As the years went by, the Cameroonians established and developed closer ties with their Peace Corps friends and their country. In fact, the Peace Corps volunteers and their services encouraged Cameroonians to learn more about the United States, a country whose people and way of life were unknown to many Cameroonians until the 1960s. Increasingly, Cameroonians became critical of the British and French systems of doing things.

Cameroonian women especially appreciated the work of the volunteers in helping to break down gender barriers. In 1964 Anna

Foncha, the wife of John Ngu Foncha, carried out lengthy discussions with the training team at Ohio University on the subject. She and other Cameroonian women saw that the female Peace Corps volunteers performed worthwhile services in Cameroon and rightly concluded that Cameroonian women had to become active in their country's development. To enhance these prospects, contacts were established with the League of Women Voters in Washington, D.C. Though little headway was made at this time, it was a step in the right direction. Looking back, these women consider those days as a time when everyone had to do something to assist the country's progress.[24]

As a result of Peace Corps services some Cameroonian elders established ties with bookstores in the United States. They hoped to improve their knowledge and also keep up with new publications coming out in their fields of study. E. T. Egbe, vice-minister of justice in Cameroon, and his colleagues developed a fresh interest in the American legal system and in legal interpretations taking place in the United States.[25] This demonstrates how volunteer services gave rise to a series of new developments not directly concerned with the Peace Corps.

A clearly positive contribution was that by spending their money in Cameroon, the volunteers continued to assist the development of the country. Economists would agree that the dollars the Peace Corps volunteers spent in the country, though few, assisted the economy. This was a marked contrast to the French, who rejected Cameroonian goods as inferior and spent their money on luxurious French goods.

Other distinctions were not so clear. Probably nothing more confused the Cameroonians in their evaluation of the Peace Corps than the race conflicts in the United States. Repeatedly, Cameroonians read about Eugene "Bull" Connor and Jim Clark, about posters reading "For Whites Only." They read about attacks on peaceful marchers, about Martin Luther King, Jr., explaining "why we [black Americans] can't wait." Given the racial strife in the United States, many would have thought that black African countries such as Cameroon would have been antagonistic toward the volunteers. But this was not the case. The Peace Corps was integrated, and both black and white Americans served in Cameroon as Peace Corps volunteers. Commenting on the existence of black Peace Corps volunteers to Cameroon, a former student of the volunteers wondered whether things were as bad for the black Americans as the papers said.[26] The

Peace Corps Agency was one of the few organizations in the United States that did not discriminate against blacks in the early 1960s.

Evidence of an integrated Peace Corps convinced Cameroonians that President Kennedy had declared a war against "apartheid" in the United States. Foncha emphasized this line of reasoning when he stated that the Peace Corps volunteers and Kennedy were winning in "their struggle to stamp out the colour bar in the United States." He noted:

> We appreciate the fact that the colour bar which has stained this great country is being gradually and systematically removed. We believe that it is only men and women like yourselves who mingle freely with us and your great leader, President Kennedy, who can eradicate the colour bar in America. Our prayers should be directed for this purpose and to the entire American nation so that they will be able to wipe out this second apartheid.[27]

For many Cameroonians, the United States was finally becoming a truly democratic nation under the New Frontier administration. Such beliefs were demonstrated in the treatment accorded the volunteers. The problems that did occur between the volunteers and their Cameroonian hosts were short lived. At no time did Cameroonians revolt against the Peace Corps volunteers, as was the case in Nigeria, Guinea, and other developing countries. Peace Corps officials Roy Fairfield, Jack Carmichael, Carl Denbow, Gilbert Schneider, and others have never forgotten the courtesy shown them in Cameroon. "It was a high point in my professional career," Jack Carmichael wrote about his experience in Cameroon.[28]

Flexibility, which was a key Peace Corps standard, was most effective in Cameroon. At a time when Cameroonians nursed strong resentment against white people because of their imperialist history and designs, the volunteers stepped in and proved to the country's people that Americans were different. Not only did Cameroonians appreciate this, but they developed momentum to challenge British and French policies. They also developed a keen interest in American affairs. Cameroonians growing up in the early 1960s will long cherish their experience with the early Peace Corps volunteers.

Conclusion

On May 20, 1972, Cameroon became a united republic. Under the strong leadership of its president, Ahmadou Ahidjo, Cameroon made tremendous political, economic, and social progress between 1960 and 1972. As a result, the country is a better place to live. While these positive changes resulted from a combination of factors, the Peace Corps volunteers did play a significant role.

Those volunteers who began serving in Cameroon in 1962 were assigned important functions. They were charged with the responsibilities of assisting the development of the country, spreading the good word about the United States, and making friends for the United States in Cameroon. Additionally, they were to serve as agents of democracy. Between 1962 and 1966, important results of their service were recorded.

Perhaps the most visible achievement was in the field of education. Cameroonian leaders understood that educational progress had to be in the forefront of economic development. More so than many other African countries, they mastered what Thomas Jefferson once said about education: "No nation can be both ignorant and free . . . education can illuminate the darkness and make men free." He added that "any society or state that ignores its humblest citizens [in education] is failing in its sacred obligations."[1] In 1960, Cameroon's educational system was on the "razor edge of danger." The country's illiteracy rate was among the highest in Africa. But with the help of Peace Corps volunteers, things changed. Though inexperienced with the Cameroonian educational system, the volunteers learned quickly and excelled in their goal of improving education.

The Peace Corps supplied a pool of volunteers to teach in schools. As school enrollments increased, more schools opened. By 1972, schools were located in every division and subdivision in the country. Thanks to the arrival of the volunteers, young Cameroonians were no longer faced with the choice of either attending and paying the high costs of mission schools or having no education. In 1973, more than a million students attended primary school, and 107,073 attended secondary school. By this time more than 65 percent of the school-age children were being educated.[2] This was a marked contrast with 1960, when too few students attended secondary school.

Despite the achievement in education, the volunteers who served in Cameroon between 1962 and 1966 only began the job in community development, a program that was born in uncertainty. The volunteers did not know what they were expected to do, nor did the Cameroonian government provide the basic financial assistance required for the programs to take off. Once in Cameroon, the volunteers operated under the most difficult circumstances: poor transportation, shortage of money, lack of knowledge of the terrain and its people, and the rejection of change by the country's people. And the volunteers and the Peace Corps Agency learned the bitter lesson that B.A. generalists could not do everything; community development projects in Cameroon were beyond the volunteers' experience. They learned from their mistakes, however, and passed this knowledge on to their successors. Not surprisingly, after 1966 the Peace Corps Agency began recruiting people with more specialized skills and also shifted the training site to Cameroon. After the 1960s, the Peace Corps Agency cut back on the recruitment of the B.A. generalists from 70 percent to 40 percent in the 1980s.[3]

Despite shortcomings in community development, the volunteers fulfilled their objective of creating friends in Cameroon. Cameroonians were beguiled by the courtesy, politeness, orthodontically perfected smiles, and friendship of the volunteers. As Gerard Rice points out, the volunteers created a new frontier for the United States in Cameroon.[4] For the Cameroonians, America became the place to visit, study, and copy. Blue jeans became the popular craze among young Cameroonians. In turn, Cameroonians visiting the United States helped reeducate Americans on Africa. The volunteers established frontiers for both countries.

The Peace Corps volunteers were part of the new direction in foreign policy Kennedy had promised in 1960. No longer willing to react to Communist initiatives, Kennedy invited young Americans to play a part in their country's foreign policy through the Peace Corps Agency. Partly as a result of the good word preached by the volunteers about the United States, some Cameroonians who were previous supporters of the Maquisards abandoned this terrorist organization funded by pro-Communist countries. By 1970 the Maquisards had almost completely disappeared. Also, the Cameroonian government restricted the travel of Cameroonians to the Soviet Union but generously granted exit visas to the United States. This trend was not reversed in later years. Though Cameroon stayed nonaligned in the Cold War, activities showed a tilt toward the United States. Significantly, the volunteers ensured that Cameroon did not fall into communism during the early years of the country's independence, when the economy tottered on the brink of collapse.

Equally important was that the volunteers who served in Cameroon and other African countries helped explode some of the myths about the so-called dark continent. Increasingly, returned Peace Corps volunteers denounced the parody of African history offered by Hollywood filmmakers and missionary slide shows. They organized conferences, associations, and lectures through which they educated Americans about Africa.[5] Americans were now told that Africans are normal human beings who are as committed to their culture as Americans are to theirs.

John Kennedy became one of the first people to notice the important achievement made by the volunteers in the Third World. In 1962, he told a group of Peace Corps volunteers that "they may ask you what you have done in the sixties for your country, and you will be able to say 'I served in the Peace Corps, I served in the United States Government.' "[6]

The Peace Corps Agency was part of a flexible response to communism. In 1961, Kennedy called on America to defend its security by closing the gap between the "have" nations and the "have nots." "If a free society cannot help the many who are poor, it cannot serve the few who are rich," Kennedy told his audience. Kennedy's ideas were based on the Cold War dogma developed during the Truman administration that economically backward areas were easily consumed by communism. Therefore, Cold War antecedents of the Peace Corps included the Marshall Plan and the Point Four program. Peace Corps volunteers were assigned a role in the Cold War. Volunteers were expected to help Third World countries leap into the twentieth century without falling prey to communism. However, the agency also had a humanitarian side. Because the Peace Corps was designed to improve human welfare, the agency was equally in line with the American tradition of caring for the less fortunate, an aspect of the Peace Corps which Kennedy and his men had also emphasized. At a press conference on March 6, 1961, Sargent Shriver stated that the Peace Corps was "going to prove that the American revolution is on the move again." He said, "When our young people go to live and work . . . in villages and schools . . . struggling to advance out of poverty, they are going to make a world contribution, I believe, to world peace."[7] Since observers of developing nations believed poverty was a major threat to peace, Peace Corps services were designed to generate economic growth, thereby eliminating poverty. Thus, the volunteers were expected to make major contributions to humanity.

By 1963, other achievements of the Peace Corps volunteers had been recorded. The new friendship established by the volunteers between the United States and developing countries contributed to the decision of Guinea and Algeria to deny Russia landing rights during the Cuban missile crisis, a generally reckless and risky time. When Kennedy was assassinated, Third World people lamented the loss of a true friend in the United States, mourning because they saw Kennedy through the eyes of the volunteers. In appreciation of Kennedy's assistance, they named schools, streets, and children after him. Third World people agreed with James Reston, who wrote:

> What was killed in Dallas was not only the President but the promise. The heart of the Kennedy legend is what might have been. All this is apparent in the faces of the people who come daily to his grave on Arlington Hill.[8]

The hospitality Peace Corps volunteers enjoyed in Cameroon was not duplicated in several other African countries. Cameroonians appreciated Peace Corps services, and the political stability in that country gave the volunteers a sense of security. It was not the situation in several African countries, especially as military takeovers became a major characteristic of postindependence Africa. This unstable political situation in certain countries caused volunteers some apprehension. Peace Corps volunteers in many African countries faced problems ranging from loneliness, insecurity, and criticism to expulsion.

The first major challenge to the Peace Corps occurred in Nigeria, a country considered by American officials as "Africa's giant." As the second country Sargent Shriver visited in 1961 to sell the Peace Corps program, Nigeria received its first contingent of volunteers in September of that year. Less than a month after the volunteers arrived in Nigeria, they were confronted with the Margery Michelmore incident. Michelmore, twenty-three and hardworking, signed up for the Peace Corps shortly after the agency was established. Formerly a schoolteacher in Massachusetts, Michelmore was assigned to work in Nigeria, where she and her thirty-six Peace Corps colleagues received in-service orientation at the University of Ibadan.

Like most volunteers in African countries, Michelmore found some of the conditions in Nigeria deplorable. Describing these conditions to a friend in the United States, she wrote on a postcard:

> With all the training we had, we really were not prepared for the squalor and absolutely primitive living conditions rampant both in the city and in the bush. We had no idea what underdeveloped meant. It really is a revelation and after we got over the initial horrified shock, a very rewarding experience. Everyone except us lives in the streets, cooks in the streets, sleeps in the streets, and even goes to the bathroom in the streets.

Unfortunately for Michelmore and her Peace Corps colleagues, the postcard dropped out of her purse as she went to the post office and ended up in the hands of the students of the University of Ibadan. The reaction to the card was immediate. Students reprinted several hundred copies and distributed them to their colleagues at the university, "where Miss Michelmore and 36 other Peace Corpsmen were in training." After reading the card, Nigerian students protested, demonstrated, and demanded the eviction of Peace Corps volunteers from their country. At a meeting organized to deal with the Michelmore crisis, the students labeled the volunteers as "America's international spies" and described the Peace Corps program as "a scheme designed to foster neo-colonialism." All over Nigeria, newspapermen chastised Michelmore. This was the first major test of the Peace Corps Agency.[9]

The volunteers in Nigeria felt insecure and thought the protestors would get their way. One of the volunteers had touched a raw nerve in that country by reporting on a "few homely truths." At a news conference, Sargent Shriver hinted that "communists had fomented the uproar." Shriver described the incident as a "big flap," adding that the press had taken a "riot of 150 people" and made it sound as if the entire Nigerian population had revolted against the Peace Corps. Questioned whether volunteers should stop writing letters to the United States, Shriver responded, "We're not sending out a bunch of correspondents to compete with the news agency." Michelmore supported Shriver's assessment of the crisis. In New York City, on October 20, 1961, Michelmore informed reporters that the crisis had been "pretty much blown up," and added that she did not know "who was behind the printing and the distribution of the postcard text."[10] Eventually the crisis subsided, and everyone affected settled back to learn the lessons.

Peace Corps volunteers were not expelled from Nigeria, but Michelmore did leave. The volunteers learned to write in their next postcards, "Having a nice time. Wish you were here." Also, the volunteers learned that no matter how terrible conditions were in African countries, they were there to improve and not criticize them. Peace Corps-Washington took measures to ensure that such a destructive episode did not recur by asking volunteers to display the utmost sensitivity in their host country. But in another incident, in October 1961, Peace Corps volunteers were attacked by the Nigerian press after journalists discovered a letter written by Craig Walker, an American who had spent the summer vacation with his Peace Corps friends. Walker wrote that "Nigeria's people live daily with poverty and disease as well as with a corrupt and irresponsible government." An enduring legacy of these episodes was the suspicion that continued to haunt the relationship between Peace Corps volunteers and Nigerians. Though the volunteers remained and performed effectively in Nigeria until 1971, their number was drastically reduced after 1966 because of the delicate political situation in that country.[11]

Another country in which the volunteers were careful not to misstep was Ghana. Kwame Nkrumah, Ghana's first leader and an alumnus of Lincoln University, was Africa's greatest critic of American foreign policy. Nkrumah never forgave Eisenhower for his support of European colonialism in Africa. Nkrumah believed that Kennedy endorsed the assassination of Lumumba. Kennedy was a "murderer," Nkrumah stated. According to Roger Hilsman, director of research and intelligence in the Kennedy administration, the events in the Congo became Kennedy's "first sustained test" in the African continent, and "history could hardly have devised a more baffling and frustrating test," for the Kennedy administration in that part of the world. When Kennedy acted as if he would reverse the decision to finance the Volta Dam, Nkrumah warned that he would distribute copies of Kennedy's promissory note to pay for the construction of the dam to other African leaders.[12]

The uneasy relations between the United States and Ghana continued until Nkrumah was overthrown in 1966. Nkrumah nursed several grievances against the United States: he never forgave the CIA for its role in the assassination of Lumumba, and he scolded America for its indecision on the issue of decolonization. While studying at Lincoln University in Pennsylvania, Nkrumah had become deeply scarred by American racism. Such were the problems volunteers assigned to Ghana were to face. Ghanaian students had been informed that the Peace Corps volunteers were "technical experts from neocolonialist nations [Britain and the United States]." Arch disciples of Nkrumah were convinced that the volunteers were in Ghana on a spy mission, much like the reaction of Peace Corps opponents in Nigeria. As a result, Ghanaians frequently bombarded the volunteers with questions such as "You are not a spy, are you?"[13]

Early in their service to Ghana, the volunteers were told how to communicate on the subject of Ghana. In September 1962, A. J. Dowuona-Hammond, Ghanaian education minister, turned a welcome address to the second batch of volunteers to his country into a series of "don'ts." He warned the volunteers to "avoid destructive criticisms" and added that "freedom in Ghana is not a license for spreading falsehood or for indulging in destructive criticism." Such warnings alerted the volunteers to the difficulties of serving in Ghana. To ease their burdens, the volunteers developed a new maxim: "The government is fine, Nkrumah is a good leader" was how the volunteers responded to questions concerning Nkrumah's regime.[14]

Adding to the volunteers' frustration was their inability to explain the continuous racial violence in America and justify their country's growing involvement in Vietnam. For many Ghanaians, these twin evils only confirmed what Nkrumah had told them about the United States. The Ghanaian press was relentless in its coverage of these events. The racial incidents were numerous: Freedom Rides; Albany, Georgia; Birmingham; the March on Washington; the assassination of Malcolm X; Selma, Alabama—it was an endless list. Each event received detailed coverage, and the stories represented a constant source of embarrassment for the volunteers. The press used these incidents to challenge America's commitment to democracy and peace. Volunteers who had gone to Ghana to assist the course of democracy in that country found the job quite challenging. Disregarding volunteer presence, Ghanaian newspapers labeled the United States the enemy of peace and cheered the Soviet Union as a country that has "always stood for peace." When China tested its first atomic bomb, the Nkrumah regime justified such action by stating that "the Chinese had discovered the bomb to increase their national defense capability and oppose the U.S. imperialist policy of nuclear blackmail and nuclear threats."[15] Few volunteers had been prepared for this anti-American attitude in Ghana.

Because of these problems, Peace Corps officials were quick to point out that the volunteers "were not having an easy time in Ghana" and tagged the entire project as being in "some danger." Volunteers realized that it was easier to perform their teaching assignments than to make friends. "Ghanaians are hard to get to know," a volunteer stated. Despite the upheavals, the volunteers remained hopeful. They devoted more time to their services and performed adequately. "Ghanaian science teaching in secondary schools depend[ed] on them [the volunteers]," a newspaperman wrote.[16] Privately, Nkrumah admitted that the only good thing the United States had done for Africa was the Peace Corps. No wonder Peace Corps volunteers have never been evicted from Ghana.

If the volunteers exercised caution in their dealings with Ghanaians, those in Sekou Touré's Guinea faced a different problem. Sekou Touré presented Peace Corps-Washington with its greatest nightmare when he became the first African leader to expel the volunteers from his country. A disciple of African nationalism, Touré denounced Charles de Gaulle's *communauté française rénovée*, took Guinea to independence, and proved de Gaulle wrong when he secured economic assistance for his country from other sources.[17] Determined not to let any single foreign power influence the affairs of Guinea, Touré secured assistance from both the United States and the Soviet Union. However, when Touré traced the source of an attempted coup against him to the Soviets, he expelled the Soviet ambassador, M. Solod, from Guinea in 1961. The following year he kicked out Soviet technicians, replacing them with American Peace Corps volunteers in 1963.

Peace Corps volunteers who went to Guinea had their first taste of the country shortly after they arrived in Conakry in 1963. "An extremely poor country as evidenced by dirty streets, homes . . . we were advised that this country would be different from the U.S. of A., what an understatement!" a volunteer wrote of his initial impression. His colleague added that "you can be prepared for how it looks but not how it feels, it smells . . . burning trash." Others complained of the humid climate and some renamed Conakry "purgatory."[18] If these were disappointments for the volunteers, severe problems were just ahead.

Sekou Touré was Nkrumah's closest ally in Africa. Perhaps as a result the two leaders held similar views on the United States. Volunteers in Guinea were reminded constantly of American imperialism and racism. Like the *Ghanaian Times*, the Guinean *Horoya* carried stories and graphic photographs of racial violence in the United States. Titles such as *"A Alabama, un jeune blanc lance un serpent vivant contre des noires,"* and *"La ≪Grande Marche≫ des noire—Américains sur Washington,"* appeared daily in the *Horoya*. Other titles focused on U.S. imperialism in the world, thereby making life quite miserable for the young volunteers. Like their colleagues in Ghana, volunteers in Guinea were totally unprepared for some of the problems they faced: Touré had won the Lenin Peace Prize in 1961; past American policy of supporting imperialism made Guineans suspicious of the volunteers; and the civil rights struggle in the United States only complicated matters for the volunteers.[19] How could they have promoted democracy in such an atmosphere?

The volunteers faced other problems in Guinea. Guinea was a country with numerous dialects, but the national language was French. Only some 15 to 20 percent of the volunteers in that country could speak fluent French or any of the dialects. As a result, several volunteers never spoke with Guineans outside their jobs. Those who did, spoke with the host country people "with signs" and a "few key French words." The inability to communicate with the host country people contributed to the misery of volunteers in Guinea. In performing their duties, the volunteers faced additional headaches: absence of textbooks and teaching aids, lack of motivation and interest on the part of the students, and the failure by students to understand the American accent. Burdened with such predicaments, the volunteers also had to deal with American embassy and AID officials in that country. Little peace existed between embassy officials and the volunteers. In 1964, Philip S. Cook, Peace Corps evaluator in Guinea, observed this troubled relationship. "There must be well over a thousand hardcore communists in Guinea but they are no match for U.S. Embassy/AID contingent when it comes to making trouble for the Peace Corps," Cook wrote.[20]

Trapped by their own weaknesses and built-in frustrations, such as the tense political climate in Guinea and other host country and embassy problems, the volunteers remained unhappy, restricted, and reserved in their service in Guinea. In 1965, several volunteers expressed their disappointments to David Hapgood, Peace Corps evaluator to Guinea. "Teaching English is only an excuse for getting the Peace Corps into Guinea—and that is not good enough for me," a volunteer anguished. Another lamented, "I've gone through hell the past two years . . . why did the Peace Corps do this to me? Why?" "All I've done is show a few Guineans that Americans ain't devils. That is nice for the State Department—but no use for Guinea," another volunteer stated.[21] Peace Corps service in Guinea was not what volunteers had hoped for.

By 1966, the volunteers had failed to achieve any of their objectives. Their years in Guinea had been unnecessarily long and lonely. If some were looking for a way out, their time came in 1966 during the United States–Guinean crisis. On October 29, 1966, nineteen Guinean delegates flying in a Pan American airliner to Addis Ababa, Ethiopia, to attend the Organization of African Unity Conference were stopped, searched, and ordered off the plane in Accra, Ghana. Refusing to disembark the plane, the Guinean officials were carried out by Ghanaian troops. In the wake of the incident, Touré accused the United States of having conspired with Lieutenant-General J. A. Ankrah, the new Ghanaian leader who overthrew Kwame Nkrumah in February 1966, to degrade Guineans. Touré held the United States "wholly responsible for the kidnapping of the Guinean delegation." Touré put Robinson McIlavine, United States ambassador to Guinea, under house arrest. Guinean troops surrounded the American ambassador's house. Some employees of the American embassy, the United States Information Agency, and the Agency for International Development were asked to leave the country.[22] The brickbats were quick to fall. American newspapers lashed out at Touré as an "avowed Marxist," an "insulting travesty of a leader," and a "ruthless tyrant" and demanded that the United States stop all assistance to Guinea. Guinean newspapermen reiterated their message of U.S. imperialism. Aid or no aid, Touré was determined to assert himself.

Tuesday, November 8, 1966, was hot and humid in Conakry, Guinea. It had rained early that morning, and crowds had gathered in the Conakry Stadium to wait for Touré. He had summoned his countrymen to inform them of his decisions about the two-week-old deterioration in United States–Guinean relations. For the American Peace Corps volunteers in that country, it was a day to sit home and wait for news from Conakry Stadium. America had had its share of problems with Guinea in the past, but this time both sides had been pushed to the brink.

Touré arrived at about 11:00 A.M. He dressed in sparkling white Guinean attire that added to his charisma. Those who had predicted his speech to be an indictment of the United States were correct. His language was firm, and the speech was brief. Touré chastised the United States, condemned continuous U.S. imperialism, and ordered the Peace Corps volunteers out of his country.[23] It was the first time a nation had ever evicted the volunteers.

The volunteers were confused, surprised, shocked, but hurried to bid farewell to their few Guinean friends. Everything had happened too quickly. They believed they were innocent bystanders unjustly caught in the cross fire of international politics. But they hurried to leave. Touré was unpredictable, and they did not know what might happen next. Responding to questions concerning Touré's decision, Peace Corps officials stated that the volunteers "simply got caught in the gears of international politics."[24] They were right. The volunteers had done nothing wrong.

Touré's decision established a precedent. One after the other, African countries expelled Peace Corps volunteers in the 1970s. In 1970, sour relations led Somalia to ask the volunteers to leave. Following Idi Amin's rise to power in Uganda, an American journalist and a Peace Corps volunteer died mysteriously. Responding to this tragedy, the United States withdrew the volunteers from that country in 1973. In 1977, when Peace Corps volunteers were found advising student protesters against the government of Colonel Mengistu Haile Mariam in Ethiopia, they were given two days to leave the country. Of the twenty-four African countries that accepted Peace Corps volunteers in the 1960s, only thirteen had not kicked out the volunteers at least once before 1980. Though volunteers returned to Guinea in 1969, they were out again in 1971 and did not return until after Touré's death in 1984.[25]

It is no surprise, then, that volunteers who served in Cameroon have continued to cherish the memory of their stay in that country. Some have even gone back to visit their old friends in Cameroon.[26] However, the expulsion of volunteers from other African countries was not the result of inadequate performance in their jobs. Peace Corps volunteers in those countries worked effectively. They had the misfortune to be caught in the tangled web of international politics.

With the Peace Corps volunteers, Kennedy revived the intellectual vitality of American foreign policy. Kennedy's Peace Corps program helped correct the Third World failures of the Eisenhower administration. But these new directions in foreign policy initiated by Kennedy have been underestimated by historians, who dismiss Kennedy as a Cold War hawk. True, he was a Cold Warrior. But as

Herbert Parmet pointed out, who in the early 1960s aspiring for the office of the presidency was not a Cold Warrior?[27] Kennedy interpreted the containment policy to provide assistance to Third World people ignored by his predecessors. In order to provide a balanced understanding of Kennedy, historians need to study how containment helped the development of the Third World.

Unfortunately, the work of the Peace Corps in Africa has not attracted much scholarly attention. Historians need to evaluate Peace Corps services in various countries. This study of the performance of the volunteers in Cameroon represents a modest start in that direction. But there are still many questions that need answers. Detailed studies are needed on Peace Corps volunteers' performance in countries such as Nigeria, Ghana, and Guinea. Why were the volunteers withdrawn in certain developing countries—Nigeria, Guinea, Chad, Ethiopia, Mauritius? Why did the Peace Corps Agency shift the training sites from the United States to the African countries? What contributions has the Peace Corps made toward the development of African nations? Scholarly biographies of the early "commanders" of the agency, such as Sargent Shriver, Warren Wiggens, and William Josephson, are also badly needed. Is Peace Corps service a guaranteed path toward a profitable and stable career? Some quantitative study is needed of those who entered the Peace Corps. All these studies are necessary for a complete evaluation of volunteer performance and to analyze the role the agency has played in the development of African nations.

The services of the Peace Corps volunteers in the Third World raise important questions about American containment policy, questions that became more urgent after the Vietnam tragedy. Today the United States has a shaky standing in many Third World countries. Many are puzzled about what the volunteers learned when they served in foreign countries in the 1960s. The volunteers were supposed to assist the United States in formulating a better foreign policy for the Third World.[28] But currently there seems to be a reversion to a one-track military solution, such as in the Persian Gulf and Central America. Each day U.S. foreign policy crises multiply. Perhaps more former volunteers need to be brought into the foreign policy-making process. They might rekindle the flexible approach and idealism that the United States employed with many of these countries during the early 1960s.

Abbreviations

C.Q.	*Congressional Quarterly Almanac*
C.R.	*Congressional Record*
Freedom of Communications	U.S. Subcommittee on *Freedom of Communications*
JFKL	John F. Kennedy Presidential Library, Boston, Massachusetts
LBJL	Lyndon Baines Johnson Presidential Library, Austin, Texas
NAB	National Archives, Buea, Cameroon
NA	National Archives, Washington, D.C.
NSF	National Security Files
OUL	Special Collections, Ohio University Library, Athens, Ohio
PCDCD	Peace Corps documents, Carl Denbow
PCDMK	Peace Corps documents, Mikell Kloeters
PCDRF	Peace Corps documents, Roy Fairfield
PCL	Peace Corps Library, Washington, D.C.
POF	President's Office Files
Public Papers	Public Papers of the Presidents of the United States
RPCV	Return Peace Corps volunteer
Statutes at Large	United States Statutes at Large

Notes

Introduction

1. Some of these studies are Gerard T. Rice, *The Bold Experiment: JFK's Peace Corps;* Robert Carey, *The Peace Corps;* Coates Redmon, *Come as You Are: The Peace Corps Story;* Morris I. Stein, *Volunteers for Peace: The First Group of Peace Corps Volunteers in a Rural Community Development Program in Colombia, South America;* Milton Viorst, ed., *Making a Difference: The Peace Corps at Twenty-five;* and Merni Ingrassia Fitzgerald, *The Peace Corps Today.* These authors focus for the most part on the idealism theory. Their discussion of the Peace Corps' activities is limited to the Latin American and Far Eastern countries; Africa is largely ignored. However, while I was working on this book, a book appeared that contained a chapter on Peace Corps activities in Ethiopia, a part of Africa toward which increasing attention has been focused (though it is only one part of a very large continent); that chapter is Gary May's "Passing the Torch and Lighting Fires: The Peace Corps," in Thomas G. Paterson, ed., *Kennedy's Quest for Victory: American Foreign Policy, 1961–1963.*

Chapter 1
The Beginning

1. Qtd. in Albert S. Miles, Kennedy's Death, Nov. 1963, Volunteer Information-Nigeria, Peace Corps Microfilm, Roll 5, Box 5, John F. Kennedy Library (hereafter cited as JFKL).

2. Mary Jo Bane, "We Have Begun," Kennedy's Death, Dec. 1963, Volunteer Information-Liberia, Peace Corps Microfilm, Roll 4, Box 4, JFKL.

3. Qtd. in "African Tributes to Kennedy," *West Africa,* Nov. 30, 1963, 1359; also in David W. and Diane McDowell, Kennedy's Death, Dec. 21, 1963, Volunteer Information-Nigeria, Peace Corps Microfilm, Roll 5, Box 5, JFKL. David W. and Diane McDowell were Peace Corps volunteers in Nigeria in 1963. Their letter describes Azikiwes's remarks and the sympathy shown by Nigerians upon Kennedy's death.

4. The quotation is from Arthur M. Schlesinger, Jr., *A Thousand Days: John F. Kennedy in the White House,* 1029. For more on the lament over Kennedy's assassination and the gratitude for his African policy, see *Africa Report,* Dec. 1963; Sanford J. Ungar, *Africa: The People and Politics of an Emerging Continent,* 59–62; Russell Warren Howe, *Along the Afric Shore: An*

Historic Review of Two Centuries of U.S.-African Relations, 130–31; "The World of John F. Kennedy," *West Africa,* Nov. 23, 1963, 1343; and ibid., Nov. 30, 1963, 1359.

5. Qtd. in Theodore C. Sorensen, *Kennedy,* 199; also in Stephen E. Ambrose, *Rise to Globalism: American Foreign Policy since 1938,* 181. John F. Kennedy's original remark is from a speech made in Tampa, Florida, at the Hillsborough County Courthouse on October 18, 1960. See U.S. Subcommittee on *Freedom of Communications,* pt. 1, The Speeches, Remarks, Press Conferences and Statements of Senator John F. Kennedy, August 1 through November 7, 1960, 658. See also John F. Kennedy, "Defremery Park, Oakland, Calif.," Nov. 2, 1960, *Freedom of Communications,* 862.

6. Qtd. in John F. Kennedy, "Remarks of Welcome to President Nkrumah of Ghana at the Washington National Airport," Mar. 8, 1961, *Public Papers of the Presidents* (hereafter cited as *Public Papers*) 1:160; Dwight D. Eisenhower, *The White House Years: Waging Peace, 1956–1961,* 582.

7. Qtd. in Richard D. Mahoney, *JFK: Ordeal in Africa,* 19; "Speech of Senator John F. Kennedy, Zembo Mosque Temple, Harrisburg, Pa.," Sept. 15, 1960, *Freedom of Communications,* 250; and also in Henry Fairlie, *The Kennedy Promise: The Politics of Expectation,* 71; "Remarks of Senator John F. Kennedy, Paducah, Ky., Airport," Oct. 8, 1960, *Freedom of Communications,* 529.

8. Qtd. in Mahoney, *JFK,* 19; Ambrose, *Rise to Globalism,* 182; Fairlie, *The Kennedy Promise,* 72.

9. John F. Kennedy, "Special Message to the Congress on the Peace Corps," Mar. 1, 1961, *Public Papers* 1:143–46.

10. John Lewis Gaddis, *The United States and the Origins of the Cold War, 1941–1947,* 353–55; qtd. in Gordon Wright, *The Ordeal of Total War, 1939–1945,* 234; Robert H. Ferrell, *Harry S. Truman and the Modern American Presidency,* 72; Thomas G. Paterson, *On Every Front: The Making of the Cold War,* 22.

11. Robert J. Donovan, *Conflict and Crisis: The Presidency of Harry S. Truman, 1945–1948,* 8.

12. Qtd. in Fraser J. Harbutt, *The Iron Curtain: Churchill, America and the Origins of the Cold War,* 153; Donovan, *Conflict and Crisis,* 81, 73; Harry S. Truman, *Memoirs: Year of Decisions.*

13. Qtd. in Harbutt, *The Iron Curtain,* 157, 185–91.

14. Ibid., 277; qtd. in Donovan, *Conflict and Crisis,* 192.

15. Harry S. Truman, "Special Message to the Congress on Greece and Turkey: The Truman Doctrine," Mar. 12, 1947, *Public Papers* 3:178–79.

16. Ambrose, *Rise to Globalism,* 86; also see Ronald Steel, *Walter Lippmann and the American Century,* 438–39; Michael H. Hunt, *Ideology and U.S. Foreign Policy,* 101, 111, 117.

17. William H. Chafe, *The Unfinished Journey: America since World War II,* 182; Arthur M. Schlesinger, Jr., *Robert Kennedy and His Times,* 72; Herbert S.

Parmet, *Jack: The Struggles of John F. Kennedy*, 208–9; John F. Kennedy, "Remarks of Senator John F. Kennedy," City Hall, Newark, N.J., Sept. 15, 1960, *Freedom of Communications*, 246.

18. Qtd. in Paterson, *On Every Front*, 71; Walter LaFeber, *America, Russia and the Cold War, 1945–1984*, 62–63.

19. Qtd. in Robert J. Donovan, *Tumultuous Years: The Presidency of Harry S. Truman, 1949–1953*, 28.

20. Harry S. Truman, "Inaugural Address," Jan. 20, 1949, *Public Papers* 5:114, 115.

21. Harry S. Truman, *Memoirs: Years of Trial and Hope*, 231–32.

22. Ibid., 232–33; also see Eric Goldman, *The Crucial Decade—And After: America, 1945–1960*, 94.

23. Truman, *Memoirs: Years of Trial*, 234.

24. Chafe, *The Unfinished Journey*, 182.

25. Qtd. in Parmet, *Jack*, 210; Chafe, *The Unfinished Journey*, 182.

26. U.S. Department of State, *Foreign Relations of the United States, 1950: National Security Affairs; Foreign Economic Policy* 1:288–92.

27. Ambrose, *Rise to Globalism*, 121. Historians have yet to come up with the final word on Washington's view of communism between 1945 and 1950. There is evidence that Washington did not perceive communism as a monolithic movement until the beginning of the Korean War. For more on this, see John Lewis Gaddis, "The Emerging Post-revisionist Synthesis on the Origins of the Cold War."

28. *United States Statutes at Large* (hereafter cited as *Statutes at Large*), Oct. 26, 1951, 82d Cong., 1st sess., vol. 65:644–45. Harry S. Truman, "Statement by the President Upon Signing the Mutual Security Act," Oct. 10, 1951, *Public Papers* 7:563–64.

29. Chafe, *The Unfinished Journey*, 108, 183; Schlesinger, *Robert Kennedy*, 99–107; Steel, *Walter Lippmann*, 521. Herbert Parmet convincingly argues that Kennedy's failure to denounce McCarthy was consistent with Kennedy's previous line of reasoning. Kennedy had accused Truman of not doing enough in the Cold War. Also, McCarthy was a friend of the Kennedy family. For more on this, see Parmet, *Jack*, 213, 300–310.

30. Steel, *Walter Lippman*, 521.

31. Fairlie, *The Kennedy Promise*, 72–73.

32. Qtd. in Hunt, *Ideology and U.S. Foreign Policy*, 164, 165.

33. Ibid., 164. Stephen E. Ambrose, *Ike's Spies: Eisenhower and the Espionage Establishment*, 293–94; Ellen Ray, William Schaap, Karl Van Meter, and Louis Wolf, eds., *Dirty Work 2: The CIA in Africa*, 70–73. The CIA cooperated fully with British intelligence. For more on this, see John Ranelagh, *The Agency: The Rise and Decline of the CIA*, 242–44, 253.

34. Qtd. in Mahoney, *JFK*, 35.

35. Vernon McKay, *Africa in World Politics*, 204–7; "Sekou Touré's Surprises," *West Africa*, Mar. 12, 1960, 287; "Communism in Africa," ibid., Jan. 13, 1962. Ibezim Chukwumerije, "The New Frontier and Africa, 1961–1963," 49; also see Schlesinger, *A Thousand Days*, 510–11; and Ungar, *The People and Politics*, 59.

36. Qtd. in Parmet, *Jack*, 226–27; also see Chafe, *The Unfinished Journey*, 182. Qtd. in Schlesinger, *A Thousand Days*, 554.

37. "Independence for Algeria," *Washington Post*, July 5, 1962, Algeria-General, 1961–63, President's Office File (hereafter cited as POF), JFKL.

38. Qtd. in Mahoney, *JFK*, 20; "Independence for Algeria," JFKL.

39. Qtd. in Mahoney, *JFK*, 22.

40. Qtd. in "The World of John F. Kennedy," *West Africa*, Nov. 23, 1963; Mahoney, *JFK*, 22.

41. William J. Lederer and Eugene Burdick, *The Ugly American*, 40.

42. Ibid., 278.

43. Joan Iversen, *"The Ugly American:* A Bestseller Reexamined," in Paul Harper and Joann P. Krieg, eds., *John F. Kennedy: The Promise Revisited*, 155–56, 157.

44. Rice, *The Bold Experiment*, 10–11; Hubert H. Humphrey, *The Education of a Public Man: My Life in Politics*, 250.

45. Carey, *The Peace Corps*, 11, 12.

46. Alan C. Elms, "New Frontier: The Peace Corps," *The Nation*, Dec. 3, 1960, Birth of the Peace Corps, Papers of Gerald W. Bush, Box 2, JFKL.

47. Rice, *The Bold Experiment*, 11.

48. John F. Kennedy, "The New Frontier," July 15, 1960, JFK Speeches, Papers of Gerald W. Bush, Box 3, JFKL; and "Remarks of Senator John F. Kennedy, San Francisco, Calif., International Airport," Sept. 3, 1960, *Freedom of Communications*, 95. Qtd. in Sorensen, *Kennedy*, 199.

49. "Speech of Senator John F. Kennedy, Citizens for Kennedy Rally, Waldorf-Astoria, New York City," Sept. 14, 1960, *Freedom of Communications*, 238; and "Speech of Senator John F. Kennedy, Portland, Maine, Portland Stadium," Sept. 2, 1960, ibid., 94; "Remarks of Senator John F. Kennedy, Eastern Carolina Stadium, Greenville, N.C." Sept. 17, 1960, ibid., 263–64.

50. Qtd. in Schlesinger, *A Thousand Days*, 554; also see Mahoney, *JFK*, 30; and Howe, *Along the Afric Shore*, 125. "Speech of Senator John F. Kennedy, Cow Palace, San Francisco, Calif.," Nov. 2, 1960, *Freedom of Communications*, 865.

51. "Speech of Senator John F. Kennedy, Cow Palace," *Freedom of Communications*, 865, 1238, 864; also see Rice, *The Bold Experiment*, 14.

52. Elms, "New Frontier," JFKL.

53. Rice, *The Bold Experiment*, 21.

54. Richard Nixon, "Statement by the Vice President of the United States, Peace Corps," Nov. 6, 1960, *Freedom of Communications*, pt. 2, The Speeches, Remarks, Press Conferences and Study Papers of Vice President Richard M. Nixon, August 1–November 7, 1960, 1061; also quoted in Harris Wofford, *Of Kennedys and Kings: Making Sense of the Sixties*, 243; and Sargent Shriver, *Point of the Lance*, 13; Elms, "New Frontier," JFKL.

55. Qtd. in Wofford, *Of Kennedys and Kings*, 257.

56. Kennedy, "The New Frontier," 6, JFKL.

Chapter 2
The Establishment of the Peace Corps

1. David Halberstam, *The Best and the Brightest*, 38–43; also see I. M. Destler, Leslie H. Gelb, and Anthony Lake, *Our Worst Enemy: The Unmaking of American Foreign Policy*, 189. Fairlie, *The Kennedy Promise*, 115, 225.

2. Qtd. in Ambrose, *Rise to Globalism*, 181; Fairlie, *The Kennedy Promise*, 102; John F. Kennedy, "Inaugural Address," Jan. 20, 1961, and "Special Message to the Congress on Foreign Aid," Mar. 22, 1961, *Public Papers* 1:1, 205.

3. Fairlie, *The Kennedy Promise*, 322, 155; also qtd. in Chafe, *The Unfinished Journey*, 196; Schlesinger, *Robert Kennedy*, 440.

4. John F. Kennedy, "Annual Message to the Congress on the State of the Union," Jan. 30, 1961, *Public Papers* 1:22–23.

5. Louise FitzSimons, *The Kennedy Doctrine*, 9; Ambrose, *Rise to Globalism*, 185; John Lewis Gaddis, *Strategies of Containment: A Critical Appraisal of Postwar American National Security Policy*, 227–28.

6. Bruce Miroff, *Pragmatic Illusions: The Presidential Politics of John F. Kennedy*, 18–19; Ambrose, *Rise to Globalism*, 203–4; "On Trial: Sargent Shriver and the Peace Corps," Newspaper Clippings, Birth of the Peace Corps, Papers of Gerald W. Bush, Box 1, JFKL.

7. Fairlie, *The Kennedy Promise*, 180, 181, 6; Chafe, *The Unfinished Journey*, 189.

8. "On Trial," JFKL.

9. Qtd. in Peter Braestrup, "Peace Corpsman No. 1—A Progress Report," *New York Times Magazine*, Dec. 17, 1961, Peace Corps July–Dec. 1961, POF, JFKL: "though the Peace Corps is still young, Director Shriver begins to look like that welcome Washington type—the fellow who gets things done."

10. Halberstam, *The Best and the Brightest*, 221.

11. Sorensen, *Kennedy*, 248; Shriver, *Point of the Lance*, 12; Harris Wofford, Oral History Transcript, May 22, 1968, JFKL; "On Trial," JFKL.

12. Wofford, Oral History Transcript, JFKL.

13. Redmon, *Come as You Are*, 48; Sargent Shriver, "The Peace Corps Speaks for Itself," *New York Herald Tribune* Youth Forum, Mar. 24, 1961, 2, Speeches of Sargent Shriver, Peace Corps Library, Washington, D.C. (hereafter cited as PCL).

14. Wofford, Oral History Transcript, JFKL; qtd. in Rice, *The Bold Experiment*, 37.

15. Roy Hoopes, *The Complete Peace Corps Guide*, 35–38; Rice, *The Bold Experiment*, 39–40. For the full text of Warren Wiggins's "The Towering Task: The National Peace Corps," see *Speeches of Warren Wiggins*, Feb. 1, 1961, PCL.

16. Kennedy, "Annual Message to Congress," Jan. 30, 1961, *Public Papers* 1:24.

17. Wiggins, "The Towering Task," PCL; qtd. in "On Trial," JFKL.

18. Wofford, Oral History Transcript, JFKL.

19. Rice, *The Bold Experiment*, 40–41.

20. "Program for the Peace Corps," Feb. 20, 1961, 1, Peace Corps, Shriver Report and Recommendations, Box 85, POF, JFKL; Rice, *The Bold Experiment*, 43.

21. Wofford, *Of Kennedy and Kings*, 261; Sargent Shriver, "Report to the President on the Peace Corps" and "Report to the President: Summary of the Next Steps," Feb. 22, 1961, Peace Corps Shriver Report and Recommendations, Box 85, POF, JFKL.

22. Shriver, "Report to the President on the Peace Corps," 19–20, JFKL.

23. Ibid., 17.

24. John F. Kennedy, "Statement by the President Upon Signing Order Establishing the Peace Corps," Mar. 1, 1961, *Public Papers* 1:134–35.

25. FitzSimons, *The Kennedy Doctrine*, 14–15.

26. Qtd. in Redmon, *Come as You Are*, 33, 36; also see Wofford, *Of Kennedys and Kings*, 268.

27. Redmon, *Come as You Are*, 37.

28. Qtd. in Wofford, *Of Kennedys and Kings*, 265.

29. Shriver, "The Peace Corps Speaks for Itself," 1–2, PCL; George Gallup, ed., *The Gallup Poll: Public Opinion, 1935–1971* 3:1704; "College Presidents Give Approval in a Poll by Margin of 9 to 1," *New York Times*, Mar. 6, 1961, 1:3. Also see Roger S. Jackson, "The Peace Corps: Political Activities and Implications during Its Pre-passage Stages" (unpublished paper), 3–4, Jan. 16, 1963, Papers of Gerald W. Bush, Box 3, JFKL. Sargent Shriver, Transcript of Background Press and Radio News Briefing, A-10, Mar. 6, 1961, Transcript of Background Press: Peace Corps Morale, Basic Design, Papers of Gerald W. Bush, Box 1, JFKL.

30. Qtd. in Rice, *The Bold Experiment*, 29.

31. John F. Kennedy to Ambassadors, May 29, 1961, Department of State, President's Letters to Ambassadors, Box 4, National Security Files (hereafter cited as NSF), JFKL.

32. Carey, *The Peace Corps*, 15–16.

33. Gaddis, *Strategies of Containment*, 224; Walter LaFeber, *Inevitable Revolutions: The United States in Central America*, 148–49.

34. University official, response to questionnaire, Oct. 20, 1987; Gilbert Schneider, interview with author, Nov. 9, 1987, Athens, Ohio. In 1965, Shriver informed President Johnson that 77 percent of American adults understood that the Peace Corps was an effective instrument of American foreign policy. For more on this, see Sargent Shriver to the President, Memorandum, Dec. 14, 1965, Peace Corps 1965, Confidential File, Agency Reports, Office of Economic Opportunity, Box 129, Lyndon Baines Johnson Library, Austin, Texas (hereafter cited as LBJL).

35. Freeman T. Pollard, response to questionnaire.

36. Harris Wofford, "Excerpts from Some Talks on the Peace Corps," Mar. 11, 1961, 5–6, Organization Folder 3 of 6, Papers of Gerald W. Bush, Box 3, JFKL.

37. Shriver, *Point of the Lance*, 12; Transcript of Background Press and Radio News Briefing, A-1, JFKL.

38. Qtd. in Robert A. Liston, *Sargeant Shriver: A Candid Portrait,* 160–62.

39. Qtd. in Redmon, *Come as You Are,* 39.

40. Liston, *Sargent Shriver: A Candid Portrait,* 151–52; Braestrup, "Peace Corpsman No. 1," JFKL.

41. Shriver, "The Peace Corps Speaks for Itself," 2, PCL; and "Commencement Address," June 7, 1961, De Paul University, Chicago, Ill., Speeches of Sargent Shriver, PCL. Shriver was asked this question in India.

42. "Speech Prepared for Delivery by Robert Sargent Shriver, Jr., Director, Peace Corps, at the Institute of Higher Education, Board of Education, Methodist Church, Nashville, Tennessee," July 24, 1961, Speeches of Sargent Shriver, PCL.

43. Wofford, *Of Kennedys and Kings,* 268; "Kennedy Sets up Peace Corps of Volunteers to Work Abroad," *New York Times,* Mar. 2, 1961, 13:1; "Youth: How About Urdu?" *Time,* Apr. 7, 1961, 24–25.

44. Qtd. in Rice, *The Bold Experiment,* 160; Transcript of Background Press and Radio News Briefing, B-7, B-8, JFKL.

45. Sargent Shriver to J. Edgar Hoover, Oct. 5, 1964, Correspondence and Memoranda, Roll 9, William Josephson Chronological File, Box 10, JFKL. The policy of contacting employers created problems for prospective volunteers who were placed in a situation of losing their jobs if not selected. These problems are discussed in an unpublished paper by Roger S. Jackson, "The Peace Corps: Problems of a New Administration," History, Papers of Gerald W. Bush, Box 3, JFKL.

46. Shriver qtd. in *Congressional Record* (hereafter referred to as *C.R.*), 87th Cong., 1st sess., 1961, 107, pt. 14:19242 (Morgan), 19247 (Curtis).

47. Moritz Thomsen, *Living Poor: A Peace Corps Chronicle,* 6–7; Josephine Ripley, "Peace Corps: Rugged Training," Feb. 10, 1962, Newspaper Clippings, Papers of Gerald W. Bush, Box 3, JFKL.

48. Roy P. Fairfield, "The Peace Corps and the University," 195; Jack Carmichael to Roy P. Fairfield, Correspondence-1963, Peace Corps Representatives, Box 2, Special Collections, Ohio University Library, Athens, Ohio (hereafter cited as OUL).

49. Fairfield, "The Peace Corps and the University," 194–95; Victor Wilson, "Peace Corps Avoids South: Negro, White Colleges Alike," *New York Herald Tribune,* June 29, 1962, Newspaper Clippings, Papers of Gerald W. Bush, Box 3, JFKL.

50. Wofford, *Of Kennedys and Kings,* 263; Rice, *The Bold Experiment,* 79; Jackson, "The Peace Corps: Problems," 11–12, and "The Peace Corps: Political Activities," 23, JFKL.

51. Jackson, "The Peace Corps: Problems," 11, JFKL; Sargent Shriver to Honorable Sam Rayburn, Mar. 15, 1961, Organizational Folder 3 of 6, Papers of Gerald W. Bush, Box 3, JFKL.

52. "On Trial," JFKL; qtd. in Braestrup, "Peace Corpsman No. 1," JFKL.

53. Qtd. in *Congressional Quarterly Almanac* (hereafter cited as *C.Q.*), 87th Cong., 1st Sess., 17:327. For the legislative history, see Carey, *The Peace Corps,* 10.

54. *C.R.*, 19244–45. The Peace Corps budget of $163.6 million in 1989 is less than half the price of one B-1 bomber.

55. *C.Q.*, 324, 327.

56. Ibid.; also see Carey, *The Peace Corps*, 16–17.

57. Kennedy, "Remarks Upon Signing the Peace Corps Bill," Sept. 22, 1961, *Public Papers*, 1:614–15; *Statutes at Large*, Sept. 22, 1961, 87th Cong. 1st sess., 75:612.

58. *Statutes at Large*, 87th Cong., 1st sess., 75:612–23.

59. Transcript of Background Press and Radio News Briefing, A-10, JFKL.

60. "Peace Corps Under Fire," *West Africa*, Apr. 15, 1961, 399; Jay Walz, "Africans Oppose Aid by the West," *New York Times*, Apr. 1, 1961, 2:8.

61. Richard D. Mahoney, *JFK*, 158–59.

62. Qtd. in Thomas J. Noer, "New Frontiers and Old Priorities in Africa," in Paterson, ed., *Kennedy's Quest for Victory*, 279; Mahoney, *JFK*, 158.

63. Qtd. in Arthur Gavshon, *Crisis in Africa: Battleground of East and West*, 71–72; also see Stephen E. Ambrose, *Eisenhower: The President*, 588–90, and *Ike's Spies*, 293, 298–302; Ranelagh, *The Agency*, 338–45.

64. Qtd. in Schlesinger, *A Thousand Days*, 571; President Nkrumah to President Kennedy, Jan. 23, 1961, Ghana 1/61, Box 99, POF, JFKL.

65. Qtd. in Wofford, *Of Kennedys and Kings*, 269.

66. Sargent Shriver, "Remarks at the Dinner of the Catholic Interracial Council at the Conrad Hilton Hotel, Chicago, Illinois," June 1, 1961, 1, Speeches of Sargent Shriver, PCL.

67. Qtd. in G. Mennen Williams to George W. Ball, memorandum, Sept. 12, 1961, Ghana–Upper Volta Projects, Box 99, POF, JFKL; also see Adu Boahen, "Ghana since Independence," in Prosser Gifford and William Roger Louis, eds., *Decolonization and African Independence: The Transfers of Power*, 216. Qtd. in Thomas W. Ottenad, "Growing Peace Corps Stepping Up Operations," undated newspaper clipping, Advanced Planning Project, Box 5, OUL.

68. Schlesinger, *Robert Kennedy*, 560–61. For more on the debate surrounding the issue of the Volta Dam, see William Attwood, Oral History Statement, Nov. 8, 1968, JFKL. Qtd. in Noer, "Africa," in Paterson, ed., *Kennedy's Quest for Victory*, 281.

69. "America in West Africa," *West Africa*, Dec. 23, 1961.

70. Qtd. in Ungar, *The People and Politics*, 358; Lansine Kaba, "From Colonialism to Autocracy: Guinea under Sekou Touré, 1957–1984," in Gifford and Louis, eds., *Decolonization and African Independence*, 229–30; Schlesinger, *A Thousand Days*, 568.

71. McKay, *Africa in World Politics*, 206; Schlesinger, *A Thousand Days*, 568. However, Kennedy's undersecretary of African affairs, G. Mennen Williams, saw Sekou Touré in a different light. Williams believed Touré was a "strong, dynamic leader against the French, a great nationalist." For more on this see G. Mennen Williams, Oral Report, Mar. 8, 1974, 12, LBJL; and Kaba, "Touré," in Gifford and Louis, eds., *Decolonization*

and African Independence, 229, 243–44.

72. William Attwood to Secretary of State, May 4, 1961, Guinea, Jan.–May 1961, Box 2, NSF, JFKL.

73. William Attwood to George Ball, memorandum, May 12, 1961, 1, 8, Guinea, Jan.–May 1961, Box 2, NSF, JFKL. Attwood believed Sekou Touré had great respect for Kennedy; he also saw Touré as a great nationalist, not as the Castro of Africa. See Attwood, Oral History Statement, 4–8, JFKL.

74. Sargent Shriver to the President and Secretary of State, memorandum, June 26, 1961, Guinea, June–Aug. 1961, Box 2, NSF, JFKL.

75. Memorandum to the Secretary of State, unsigned and undated, Guinea, Jan.–May 1961, Box 2, NSF, JFKL.

76. Harris Wofford to the President, memorandum, Jan. 20, 1962, 1–3, PC Peace Corps Program Aug. 16, 1961–Apr. 8, 1962, White House Central Subject File, Box 670, JFKL.

Chapter 3
Cameroon and Its Problems

1. Tikum Mbah Azonga, "Cameroon: A friend in need . . . ," *West Africa*, May 18, 1987, 954–55; Richard Everett, "Cameroon: Cushioning the Shock," *Africa Report*, May–June 1986, 77–80; "Le Chef de l'Etat prescrit une application stricte du Pas" and Jean Ngandjeu, "L'affaires de tous," *Cameroun Tribune*, Aug. 23, 1990; "Cameroon: Facing the Challenge," *West Africa*, July 27, 1987, 1439–40.

2. Willard R. Johnson, "Foreword" to Ndiva Kofele-Kale, ed., *An African Experiment in Nation Building: The Bilingual Cameroon Republic since Reunification*, xiii; Victor T. Le Vine, *The Cameroon Federal Republic*, 30; Neville Rubin, *Cameroon: An African Federation*, 3–6.

3. Ralph A. Austen, "Slavery among Coastal Middlemen: The Douala of Cameroon," 305–7.

4. Harry R. Rudin, *Germans in the Cameroons, 1884–1914: A Case Study in Modern Imperialism*, 19–20; Robert Cornevin, "The Germans in Africa before 1918," in L. H. Gann and Peter Duignan, eds., *Colonialism in Africa, 1870–1914*, 397–99.

5. Rudin, *Germans in the Cameroons*, 160–63; Cornevin, "The Germans in Africa," 401–3.

6. Mark W. DeLancey, *Cameroon: Dependence and Independence*, 9–10, 13–14; Victor T. Le Vine, *The Cameroons: From Mandate to Independence*, 24, 30.

7. Christraud M. Geary, *Images from Bamum: German Colonial Photography at the Court of King Njoya, Cameroon, West Africa, 1902–1915*, 25–26, 37–42; Elizabeth M. Chilver, "Paramountcy and Protection in the Cameroons: The Bali and the Germans, 1889–1913," in Prosser Gifford and William Roger Louis, eds., *Britain and Germany in Africa: Imperial Rivalry and Colonial Rule*, 480–511; Cornevin, "The Germans in Africa," 400.

8. Rudin, *Germans in the Cameroons*, 289–90, 254–55, 261, 264; Cornevin, "The Germans in Africa," 400–401.

9. Le Vine, *The Cameroon Federal Republic*, 5. Most of the government offices and houses available today in the city of Buea, Fako division, were constructed during the German colonial era in Cameroon.

10. Rubin, *An African Federation*, 38.

11. Ndiva Kofele-Kale, "Reconciling the Dual Heritage: Reflections on the Kamerun Idea," in Kofele-Kale, ed., *An African Experiment*, 16–17.

12. Rudin, *Germans in the Cameroons*, 307, 419.

13. Qtd. in David E. Gardinier, *Cameroon: United Nations Challenge to French Policy*, 6; Le Vine, *The Cameroon Federal Republic*, 11.

14. Willard R. Johnson, *The Cameroon Federation: Political Integration in a Fragmentary Society*, 117–28; Le Vine, *The Cameroons*, 199, 202; Gardinier, *Cameroon*, 36–37.

15. Gardinier, *Cameroon*, 44–45; Le Vine, *The Cameroons*, 142–48.

16. Gardinier, *Cameroon*, 44–45; the French version is quoted in Richard Joseph, "Radical Nationalism in French West Africa: The Case of Cameroon," in Gifford and Louis, eds., *Decolonization and African Independence*, 331. Johnson, *The Cameroon Federation*, 138; Le Vine, *The Cameroons*, 146–48.

17. Joseph, "Radical Nationalism," in Gifford and Louis, eds., *Decolonization and African Independence*, 334–37; Gardinier, *Cameroon*, 68–70.

18. Gardinier, *Cameroon*, 80–93; Elizabeth S. Landis, "Cameroon in Chaos," *Africa Today* 7 (Mar. 1960): 7–8; Rubin, *An African Federation*, 97–98. Because Ghana and Guinea supported the UPC, these two countries openly rejected Ahmadou Ahidjo and did not send representatives to Cameroon on Independence Day. See "The Two Cameroons Today," *West Africa*, Jan. 9, 1960, 41–42; Helen Kitchen, "Cameroon Faces Troubled Future," *Africa Report*, Jan. 1960, 2–3, 7.

19. DeLancey, *Cameroon*, 34.

20. Nationalism in British Cameroon is discussed in Le Vine, *The Cameroons*, 193–214; and Johnson, *The Cameroon Federation*, 116–34. These two books, though published in 1964 and 1970, respectively, are still the authoritative works on the subject.

21. "Cameroons After Foncha: 1," *West Africa*, Aug. 15, 1959, 603; "Cameroons After Foncha: 2," ibid., Aug. 22, 1959, 637; Michael Crowder, "Independence and the Cameroons," ibid., Jan. 3, 1959, 3.

22. "Nigeria or Trusteeship?" and "Northern Cameroons Surprise," *West Africa*, Nov. 7, 1959, 931, and Nov. 14, 1959, 975.

23. "Terrorism at Cameroons Celebrations," ibid., Jan. 9, 1960, 35; Landis, "Cameroon in Chaos," 7–8. In his open letter titled "Dr. Moumie and M. Ahidjo," *West Africa*, Jan. 2, 1960, 14, Moumie stated that Ahidjo did not have support of the Cameroonians. "Cameroon's Fulani Premier," ibid., Jan. 2, 1960, 5–6; "Cameroon Plebiscite Results," ibid., Feb. 18, 1961, 187; Rubin, *An African Federation*, 109. The results of the plebiscite in Northern Cameroon were severely protested on the grounds that the Nigerian police "intimidated" the voters. " 'P'Day in the Cameroons: 2,"

West Africa, Mar. 11, 1961, 265; also see Victor T. Le Vine, "Calm before the Storm in Cameroon?" 3–4.

24. There are several studies on the Cameroonian constitution, which came into being in 1961. Some scholars have accused Ahidjo of using the constitution to establish a dictatorship. See Mbu Etonga, "An Imperial Presidency: A Study of Presidential Power in Cameroon," in Kofele-Kale, ed., *An African Experiment,* 133–55; Sammy Kum Buo, "How United Is Cameroon?" *Africa Report,* Nov.–Dec. 1976, 17–20.

25. "The Federal Republic of Cameroon," Dec. 13, 1961, Cameroon-Ahidjo's visit, Mar. 22, 1962, Box 112a, POF, JFKL; Kofele-Kale, "Reconciling the Dual Heritage," in Kofele-Kale, ed., *An African Experiment,* 3; Le Vine, *The Cameroon Federal Republic,* 30–32.

26. Rubin, *An African Federation,* 188; Kum Buo, "How United Is Cameroon?" 17–20; "Cameroon: Opposition in Parliament," *Africa Digest,* Oct. 1962, 105; "Cameroon: Two Views of One Party State," ibid., Apr. 1963, 168–69.

27. Rubin, *An African Federation,* 158–61.

28. Ibid., 183–84; Le Vine, *The Cameroon Federal Republic,* 34–36, and "The New Cameroon Federation," 8, 10.

29. I experienced the long hours on the Mamfe road at a later date, but I have also listened to many elderly people comment on the status of the road in the early years of independence. It was in the mid-1970s that the road was finally opened to traffic coming in opposite directions on the same day. Before then, Mondays, Wednesdays, and Fridays were the days when vehicles went to Mamfe; while on Tuesdays, Thursdays, and Saturdays vehicles returned to Kumba. Sunday was a day of rest.

30. Kitty and Andy Edwards, "Bojongo, A Case Study," Southern Cameroon: American Mission and the Peace Corps, 1962, National Archives, Buea, Cameroon (hereafter cited as NAB); also see documents presented by Carl Denbow for this study (hereafter cited as PCDCD). Professor Denbow directed the Peace Corps training program for volunteers going to Cameroon in 1964.

31. Le Vine, *The Cameroon Federal Republic,* 42; Peace Corps Project Description (104), 1, Peace Corps Documents, Box 8, OUL. In 1959, the whole of Cameroon had approximately 5,668 pupils in preschool, 435,497 in primary schools, 9,305 in secondary schools, 4,553 in technical schools, and 1,417 in teacher training schools. For more on these figures, see United Nations, *Statistical Year Book, 1962,* 625. The literacy rate in Cameroon as a whole was 15 percent. "A Long Way from Modern Civilization," *Time,* Aug. 3, 1962, 21.

32. Stanford Research Institute, *Education and Manpower,* 14–20, 35–36 (copies in the PCL and NAB). Also see Ako D. Mengot, "Pressures and Constraints on the Development of Education in West Cameroon," 19.

33. Stanford Research Institute, *Education and Manpower,* 22.

34. Ibid., 4, 64; Mengot, "Pressures and Constraints," 20.

35. Stanford Research Institute, *Education and Manpower,* 26.

36. There are thousands of students in Cameroon who were trapped

because they could not pass the GCE exams, thus giving up any other educational endeavors. A retired secondary schoolteacher commented that "once you fail[ed] the GCE, you receive[d] a new Christian name, 'dull.' " Of course, the psychological impact of such labels can hardly be overstated. Interviews conducted by author, Dec. 1987, Cameroon. For efforts to improve student performance on the GCE, see Mengot, "Pressures and Constraints," 19–20; L. M. Ndamukong, "Are West Cameroonians' Educational Standards Falling?" *West Cameroon Teachers' Journal* (Dec. 1964): 9–11, NAB.

37. A middle-class Cameroonian at this time made roughly 135,000 francs CFA ($540) in a year. Annual tuition for the primary schools averaged 1,600 francs CFA ($5), while that of secondary schools was as much as 25,000 francs CFA ($100). For more on this, see Stanford Research Institute, *Education and Manpower*, 28, 112. The country's average per capita income was $70 in 1962. "A Long Way from Modern Civilization," *Time*, Aug. 3, 1962, 21.

38. Stanford Research Institute, *Education and Manpower*, 20.

39. "Cameroon: Financial Position," *Africa Digest*, Aug. 1962, 30; "London Log: No Aid for Cameroon," *West Africa*, Nov. 19, 1960, 1321; "Cameroon Loses Commonwealth Preference," ibid., July 13, 1963, 791; Le Vine, *The Cameroon Federal Republic*, 43.

40. "Possible Points for Discussion with the new Cameroonian Ambassador," unsigned, undated memorandum, declassified Mar. 1990; and L. D. Battle to Kenneth O'Donnell, memorandum, Nov. 18, 1961, declassified Mar. 1990, copies in author's possession.

41. Memorandum to the President, Mar. 13, 1962, unsigned, Cameroon-Ahidjo Visit, Mar. 1962, Box 112a, POF, JFKL. For more on Ahidjo's appeal for help against the pro-Communist terrorist group, see "Head of Cameroon Says Reds Aid Foes," *New York Times*, Mar. 15, 1962.

42. "Dinner Speech, July 5, 1963, by U.S. Assistant Secretary of State for African Affairs, Governor G. Mennen Williams," Press Release No. 2530, July 8, 1963, and "U.S. Grants to Cameroon 120 Million Francs for Social Development," August 8, 1963, Press Release No. 2615, NAB.

43. "U.S. Grants to Cameroon 120 Million Francs," NAB.

44. "Ambassador Barrows Presents U.S. Plane to Cameroon," Press Release No. 2641, Sept. 2, 1963, NAB.

45. "Cameroon, United States Sign Loan Agreement," Press Release No. 2658; and "More U.S. Aid for West Cameroon," Press Release No. 2776, Oct. 31, 1963, NAB.

46. Peace Corps Project Description (104), 3, OUL.

47. A. D. Mengot to Honorable Minister, memorandum, Jan. 11, 1962, Southern Cameroon: American Aid Mission and Peace Corps, NAB; Memorandum to the President, unsigned, Mar. 12, 1962, JFKL.

48. Letter to American Embassy, Yaounde, unsigned draft, May 8, 1962, Roll 9, William Josephson Chronological File, Jan. 1961–Dec. 1962, Box 9, JFKL.

49. U.S. Department of State, *United States Treaties and Other International Agreements*, vol. 13, pt. 2:2114–19.

Chapter 4
Recruitment, Training, and Selection

1. Mert Guswiler, "Ohio University Peace Corps Volunteers May Continue Studies on Assignment," Aug. 4, 1962, *Cincinnati Enquirer*, Publicity, Box 9, Peace Corps Documents, OUL. *Peace Corps Training for Federal Republic of Cameroon, 1962;* and Roy P. Fairfield, *Training Plan for West Cameroon Peace Corps Project,* July 5–Aug. 31, 1962, Ohio University, Athens, Ohio, Peace Corps documents provided by Roy P. Fairfield (hereafter cited as PCDRF).

2. These quotations are responses to the questionnaire I administered to former Peace Corps volunteers.

3. Edward Kernan, "56 in Peace Corps to Attend Ohio U," *Plain Dealer*, and "OU to Begin Training for 56 Peace Corpsmen," *The Messenger*, Apr. 30, 1962, Publicity, Box 8, OUL. In a telephone interview, on Feb. 22, 1988, Roy Fairfield, who was project director, stated that fifty volunteers showed up for the training, not fifty-six as planned. But while some newspapers continued to write that fifty-six came for the training, others wrote forty-nine and fifty-five. Rice, *The Bold Experiment,* 143–44. "Mikell Joins the Peace Corps" 1:1–2, 9. Mikell Kloeters, a volunteer in 1962–64, kept a diary, later edited by Mary C. Thierer, titled "Mikell Joins the Peace Corps and Goes to Africa." This diary is divided into two parts and has provided a great deal of information on Peace Corps life: it is found in Peace Corps documents provided by Mikell Kloeters (hereafter cited as PCDMK).

4. "Oberlin's 54 Peace Corps Trainees Vow Racial Truth," *Plain Dealer,* 1963, newspaper clipping, PCDMK; Victor Wilson, "Peace Corps Avoids South, Negro, White Colleges Alike," *New York Herald Tribune,* June 29, 1962, Newspaper Clippings, Papers of Gerald W. Bush, Box 3, JFKL; Shriver, "Remarks at the Dinner of the Catholic Interracial Council," PCL.

5. Fairfield, *Training Plan,* 1, PCDRF; Russell Milliken, *Proposal: Peace Corps Cameroon Project,* Mar. 22, 1963, 2, PCDRF.

6. Ohio University/Cameroon PC-(W)-76, Peace Corps, 1963, Box 1, Peace Corps Documents, OUL; "Peace Corps Director Shriver Helps Get Ohio U. Training Program Started," July 1, 1962, Publicity, Box 9, Peace Corps Documents, OUL.

7. Qtd. in Fairfield, *Training Plan,* unnumbered page, PCDRF.

8. Ibid., 78–87.

9. Thomsen, *Living Poor,* 6.

10. Milliken, *Proposal,* 18–19, PCDRF. This material came from Roy Fairfield in a July 3, 1987, questionnaire response. Fairfield described Carmichael as a fellow who understood the craft of his assignment. There are countless letters on file at OUL written by Carmichael to volunteers. Most of these letters pointed out the strengths and weaknesses of volunteer performance.

11. Fairfield, *Training Plan,* 3, 4, PCDRF.

12. Ibid. Some of the quotations are from questionnaire responses. Also see Roy Fairfield, "Fairfield's Fiendish Field Day," lecture, Aug. 11, 1962, Archives-General, Box 5, Peace Corps Documents, OUL.

13. Fairfield, *Training Plan*, 5–6, PCDRF. The volunteers' remarks are from questionnaire responses. Freeman T. Pollard, a former volunteer, specifically emphasized that there was "[a] lot of 'Cold War' propaganda on [the] danger of Communism."

14. Fairfield, *Training Plan*, 14, PCDRF.

15. Ibid., 15, 16.

16. Ibid., 16.

17. Ibid.; Robert C. Clapp, "Peace Corps Coach Finds Rookies Poorly Equipped," Sept. 6, 1962, 1, Publicity, Box 9, Peace Corps Documents, OUL.

18. Clapp, "Peace Corps Coach," OUL; Roy P. Fairfield, Jack J. Carmichael, Russell A. Milliken, *Second Quarterly Report: Ohio University/ Peace Corps West Cameroon Project*, Mar. 31, 1964, 21, Ohio University, Athens, Ohio, PCDRF. Fairfield, *Training Plan*, 14, PCDRF; and Paul Gebauer to David Arnold, report, Oct. 31, 1964, 1–2, Budget-Misc., 1961–66, Box 1, Peace Corps Documents, OUL.

19. Gebauer to Arnold, report, 1–2, OUL.

20. Qtd. in Guswiler, "Ohio University Peace Corps Volunteers May Continue Studies on Assignment," OUL; Clapp, "Peace Corps Coach," OUL.

21. Fairfield, *Training Plan*, 17, PCDRF.

22. The early experience of bilingualism was marked with language confusion. People mixed dialects, English, Pidgin English, and French in conversations.

23. Fairfield, *Training Plan*, 39–41, PCDRF; "Exercise in Critical Thinking," 2, American and World, Box 10, Peace Corps Documents, OUL.

24. Charles Goslin, "Peace Corps Trainees Hike over Buckeye Trail," Aug. 2, 1962, *Daily News,* and "Hocking Section of Buckeye Trail Is Now Complete," Press Releases Misc., Peace Corps Documents, Box 9, OUL.

25. Qtd. in Thomsen, *Living Poor,* 5. Some former volunteers have expressed profound dismay with this testing. In his October 31, 1964, report to David Arnold, Paul Gebauer described the nervousness of students when the psychiatrist came.

26. Fairfield's remarks about the opinions of the psychiatrists are from a telephone interview, Feb. 22, 1987; the quotation is from a letter from Fairfield to Amin, July 3, 1987.

27. Philip S. Cook to Director and Authorized Eyes Only, "Evaluation Report: Ohio University, West Cameroon," July 26–27, 1962, 2, 6–7, National Archives, Washington, D.C. (hereafter cited as NA).

28. Fairfield, telephone interview, Feb. 22, 1987; Cook, "Evaluation Report," 7, NA.

29. Thomsen refers to "deselection" in *Living Poor* (7), from which the longer quotation is also taken.

30. Roy Fairfield, "Quarterly Report: Cameroon Peace Corps Project, Jan. 5, 1963," 17, PCDRF; also see Clapp, "Peace Corps Coach," OUL.

31. Qtd. in Charles A. Caldwell, "Cameroons Evaluation Report," Nov. 19–Dec. 15, 1963, 72–73, PCL; Fairfield, "Quarterly Report," Jan. 5, 1963, 19, PCDRF; Fairfield to Rogers Finch, International Center, Sept. 28, 1962, 1–4 Budget-Misc., 1961–66, Box 1, Peace Corps Documents, OUL.

32. Fairfield to Finch, Sept. 28, 1962, 1–2, OUL; Fairfield, "The Peace Corps and the University," 192–201.

33. Fairfield to Finch, Sept. 28, 1962, 3, OUL.

34. Ibid.

35. Ibid., 2.

36. Gebauer to Arnold, report, 7–8, OUL; Carmichael to Fairfield, Aug. 22, 1963, OUL.

37. Fairfield to Finch, Sept. 28, 1962, 3, OUL.

38. Volunteers complained from the field about their inadequacy in Pidgin English, which Paul Gebauer thought was a weakness of the first training program. Gebauer to Arnold, report, 1–8, OUL.

39. Quotation obtained from one of the returned Peace Corps volunteer-Cameroon (hereafter cited as RPCVC) responses to questionnaires, Jan. 24, 1988.

40. Jack Carmichael's response to questionnaire, Oct. 14, 1987.

41. Cook, "Evaluation Report," 5, NA; Jack Carmichael to Roy Fairfield, Apr. 18 and May 1, 1964, Jack Carmichael, Box 1, OUL.

42. "Ohio University to Sponsor Peace Corps Project in Africa," Apr. 30, 1962, *Logan Daily News*, newspaper clipping, Press Releases-Misc., Box 9, Peace Corps Documents, OUL. There are countless letters of recommendation written by Fairfield for the volunteers on file at the Special Collections, Ohio University Library. Fairfield said in a telephone interview on Feb. 22, 1988, that the volunteers could not effectively take the correspondence courses because they were more than busy with their ten-hour days and accompanying assignments. During vacation, however, they expanded their education as they traveled all over Cameroon; some went to other African countries as well.

43. Gilbert Schneider, interview with author, Nov. 9, 1987, Athens, Ohio.

44. Carl Denbow, interview with author, Nov. 10, 1987, Athens, Ohio; Carl H. Denbow, "Final Report of the Third Ohio University Corps Training Program for the Federal Republic of Cameroon, June 21–Sept. 5, 1964," PCDCD. Denbow also worked effectively with Fairfield, who was project coordinator when Denbow was director.

45. Gebauer to Arnold, report, 1, OUL; the names appear in PCDCD.

46. Milliken, *Proposal*, 3, PCDRF.

47. Gilbert Schneider, interview, Nov. 9, 1987.

48. Ibid.

49. Carl Denbow to Prof. Paul Roaden, Jan. 30, 1965, Advanced Planning Project, Box 5, Peace Corps Documents, OUL.

50. Grover A. Smith to Dr. O. Paul Roaden, report, Aug. 9, 1965, Education Conference, Box 5, Peace Corps Documents, OUL.

51. Numerous letters written by Cameroonian secondary students are available in Special Collections, Ohio University Library. Denbow and Schneider, in previously cited interviews, recalled the wonderful times they had with Foncha. Denbow, "Final Report," 6, PCDCD. Denbow stressed the "series of authoritative lectures given by Honorable A. D. Mengot." See also commentary on the returning volunteers.

52. Denbow, "Final Report," 6–8, 10, PCDCD.

53. Denbow to Amin, Nov. 17, 1987; and Tyrolt to Denbow, Labor Day, 1964, PCDCD.

54. Denbow, interview, Nov. 10, 1987.

55. Gebauer to Arnold, report, 5, OUL.

56. "Oberlin's 54 Peace Corps," PCDMK.

57. Andy Ruckman, "It's Groan and Grind as Peace Corps Trainees Seek Goal Here; But Smiles Keep Coming Through," 1963 (Reich is quoted here), and Bud Weidenthal, "Day in Peace Corps Seems like a Week," 1963, newspaper clippings, PCDMK.

58. "Mikell Joins the Peace Corps," 1:15, PCDMK.

59. Qtd. in Weidenthal, "Day in Peace Corps," PCDMK.

60. Among the factors that led to this decision was Ohio University's lack of a suitable environment for the practical training of the volunteers. For more on this see Stanley Meisler, "Overseas Evaluation-Cameroon," Jan. 13, 1966, 60–62, PCL. "Peace Corps Contracts," Interoffice communication to Jack W. Dumond, Nov. 23, 1964, 3, Budget-Misc., 1961–66, Box 1, Peace Corps Documents, OUL.

61. Gilbert Schneider, interview, Nov. 9, 1987. Carl Denbow to Amin, Sept. 28, 1987; similar feelings confirmed in an interview on Nov. 10, 1987.

Chapter 5
The Volunteers as Teachers

1. Fairfield, "Quarterly Report," 3, PCDRF.

2. Ibid.

3. "Mikell Joins the Peace Corps," 25–26, PCDMK.

4. Mary Asmundson Dunbar to Amin, Jan. 24, 1988.

5. Margery Michelmore, a Peace Corps volunteer in Nigeria in 1961, wrote a postcard to a friend in which she described the poor conditions in Nigeria. Unfortunately, the card ended up in the hands of Nigerian students, who rose in anger against the Peace Corps. For more on the Michelmore affair, see Harris Wofford, "Excerpts from Some Talks on the Peace Corps," Oct. 24, 1961, 7–12, JFKL; "Peace Corps Girl Stirs Anger in Nigeria," *New York Times*, Oct. 21, 1961, 10:4; Roy Fairfield, "Progress in the Cameroons," report, Apr. 16, 1963, 2, PCDRF.

6. Fairfield, "Quarterly Report," 9, PCDRF. When the Jeeps did arrive, they were totally inadequate, especially as the five Jeeps could not satisfy

the "American propensity for using an automobile." For more on this, see Lawrence E. Williams, "African Republic Unifies British, French Backgrounds," *Peace Corps Volunteer* 2 (Mar. 1964): 14.

Mami wagons were large buses used in Cameroon for public transportation. These buses were painted outlandish colors and carried as many passengers as possible, and whatever luggage passengers could not fit in the carriage was carried inside the vehicles where the passengers sat. Passengers often traveled with goats, pigs, and chickens. For further description, see Mary-Ann Tirone Smith, *Lament for a Silver-eyed Woman*, 115. Smith's novel contains vivid descriptions of aspects of Cameroonian culture—especially the life-style in the city of Buea, where she served.

7. Fairfield, "Quarterly Report," 2; and Fairfield, Carmichael, and Milliken, "First Quarterly Report," Feb. 1963, 7–9, PCDRF.

8. Fairfield, "Quarterly Report," 2, 6–7, PCDRF.

9. Ibid., 5–7.

10. Ibid.

11. On the problem of no textbooks, see Grover A. Smith to O. Paul Roaden, report, Oct. 29, 1965, 3, Corr. Smith, Grover, 1965, Box 4, Peace Corps Documents, OUL. Peace Corps-Washington provided no budget for such emergencies, and it was too expensive to mail heavy luggage by air. Roy Fairfield took a few books with him when he went for an inspection tour of the Peace Corps services in December 1962.

12. Wilson McCarthy, "Overseas Evaluations—Cameroon," Dec. 6–20, 1962, 2, Peace Corps Cameroon, PCL; Fairfield, "Quarterly Report," 8, PCDRF; Jack J. Carmichael to Russell Milliken, Jan. 31, 1964, 1, Correspondence 1963, Peace Corps Representative, Box 2, Peace Corps Documents, OUL.

13. Fairfield, "Quarterly Report," 10–11, PCDRF; "U.S. Peace Corps-Cameroon: Notes from Your Rep.," report, Nov. 29, 1962, 1–3, Correspondence-General, Box 4, Peace Corps Documents, OUL.

14. Fairfield, "Quarterly Report," 14, PCDRF.

15. Ibid., 13. A volunteer serving at the Queen of the Holy Rosary secondary school in Okoyong was one of the earliest volunteers to quit service in Cameroon. For more on this, see McCarthy, "Overseas Evaluations," 12, PCL; Fairfield, Carmichael, and Milliken, "Third Quarterly, Report: Ohio University/Peace Corps West Cameroon Project," Aug. 1963, 10, PCDRF. For the names of the volunteers who dropped out of the Peace Corps in Cameroon and the dates when they did so, see "Peace Corps Volunteers Who Served in Cameroon between 1961 and 1982," Office of Administrative Services, Peace Corps, Washington, D.C.

16. Fairfield, "Quarterly Report," 7, PCDRF.

17. In the telephone interview of Feb. 22, 1988, Roy Fairfield emphasized the continuous effort of Ohio University in sending books to volunteers. The University also worked with Jack Carmichael in Cameroon to raise the morale of the volunteers. This was very important in providing the volunteers with "emotional equilibrium." For more on this, see Fairfield, Carmichael, and Milliken, "Second Quarterly Report," Apr. 1963, 7, 15, and Fairfield "Quarterly Report," 14, PCDRF. Books also

came from sources other than Ohio University. Individual volunteers requested and obtained books from their alma maters. For example, Tirone received 3,000 books from various agencies in the United States to equip the library she established. In a telephone interview on May 12, 1991, she stated that about 75 percent of the books were collected by Connecticut General Life Insurance, where she worked before joining the Peace Corps.

18. Stanford Research Institute, *Education and Manpower* 2:20–22; E. D. Quan to Doo Kingue, memorandum, Mar. 15, 1962, Southern Cameroon, American Aid Mission and Peace Corps, NAB. For his services at Ombe, see McCarthy, "Overseas Evaluations," 11, PCL; Fairfield, Carmichael, and Milliken, "First Quarterly Report," Feb. 1963, 7–8, PCDRF.

19. Fairfield, Carmichael, and Milliken, "First Quarterly Report," Feb. 1963, 11, PCDRF.

20. Stanford Research Institute, *Education and Manpower,* 2:22; Fairfield, "Quarterly Report," 4, PCDRF.

21. Fairfield, "Quarterly Report," 12, PCDRF; qtd. in McCarthy, "Overseas Evaluations," 12, 15 PCL.

22. Fairfield, "Quarterly Report," 3, PCDRF; responses to questionnaires.

23. This credential was greatly appreciated by the Cameroonian students, especially as the volunteers replaced the less-qualified British expatriates.

24. Caldwell, "Cameroons Evaluation Report," 16–17, PCL; responses to questionnaires.

25. The Peace Corps-Cameroon project requested the volunteers in Cameroon to evaluate a "typical Cameroonian student" on the basis of general ability, motivation, study and classroom habits, personal and career objectives, temperament, and prejudices. The responses were varied, but all the volunteers agreed that the Cameroonian student was generally disciplined and hardworking. For the complete evaluation, see Smith to Roaden, report, Aug. 9, 1965, 1–9, OUL.

26. Ibid., 3; Stanley Meisler, "Overseas Evaluation: Cameroon," Feb. 10, 1965, 6, Peace Corps Cameroon, PCL.

27. Roy Fairfield, "Ohio Volunteers Render Service Beyond Community," 16–17.

28. Caldwell, "Cameroons Evaluation Report," 45, PCL; Fairfield, Carmichael, and Milliken, "Second Quarterly Report," Apr. 1963, PCDRF. My own class, incidentally, was the last to write the GCE ordinary- and advanced-level exams administered and graded by the University of London in 1974 and 1976, respectively.

29. Stanford Research Institute, *Education and Manpower* 2:20–22, 28, 88, 90, 98.

30. Ibid., 2:98; "Summary: Peace Corps Program in Cameroon," unsigned, undated report, Oct. 18, 1965, 3, Peace Corps Cameroon, PCL.

31. Meisler, "Overseas Evaluation," 1966, 11, PCL; Stanford Research Institute, *Education and Manpower,* 120; E. A. Ekiti, "Basel Mission Education Development in West Cameroon," *West Cameroon Teachers' Journal* 2 (Dec. 1964): 39.

32. Ekiti, "Basel Mission Education," 40; Meisler, "Overseas Evaluation," 1965, 7, PCL. D. P. Hayden to Le Directeur de Cabinet, memorandum, Jan. 14, 1963, American Aid Missions and Peace Corps, Southern Cameroon, NAB; George W. Lang to the Permanent Secretary, the Ministry of Education and Social Welfare, Buea, Nov. 3, 1964, Application for Peace Corps Volunteers, Secretariat of State for Interior, NAB.

33. The group was originally larger, but some members resigned from the Peace Corps services in Cameroon for various reasons. While some could not adjust to the cultural differences, others simply could not stand being away from the United States. Still, some were pressured into resigning by the Peace Corps because of alcohol abuse or apparent psychological problems. For the specifics on who resigned when, see "Peace Corps Volunteers Who Served in Cameroon Between 1964 and 1982." For more on some of the reasons for resignation, see Caldwell, "Cameroons Evaluation Report," 23–23, PCL; and Smith, *Lament for a Silver-eyed Woman*, 91. Some RPCVC stated in interviews that some of their colleagues withdrew very early from the Peace Corps because they found it almost impossible to adjust to life in Cameroon. Mikell Kloeters, telephone interview, Feb. 21, 1988. I have also picked up some of this material from questionnaire responses.

34. The bilingual issue in Cameroon has been troublesome throughout the country's history. Some competent observers continue to stress the systematic attempts by the French-speaking people to do away with English. It is unclear whether the problem has been resolved even today. The nation's university is in principle supposed to be bilingual, but almost 85 percent of its staff is French speaking, and few speak or write English.

35. U.S. Department of State, "GFRC Criticism of Peace Corps in Cameroon," Dec. 30, 1965, declassified Apr. 14, 1988, through Freedom of Information Act; Meisler, "Overseas Evaluation," 1966, 33–34, PCL.

U.S. Department of State, "Text of the Diplomatic Note from [Cameroon] Foreign Ministry," undated, declassified Apr. 11, 1988 (translated by Amin):

> At the level of the technical assistance from the American government to developing countries, the Cameroon government has gained enormously from the knowledge of a group of Peace Corps volunteers assigned to teach English in Cameroonian schools. While these young volunteers have good intentions, unfortunately they possess a very rudimentary knowledge of French, and as a result they have problems communicating with their students. Despite the numerous assurances given to us by the American authorities, no solution has yet been provided to this problem. Additionally, their teaching method shows a complete absence of effective pedagogy. These two weaknesses, in the long run, tend to discourage the students. Based on the difficulties stated above, the government of the Federal Republic of Cameroon suggests that in the future the work of the Peace Corps volunteers should be geared toward the teaching of physical education and sports, where they are more efficient.

36. Meisler, "Overseas Evaluation," 1966, 35, PCL. Though the "nasty note" was partially approved by William-Aurélien Eteki Mbouma, then minister of education, his technical adviser later submitted a "confidential report" to him stating that the volunteers were doing an adequate job. They were assisting Cameroon's drive to achieve total bilingualism. For more on this, see U.S. Department of State, "GFRC Criticism of Peace Corps in Cameroon."

37. Caldwell, "Cameroons Evaluation Report," 7, PCL; Meisler, "Overseas Evaluation," 1966, 36–40, PCL; also see Sam McPhetres and Eric Stevenson, "Completion of Service Conference," July 7, 1967, 12; and Department of State, "Text of [American] Embassy's Note to Foreign Ministry," Nov. 22, 1965, declassified Apr. 14, 1988.

38. Meisler, "Overseas Evaluation," 1965, 25–27, PCL. Meisler documents some of the problems the volunteers had with French expatriates. Overall, the story of the French in Cameroon has always troubled Cameroonians, who have not forgotten the rigid exploitation policy France implemented in Cameroon during colonialism. Moreover, the exclusive and ostentatious life-style of the French in postindependent Cameroon was highly resented. As early as 1962, Ahmadou Ahidjo, Cameroon's president, complained to President Kennedy about the behavior of French people in Cameroon. For more on this, see Memorandum to the President, Mar. 13, 1962, JFKL.

The French lived ostentatiously in Cameroon, and they needed money to support this life-style. Observing them, Mary-Ann Tirone Smith wrote in her novel that "all they [Frenchmen] do is make love and drink wine." For more on this, see Smith, *Lament for a Silver-eyed Woman*, 105; and Gardinier, *Cameroon*, 101–2. Smith, in a telephone interview and in her response to questionnaires, emphasized her friendship with Cameroonians. "They [Cameroonians] were like family," she wrote in her questionnaire. Volunteers generally were most relaxed with the Cameroonians. For more on this see Smith, *Lament for a Silver-eyed Woman*, 92, 98, 101. In "Mikell Joins the Peace Corps," Dec. 1963 to Sept. 1964, 2:7–12, PCDMK, this is also discussed, as it is in entries of Caldwell, "Cameroons Evaluation Report," 24, PCL. All the responses to questionnaires expressed similar feelings.

39. Ako D. Mengot, "Are West Cameroon Education Standards Falling?" *West Cameroon Teachers' Journal*, 17, NAB.

40. Qtd. in Caldwell, "Cameroons Evaluation Report," 31, PCL.

41. Ibid., 30.

42. Freeman Pollard, response to questionnaire.

43. Meisler, "Overseas Evaluation," 1965, 20–21, PCL.

44. I attended a mission school and witnessed firsthand how Cameroonian teachers were relegated to inadequate conditions. Missionaries had their own way of life, and they were always together at social events. Accommodations assigned to Cameroonian teachers in that school were horrible. For additional information on the Peace Corps goal of destroying "elitism," see Stanley Meisler, "Peace Corps Teaching in Africa," 16–20.

45. "Peace Corps Aids Sectarian Expansion," *Christianity Today,* Aug. 24, 28, 1964, Budget-Misc., 1961–66, Box 1, OUL.

46. "Peace Corps Aids Sectarian Expansion," OUL; Gebauer to Arnold, report, Oct. 31, 1964, 7–8, OUL.

47. There is no evidence in the Cameroon National Archives showing that the men in charge in Cameroon ever seriously considered the complaints against the volunteers. Country Report-Republic of Cameroon, memorandum, Mar. 22, 1963, Cameroon Peace Corps, PCL. For more on the positive achievement of the volunteers, see "Prime Minister Honours New Peace Corps Volunteers," Press Release No. 2714, Sept. 26, 1963, West Cameroon Press Release, NAB; "Address by His Excellency the Prime Minister at the Cocktail Party on 25/9/63 in Honour of the Second Group of Peace Corps Volunteers," Budget-Misc., 1961–66, Box 1, Peace Corps Documents, OUL. Smith to Roaden, report, OUL.

48. Smith to Roaden, report, OUL; Minutes, Jan. 22 and 29, 1966, 7, Education Conferences, Box 7, Peace Corps Documents, OUL.

49. Minutes, Education Conferences, OUL; Smith to Roaden, report, OUL; "Quarterly Report of the Contractor's Overseas Representative, Peace Corps Project, West Cameroon," Apr. 6, 1965, 3, COR-Grover, Smith, 1965, Box 4, Peace Corps Documents, OUL; Peggy Anderson, "Overseas Evaluation-Cameroon," Jan. 26, 1967, 16–17, PCL; Jack J. Carmichael to Roy Fairfield, May 1, 1964, Jack Carmichael, Box 1, Peace Corps Documents, OUL.

50. Minutes, Education Conferences, 3, OUL.

51. Meisler, "Overseas Evaluation," 1966, 22–23, PCL.

52. Ibid., 24.

53. Barbara Psarakis to Amin, June 29, 1987; Dick Weber to Miss Gloria Gaston, June 6, 1963, Volunteer Information, Cameroon/Ceylon, Peace Corps Microfilm, Roll 3, JFKL; responses to questionnaires; Minutes, Education Conferences, 2, OUL.

54. Meisler, "Overseas Evaluation," 1966, 22, PCL; also mentioned in responses to questionnaires. These remarks are from interviews conducted in Cameroon during December 1987 and January 1988.

55. Responses to questionnaires; Fairfield, "Progress in Cameroon," April 16, 1963, 2, PCDRF.

56. Meisler, "Overseas Evaluation," 1966, 6–10, PCL. Meisler alludes to the belief that the British system was the cause for rote learning.

57. Meisler, "Overseas Evaluation," 1965, 14, PCL.

58. Ibid., 19.

59. Alfred Mimba, "A Farewell Address Presented to the Peace Corps Volunteers by the Students of the Baptist Teacher Training College Great Soppo Buea on the Occasion of Their Departure, July 4, 1964"; copy of speech supplied by Richard W. Weber, former Peace Corps volunteer at BTTC.

Chapter 6
Volunteers in Community Development

1. Uma Lele, *The Design of Rural Development: Lessons from Africa*, 20; David K. Leonard, "Interorganizational Linkages for Decentralized Rural Development: Overcoming Administrative Weaknesses," in G. Shabbir Cheema and Dennis A. Rondinelli, eds. *Decentralization and Development: Policy Implementation in Developing Countries*, 271–72; G. Shabbir Cheema, "The Role of Voluntary Organizations," in ibid., 203.

2. Director of Land and Survey-West Cameroon to the Permanent Secretary, Ministry of Local Government, Land and Survey, Jan. 15, 1964, NAB; Secretary of State for Local Government, Land and Survey, "Application for Assistance by the United States Peace Corps Volunteers for Town Planning, Survey, Administrative Land Officers," unsigned, undated memorandum, NAB; Secretariat of State for Interior, Application for Peace Corps Volunteers, 1964, NAB; Milliken, *Proposal*, 3, PCDRF; "Summary: Peace Corps Program in Cameroon," PCL. Meisler, "Overseas Evaluation," 1965, 2; and 1966, 4, PCL.

3. Fairfield, Carmichael, and Milliken, "Third Quarterly Report," Aug. 1963, 5–7, PCDRF; Carmichael to Fairfield, June 26, 1963, OUL.

4. Fairfield, Carmichael, and Milliken, "Fourth Quarterly Report," Sept. 1963, 36–38, PCDRF.

5. Martin Akong, interview with author, Dec. 30, 1987, Cameroon; Andy Edwards, "Bojongo Gets Its Fence," *Peace Corps Volunteer* 2 (Mar. 1964): 20–21; Kitty and Andy Edwards, "Bojongo: A Case Study," PCDCD.

6. Kitty and Andy Edwards, "Bojongo: A Case Study," PCDCD; Andy Edwards, "Bojongo Gets Its Fence," 20.

7. Andy Edwards, "Bojongo Gets Its Fence," 20–21; Kitty and Andy Edwards, "Bojongo: A Case Study," PCDCD.

8. Fairfield, Carmichael, and Milliken, "Third Quarterly Report," Aug. 1963, 5–7, and "First Quarterly Report," Dec. 1963, 4–6, PCDRF; Fairfield to Peace Corps Faculty and Friends, "Progress in Cameroon," report, Feb. 11, 1963, 3, PCDRF.

9. Foncha and Lafon qtd. in Andy Edwards, "Bojongo Gets Its Fence," 20.

10. Ibid.

11. Roger Schneier to Amin, June 2, 1987; Meisler, "Overseas Evaluation," 1965, 41, PCL. Following the Peace Corps example, efforts were made in several divisions to establish cooperatives.

12. Meisler, "Overseas Evaluation," 1966, 52, PCL.

13. Ibid., 1965, 41; 1966, 51.

14. Fairfield, Carmichael, and Milliken, "Third Quarterly Report," Aug. 1963, 21–26, PCDRF; Edith Pana and Elizabeth Ann Hughes, "Banso Corn Mill Society Tour/Peace Corps," 30 Apr.–May 7, 1963, report, 1–4, Advanced Planning Project, Box 5, Peace Corps Documents, OUL.

15. Fairfield, Carmichael, and Milliken, "Third Quarterly Report," Aug. 1963, 23–25, PCDRF; Caldwell, "Cameroons Evaluation Report," 64, PCL.

16. Pana and Hughes, "Banso Corn Mill Society," 1–9, OUL. For a general overview of how the Peace Corps volunteers were able to encourage mass participation among the various countries' people, see Gerard T. Rice, *Twenty Years of Peace Corps*, 62–64.

17. Pana and Hughes, "Banso Corn Mill Society," 7, OUL.

18. Questionnaire responses; interviews with the author, 1987–88, Cameroon.

19. Fairfield, Carmichael, and Milliken, "Third Quarterly Report," Aug. 1963, 24–26, PCDRF. For additional information on Cameroonian responses and attitudes toward cooperatives involving Peace Corps volunteers, see Mark W. DeLancey, "The U.S. Peace Corps Program for Credit Union and Cooperative Development in Cameroon, 1969–1976," 92–123. Only four volunteers were involved with the organization of corn mill societies.

20. Peace Corps Project Description, Jan. 18, 1962, 1, P.C. Project Draft 104, OUL; "Summary: Peace Corps Program in Cameroon," 3–5, 6, 9 PCL; "Williams Re-affirms Friendly Cameroon United States Relations," Press Release No. 2527, July 6, 1963, and "More U.S. Aid for West Cameroon," Press Release No. 2776, Oct. 31, 1963, West Cameroon Press Releases 1963, NAB; J. Thrupp, Permanent Secretary, Ministry of Local Government to L. E. Williams, Esq., Peace Corps Representatives, May 15, 1964, Secretariat of State for Interior, Application for Peace Corps Volunteers, NAB; "Notes on Activities of Lands and Surveys Department for U.S.A. Peace Corps Volunteers in West Cameroon," unsigned, undated memorandum, Secretariat of State for Interior, Application for Peace Corps Volunteers, 1964, NAB; J. Thrupp, Permanent Secretary, to J. R. Harris, Esq., Field Officer, United States Peace Corps, Dec. 5, 1964, American Aid Mission and Peace Corps Volunteers, NAB; Town Planning Officer to Permanent Secretary, Secretariat of State for Interior, "Peace Corps Volunteers for December, 1966," Application for Peace Corps Volunteers, NAB; Ministry of Local Government, to James Kelly, Deputy Director, Peace Corps-Buea, "Town Planning Programme, West Cameroon," Mar. 5, 1966, NAB.

21. "Summary: Peace Corps Program in Cameroon," 2, PCL; Caldwell, "Cameroons Evaluation Report," 67, PCL. In Buea, Mary-Ann Tirone Smith also presented a positive image of Americans. The responses in the questionnaires confirm that the volunteers established better relations when they undertook joint projects with Cameroonians. In Foumban, the work of Mikell Kloeters made the residents of that city conclude that Americans were hardworking and friendly.

22. Meisler, "Overseas Evaluation," 1965, 39, PCL; "More U.S. Aid for West Cameroon," Press Release No. 2776, Oct. 31, 1963, NAB.

23. Qtd. in McPhetres and Stevenson, "Completion of Service Conference," 6.

24. Meisler, "Cameroon Evaluation," 1965, 52–54, PCL. AID'S primary purpose was to represent America's interest.

25. Ibid., 56; McPhetres and Stevenson, "Completion of Service Conference," 6.

26. Meisler, "Overseas Evaluation," 1965, 58–59, PCL; McPhetres and Stevenson, "Completion of Service Conference," 5–7.

27. Responses to questionnaires. A returned Peace Corps volunteer from Cameroon emphasized that though his group did road surveying, bridge work, and community development services, its members knew very little about the country: "We didn't have the slightest idea of what we were going to do—the organization of the C.D. Dept., skills needed, etc., but we knew something about the country and could use Pidgin." Perhaps it is important to point out that this volunteer, with a B.A. in one of the social science disciplines, was just one of the examples of the agency's misdirection of talent, as he was assigned to road surveying and bridge construction in the Nkambe and Njinikon area.

28. "Program for the Peace Corps," 2, JFKL; Rice, *The Bold Experiment,* 150; Meisler, "Overseas Evaluation," 1965, 30–31, PCL.

29. The projects of introducing new crops and organizing youth clubs and poultry farms were quite ambitious. To introduce new crops, the volunteers had to study the soil types of their regions, a task that was possible only in the United States, for West Cameroon had no documentation on the various soil types. Soil samples sent back to the U.S. for testing were never done on time; bureaucratic red tape slowed everything. See Anderson, "Overseas Evaluation," 34–37, PCL.

30. Ibid., 36. One of the reasons that the volunteers arrived in the late mornings in the villages was because of the poor means of transportation linking the villages to the senior service residential areas.

31. Lele, *The Design of Rural Development,* 62–66. Lele provides a detailed account of the problems extension workers faced in Africa. For more on the problems of the volunteers in community development, see DeLancey, "The U.S. Peace Corps Program," 112, 116–18.

32. Anderson, "Overseas Evaluation," 34, 36, PCL. Anderson wrote that "it would be ridiculous to even consider replacing the ag[riculture] volunteer next January."

33. B. James Kellenberger, William J. Kane, and Richard L. Brennan to Community Development Headquarters, report, July 23, 1963, 1–7, OUL.

34. "Summary: Peace Corps Program in Cameroon," 6–7, PCL.

35. "The Combined Work Report of the American Peace Corps Volunteers in Public Health: Cameroon, Feb. 1968 to Apr. 1969," PCL; Jean Pierre Nkandem, interview with author, Jan. 6, 1988, Cameroon.

36. *Training Manual, Public Health Program-Cameroon,* 1968. B-A7, PCL.

37. During the early 1960s, various theories of modernization emerged, including David C. McClelland, "The Achievement Motive of Economic Growth," and Simon Kuznet, "The Economic Growth and Income Inequality," both in Mitchell A. Seligson, ed., *The Gap between Rich and Poor: Contending Perspectives on the Political Economy of Development.* Volunteers

understood the theories of the 1960s, but it was not until the late 1970s that the so-called developmentalists began realizing that these theories were inapplicable to African countries. Tony Smith, in criticizing the developmentalist view of the Third World, states that "Third World studies is in a state of crisis." For more on this, see Tony Smith, "Requiem or New Agenda for Third World Studies," *World Politics* 37 (July 1985): 532–61.

Howard J. Wiarda also blasted the approach of developmentalists towards developing countries, documenting his assertion that "Western Political Sociology . . . assumes that . . . institutions as tribes, castes, clans, patrimonialist authority, and historic cooperate units must either yield . . . under the impact of modernization or be overwhelmed." Additionally, he states, "The Eurocentrism of the major development models has skewed, biased, and distorted their own and the outside world's understanding of Third World Societies and has made them into something of a laughing-stock, the butt of cruel, ethnic, and sometimes racial gibes." For more on this, see Wiarda, "Toward a Nonethnocentric Theory of Development: Alternative Conceptions from the Third World," *Journal of Developing Areas* 17 (July 1983):433–52. Like the volunteers, developmentalists did not understand the chemistry or makeup of Third World societies.

38. Meisler, "Overseas Evaluation," 1965, 33, PCL.

39. Qtd. in Arthur Schlesinger, Jr., *Robert Kennedy*, 745–46.

40. Kennedy, in his inaugural speech in 1961, stressed a beginning when he said: "All this will not be finished in the first one hundred days. Nor will it be finished in the first one thousand days, nor in the lifetime of this administration, nor even perhaps in the lifetime on this planet. But let us begin." For the full speech, see Kennedy, "Inaugural Address," *Public Papers* 1:1–3. For more on the feelings of Africans about Kennedy, see Howe, *Along the Afric Shore*, 131; "African Tribute to Kennedy," *West Africa*, Nov. 30, 1963, 1359; "The World of John F. Kennedy," ibid., Nov. 23, 1963, 1343.

Chapter 7
Living in Cameroon

1. All the volunteers who responded to my questionnaire discussed their treatment in Cameroon. Failure to adjust to conditions in Cameroon, combined with the number of volunteers sent back by Peace Corps officials as a result of poor behavior, accounted for less than 10 percent of the early volunteer returns from the two-year Peace Corps term of service.

2. Some observers, including the volunteers themselves, have indicated that the volunteers were underemployed in Cameroon. For more on this, see Meisler, "Overseas Evaluation," 1965, 16–20, and 1966, 10, PCL; questionnaire responses reflect the same. There were towns in East Cameroon with only one volunteer; Mikell Kloeters, for example, was the only volunteer in Foumban.

3. On the overall situation, see Rubin, *An African Federation*, 94–95, 188–89; Gardinier, *Cameroon*, 95–96; and Le Vine, *The Cameroon Federal*

Republic, 121–28. Caldwell, "Cameroons Evaluation Report," 4, PCL, reports on the shootings at the two Americans.

4. "Mikell Joins the Peace Corps" 1:27, PCDMK.

5. Denbow, "Final Report," 2, PCDCD; Paul Gebauer, "West Cameroon: Outline of Paul Gebauer's Lectures," July 11–18, 1962, lecture notes, 13–14, Advanced Planning Project, Box 5, Peace Corps Documents, OUL.

6. Fairfield, *Training Plan,* 14, PCDRF.

7. "Mikell Joins the Peace Corps" 1:37, PCDMK; Eric Swenson to "Folks," Oct. 28, 1963, copy provided by Eric Swenson.

8. Eric Swenson to "Folks," Oct. 28, 1963; Mary-Ann Tirone Smith, telephone interview, Jan. 28, 1988, and *Lament for a Silver-eyed Woman,* 109–11; responses to questionnaires.

9. "Mikell Joins the Peace Corps" 1:42, PCDMK; responses to questionnaires.

10. *Training Manual, Public Health Program: Cameroon,* 1968, D-A14, PCL.

11. In several questionnaire responses, volunteers referred to the dislike of the volunteers by the French. A returned volunteer stated that he "didn't care much for the French, they hated my guts." Mary-Ann Tirone Smith wrote that "the French military personnel didn't like Americans."

12. "Mikell Joins the Peace Corps" 2:1, 4, PCDMK; Eric Swenson to "Folks," Oct. 28, 1963; responses to questionnaires.

13. Fairfield, "Progress in Cameroon," Dec. 11, 1963, 2, PCDRF; qtd. in Fairfield, Carmichael, and Milliken, "First Quarterly Report," Dec. 1963, 32, PCDRF. The "juju" dance mentioned in the passage was a form of native dance in which the main dancer uses a mask. Young and old participated in this dance, a form of entertainment on Christmas Day. However, it was outlawed by the government in the early 1980s. Government officials, who spent most of their time in the capital cities, erroneously assumed that juju dances on Christmas Day encouraged children to grow up as beggars. Additionally, they added that children crossing the roads on Christmas Day unescorted often led to accidents. As a result, juju was banned, and it is still missed on Christmas Day in Cameroon.

14. McPhetres and Stevenson, "Completion of Service Conference," 12–13.

15. William E. Leuchtenburg, *A Troubled Feast: American Society since 1945,* 189; Chafe, *The Unfinished Journey,* 327.

16. Betty Friedan, *The Feminine Mystique,* 282; anonymous volunteer, personal Peace Corps notes, undated.

17. Gebauer, "Lectures," 13, OUL. In a questionnaire response a volunteer wrote, "I . . . felt at a disadvantage following a vol[unteer] who'd been very popular and had made a lot of friends." The Peace Corps was vague on dating and unanticipated pregnancy. For debates over the pregnancy issue, see Redmon, *Come as You Are,* 96–98, 112–14.

18. Meisler, "Overseas Evaluation," 1965, 66–67, PCL. It is unclear whether any marriages among Peace Corps volunteers resulted from this social situation in Cameroon. Meisler also notes that female volunteers

informed him that during the training they were warned to "stay away from African men."

19. McPhetres and Stevenson, "Completion of Service Conference," 13; Caldwell, "Cameroons Evaluation Report," 22, PCL.

20. "Mikell Joins the Peace Corps" 2:15, PCDMK.

21. McPhetres and Stevenson, "Completion of Service Conference," 13.

22. Volunteers traveled to Nigeria, Ivory Coast, and other neighboring countries for rendezvous. This information was obtained from telephone interviews with some of the RPCVC.

23. Caldwell, "Cameroons Evaluation Report," 14, PCL; Mary-Ann Tirone Smith, telephone interview, May 12, 1991. Some returned female volunteers have asked me to locate the addresses of their former boyfriends in Cameroon.

24. Responses to questionnaires; "Mikell Joins the Peace Corps" 2:13, PCDMK; Smith, *Lament for a Silver-eyed Woman*, 102. In a telephone interview with Mary-Ann Tirone Smith on May 12, 1991, she confirmed that she was asked some of the questions in her novel. Some of the quotations are from her response to questionnaires.

25. Qtd. in Melvin Drimmer, *Issues in Black History: Reflections and Commentaries on the Black Historical Experience*, 6. For detailed surveys of these racial uprisings, see Harvard Sitkoff, *The Struggle for Black Equality, 1954–1980;* David J. Garrow, *Protest At Selma: Martin Luther King, Jr., and the Voting Rights Act of 1965;* Chafe, *The Unfinished Journey*, 302–42. "The Colour Bar Problems in America," *Cameroon Times*, May 21, 28, 1963; ETATS-UNIS: LA GRANDE MARCHE," *Jeune Afrique*, June 26, 1966.

26. John F. Kennedy denounced the treatment of African officials in American restaurants. In 1962 he was astonished when told that the child of an African diplomat was denied water in a white restaurant in Maryland. To avoid similar embarrassments, Kennedy wished African ambassadors could "avoid Route 40 and fly from New York to Washington." Chafe, *The Unfinished Journey*, 207.

27. Caldwell, "Cameroons Evaluation Report," 31, PCL; responses to questionnaires.

28. Caldwell, "Cameroons Evaluation Report," 31, PCL.

29. Fairfield, Carmichael, and Milliken, "First Quarterly Report," Dec. 1963, 32, PCDRF. Fairfield compiled the text from letters written to him by volunteers in Cameroon; in the letters they explained and described their experiences in Cameroon.

30. Many volunteers indicated in questionnaires that one of the reasons they joined the Peace Corps was to have the opportunity to travel. Fairfield, Carmichael, and Milliken, "First Quarterly Report," Dec. 1963, 6, PCDRF.

31. Responses to questionnaires.

32. "Mikell Joins the Peace Corps" 2:6, PCDMK; responses to questionnaires.

33. Meisler, "Overseas Evaluation," 1965, 25–27, PCL; McCarthy, "Overseas Evaluation," 3, PCL; Anderson, "Overseas Evaluation," 19, PCL.

34. Meisler, "Overseas Evaluation," 1966, 27, PCL. Some volunteers received additional money from their families in the United States.

35. McCarthy, "Overseas Evaluation," 3, PCL. See also Meisler, "Overseas Evaluation," 1966, 25, PCL, who remarks after visiting a volunteer, "I soon found out that this volunteer tinkles a bell three times a day. A steward rushes in and clears away the dishes from the dinner table." See also McPhetres and Stevenson, "Completion of Service Conference," 7.

36. I will never forget a personal experience at the Buea Mountain Club while I was teaching at Government High School in Limbe. It was foggy on that May day in 1980 in Buea when I invited some friends to the club for a drink. I assumed that the Buea Mountain Club was open to the public, and my guests and I sat waiting to be served. When I asked if we could be served, a low-level functionary snapped, "You are not a member." Sitting there, unsure of what to tell my guests, I asked again, and the response was the same. Finally my group walked out in shame—my own at having been treated so meanly in my own hospitable country, and my guests' mortification coming from having been helpless witnesses. It was not until December 1987 that I went there again, to honor an interview appointment with a senior government official.

37. Meisler, "Overseas Evaluation," 1965, 43, PCL.

38. Anderson, "Overseas Evaluation," 1967, 53–55, PCL; Fairfield, "Progress in Cameroon," Feb. 11, 1963, 1, PCDRF.

39. Stein, *Volunteers for Peace*, 237–38. About 98 percent of the volunteers who responded to my questionnaires emphasized the cultural aspect of what they learned from their Peace Corps experience in Cameroon.

40. Responses to questionnaires.

41. In a survey conducted at one of the Peace Corps conferences in Cameroon, the volunteers were asked, "Have you changed . . . your attitude toward the U.S.?" Thirty-five volunteers responded yes, and ten responded no. McPhetres and Stevenson, "Completion of Service Conference," 7. Mary Asmundson Dunbar, questionnaire response; RPCVC responses to questionnaires.

42. Freeman T. Pollard, questionnaire response; David J. Dwyer to Amin, June 17, 1987.

Chapter 8
Cameroonians Evaluate Volunteer Services

1. Responses to questionnaires; interviews, Cameroon, Dec. 1987 to Jan. 1988. Almost all RPCVC interviewed agreed that send-off occasions were highly emotional. Though I did not attend secondary school in the early 1960s, I have a vivid memory of a similar occasion when, as a first-year secondary school student in the late 1960s, I sang in the choir charged with the responsibility for performing the farewell song for returning volunteers. On this particular occasion the volunteers were presented with all sorts of prizes and gifts from various groups in the school. The gifts ranged from chieftaincy hats to other Cameroonian handicrafts;

all types of souvenirs from Cameroon were presented. It was an emotional ceremony for both the volunteers and the students.

The Truman Doctrine reiterated the American foreign policy of containment for generations to come. Stephen Ambrose states that Truman's statement "I believe that it must be the policy of the United States to support the free people who are resisting attempted subjugation by armed minorities or by outside pressures" summarized these goals in American foreign policy. Ambrose added, "In a single sentence Truman had defined American policy for the next generation." For more on this, see Ambrose, *Rise to Globalism*, 86.

2. Qtd. in Roy P. Fairfield, "Service Beyond Community," Apr. 1964, 16, OUL; J. Thrupp to J. R. Harris, Esq., Dec. 5, 1964, Secretariat of State for Interior, Application for Peace Corps Volunteers, NAB; "Mami" Angela Tanyi, interview with author, Jan. 3, 1988, Cameroon.

3. Martin Njang, interview with author, Dec. 28, 1987, Cameroon.

4. Qtd. in Fairfield, Carmichael, and Milliken, "Third Quarterly Report," Aug. 1963, 26, PCDRF.

5. For the full text of the speech, see Kennedy, "Annual Message to the Congress on the State of the Union," *Public Papers* 1:24.

6. Mengot, "Are West Cameroonian Educational Standards Falling?" 17–18.

7. Qtd. in Viorst, ed., *Making a Difference*, 182–83.

8. Qtd. in Rice, *Peace Corps in the 80's*, 57.

9. John Ngu Foncha, "Address by His Excellency, the Prime Minister at the Cocktail Party on 25/9/63 in Honour of the Second Batch of Peace Corps Volunteers," Budget-Misc., 1961–66, Box 1, Peace Corps Documents, OUL.

10. Ibid. "More U.S. Peace Corps Volunteers Will Arrive on Monday," Sept. 2, 1963, Press Release No. 2695; "Prime Minister Honours New Peace Corps Volunteers," Sept. 26, 1963, Press Release No. 2704; "Second Set of U.S. Peace Corps Volunteers Arrives, the Federal Republic of Cameroon," Sept. 26, 1963, Press Release No. 2705; West Cameroon Press Releases, 1963, NAB. Jacques Kuoh Moukori to Sargent Shriver, Apr. 15, 1964, No. 270/AWA/3, PCL; also see U.S. Department of State, "Note of Thanks for Peace Corps Assistance," Aug. 20, 1963, declassified Apr. 14, 1988 (translated by Amin): "Let me use this opportunity to inform you of my government's satisfaction of the positive contributions the Peace Corps volunteers are making in Cameroon."

11. "*New York Times* Story Considered Inaccurate," *Messenger*, Aug. 9, 1964, 3, Publicity, Box 8, Peace Corps Documents, OUL. For the full text of the article Mengot challenged, see Lloyd Garrison, "Cameroon Woes Mirror Africa's: Tribalism and Dual Culture Temper Hope for Unity," *New York Times*, Aug. 24, 1964, 6:3.

12. George W. Lang to the Permanent Secretary, the Ministry of Education and Social Welfare, 3 Nov. 1964, Ministry of Education, West Cameroon, NAB; "Peace Corps Aids Sectarian Expansion," unsigned,

undated article, ibid.; Gebauer to Arnold, report, OUL; Franklin C. Salisbury to Dean Rusk, Oct. 22, 1964, RG59, General Records of the Department of State, Records of G. M. Williams, 1961–66, NA.

13. Sargent Shriver, "The Peace Corps," *Christianity Today*, July 31, 1964, 31.

14. George Lang to Permanent Secretary, Nov. 3, 1964, NAB.

15. "Peace Corps in West Cameroon," *Christianity Today*, Jan. 1, 1965; and the Reverend Flavius Martin, "My Return to Africa," *Baptist Herald*, undated, Budget-Misc., 1961–66, Box 1, Peace Corps Documents, OUL. John Ngu Foncha to the Federal Minister of Foreign Affairs, Yaounde, memorandum, the Federal Minister of National Education-Yaounde, Dec. 10, 1964, NAB.

16. In the Peace Corps Documents, OUL, there are numerous letters written by Cameroonian secondary school students in 1963 and 1964. This information is from interviews I conducted in December 1987 and January 1988 with about thirty Cameroonians who were in secondary school in the early 1960s.

17. Mimba, "A Farewell Address," July 1964.

18. In December 1987 and January 1988, I visited the libraries of Bishop Rogan College, Saint Joseph's College, Sasse, and the former BTTC. In these libraries, there are books, though old, with the Peace Corps mark. Though time did not permit visits to other schools, I found it significant that the three libraries I visited still had donated Peace Corps books.

19. Questionnaire responses; Mikell Kloeters, "Mikell Joins the Peace Corps" 2:15, and (on the soccer tickets) 1:29, PCDMK; Smith, *Lament for a Silver-eyed Woman*, 95–105. Smith told the author in an interview on May 12, 1991, that "the card catalogue was very beautiful." For more on appreciation shown by Cameroonians, see Kitty and Andy Edwards, "Bojongo: A Case Study," NAB.

20. Louis Durbin, "Sultan Collects Art: Cameroon Royal Couple Visiting," *Washington Post*, 1964, PCDMK.

21. Anonymous Peace Corps volunteer to family in the United States, undated letter; this former volunteer is one who asked for anonymity upon lending documents. Carl W. Stinson to Amin, June 4, 1987, explains how interested Cameroonians were in American politics.

22. *Cameroon Times*, Apr. 27, 1965, 1; anonymous Peace Corps volunteer to friend in the United States, Apr. 18, 1967.

23. Responses to questionnaires. "High-life" is a form of dance that was quite popular in bars in West African countries. Roger Schneier to Amin, June 2, 1987; Victor Atem, interview with author, Jan. 8, 1988, Buea, Cameroon.

24. Russell A. Milliken to Mrs. Anna Foncha, July 2, 1964, Cameroon, 1964–65, Box 1, Peace Corps Documents, OUL. Perdita Huston conducted interviews in Africa in 1981, traveling to several countries. In a telephone interview in Nov. 1987, she said that Cameroonian women were gratified

to see female volunteers at work. The service of these volunteers encouraged the Cameroonian women to take initiative and participate in the development of their country.

25. Roy P. Fairfield to Emmanuel Tabi Egbe, June 11, 1964, Cameroon, 1964–65, Washington, D.C., Box 1, Peace Corps Documents, OUL.

26. "America and Freedom," *Cameroon Times,* June 6, 1963; "Le Président des Etat-Unis Lyndon B. Johnson: *LE NOIR DEMANDE JUSTICE,* Les Américains, noirs et blancs, doivent travailler à résoudre le problème qui nous confronte," ibid., Nov. 28, 1963; "LA QUESTION RACIALE," *La Presse du Cameroun,* Nov. 12, 1966; interviews, Cameroon, Dec. 29, 1987.

27. Foncha, "Address by His Excellency," OUL; also see Ministry of Education, NAB. It is no surprise that some Cameroonians assumed that Kennedy was assassinated because "he was trying to help the Negroes or that President Johnson directed the assassination." The quoted portion of the note is from McPhetres and Stevenson, "Completion of Service Conference," 15. Foncha is quoted in "Prime Minister Honours New Peace Corps Volunteers," West Cameroon Press Releases, Press Release No. 2704, Sept. 26, 1963, NAB.

28. Gilbert Schneider, interview, Nov. 9, 1987; Carl Denbow, interview, Nov. 10, 1987; Roy Fairfield, telephone interview, Feb. 22, 1988; Jack Carmichael, response to questionnaire.

Conclusion

1. Qtd. in F. N. Hamblin, "The Function of Education in Underdeveloped Countries," Sept. 15, 1959, 13, Advanced Planning Project, Box 5, Peace Corps Documents, OUL.

2. United Nations, *Statistical Year Book, 1975,* 863; Rubin, *Cameroon,* 179.

3. Rice, *Peace Corps in the 80's,* 2; T. Zane Reeves, *The Politics of the Peace Corps and VISTA,* 44.

4. Rice, *The Bold Experiment,* 302.

5. Several returned Peace Corps volunteer organizations have been formed. In 1988, returned Peace Corps volunteers from Cameroon established the Friends of Cameroon. The largest Peace Corps organization is the National Council of Returned Peace Corps Volunteers.

6. "Remarks of the President at Peace Corps Meeting in Chamber of Commerce Auditorium, Washington, D.C.," June 14, 1962, JFK Speeches, Papers of Gerald W. Bush, Box 3, JFKL.

7. Kennedy, "Inaugural Address," *Public Papers* 1:1, qtd. in Serapio R. Zalba, "The Peace Corps—Its Historical Antecedents and Its Meaning for Social Work," *Duquesne Review* 11 (Fall 1966): 127, 128–29; Transcript of Background Press and Radio News Briefing, JFKL.

8. Qtd. in Chafe, *The Unfinished Journey,* 220; also see Kenneth P. O'Donnell, David F. Powers, and Joe McCarthy, *"Johnny, We Hardly Knew Ye": Memories of John Fitzgerald Kennedy,* 414.

9. Wofford, "Excerpts from Some Talks on the Peace Corps," Mar. 11, 1961, 7–12, JFKL. A copy of the postcard is posted in the Peace Corps Library in Washington, D.C. For more on the incident, see Rice, *The Bold Experiment*, 241–42. "Peace Corps Girl Stirs Anger in Nigeria by Alledging 'Squalor,' " *New York Times*, Oct. 4, 1961, 10:2; also qtd. in "The Peace Corps Suffers from Growing Pains," *U.S. News & World Report*, Oct. 30, 1961, 4.

10. "The Peace Corps Suffers from Growing Pains," 4; qtd. in *West Africa*, Jan. 6, 1962, 26; *New York Times*, Oct. 21, 1961.

11. Wofford, "Excerpts from Some Talks on the Peace Corps," Mar. 11, 1961, JFKL; Walker qtd. in "Incident 'Blown up,' Corps Member Says," *New York Times*, Oct. 16, 1961, 9:6. "Peace Corps Recoups in Nigeria," *Christian Science Monitor*, May 25, 1962, News Clippings, Papers of Gerald W. Bush, Box 3, JFKL; Rice, *Peace Corps in the 80's*, 41.

12. Roger Hilsman, *To Move a Nation: The Politics of Foreign Policy in the Administration of John F. Kennedy*, 233; Noer, "New Frontiers and Old Priorities in Africa," in Paterson, ed., *Kennedy's Quest for Victory*, 260, 280–81.

13. Qtd. in Richard Richter, "Ghana: Overseas Evaluation," January 6, 1965, 7, RG Peace Corps, NA.

14. Qtd. in "U.S. Peace Corps told: Avoid destructive criticisms," *Ghanaian Times*, Sept. 4, 1962, 3; Richter, "Overseas Evaluation," 7, NA.

15. For the newspaper coverage of the racial crisis in the U.S., see "Young African-American on trial today: The Crimes of William Worthy," *Evening News*, Aug. 7, 1962, 4; "Jim Crow and Apartheid," ibid., July 26, 1962, 6; "Negroes demonstrate against racialism," ibid., July 4, 1962, 4; "Meredith, object for crisis in U.S. Varsity gets protection," *Ghanaian Times*, Oct. 6, 1962, 3. Qtd. in Richter, "Overseas Evaluation," 2, NA.

16. "Preliminary Evaluation Report on Ghana," Apr. 4, 1962, unsigned report, 1–2, RG Peace Corps, NA. The letters from Peace Corps volunteers in Ghana focused mostly on their jobs. The political and social gossip of the letters from volunteers in Cameroon was almost entirely absent. For more on letters from Peace Corps volunteers who served in Ghana, see Volunteer Information—Ghana (1), Peace Corps Microfilm, Roll 4, JFKL. "The U.S. in West Africa," *West Africa*, Nov. 30, 1963, 1343; also see Rice, *The Bold Experiment*, 277–79.

17. Kaba, "From Colonialism to Autocracy: Guinea under Sekou Touré, 1957–1984," in Gifford and Louis, eds., *Decolonization and African Independence*, 225–27.

18. Responses to questionnaires. Of the sixty-five returned Peace Corps volunteers from Sekou Touré's Guinea to whom I sent a nine-page questionnaire, twenty-five responded.

19. "Le problème racial aux Etats-Unis," *Horoya*, Sept. 21, 1963, 5, 6; "Le Président Kennedy évoque la ségrégation qui sévit dans l'Etat d'Alabama," ibid., May 11, 1963, 4; "La ≪Grande Marche≫ des noirs-américains sur Washington," ibid., Aug. 17, 1963, 5, 6; "Le Président Kennedy et Birmingham," ibid., May 14, 1963, 3; "La lutte raciale au USA: Le Président Kennedy reçoit les leaders noirs," ibid., Sept. 21, 1963, 5, 6; "Le racisme

en Afrique du sud et aux Etats-Unis," June 22, 1963, 5. Between 1961 and 1968, the *Horoya* carried detailed accounts of the civil rights struggle in the United States. "Éditorial: Prix Lénine de la Paix," ibid., May 6, 1961.

20. Responses to questionnaires by returned volunteers from Ghana; Philip S. Cook, "Guinea: Overseas Evaluation," Apr. 17–May 11, 1964, 23–24, RG Peace Corps, NA.

21. Qtd. in David Hapgood, "Guinea: Overseas Evaluation," July 23, 1965, 28–29, RG Peace Corps, NA.

22. Neil Sheehan, "Guinea Holds U.S. Envoy to Protest Ghana Arrest," *New York Times*, Oct. 31, 1961, 1:4, 14:2; "Ghana, Guinea, OAU Crisis over Arrests in Accra," *West Africa*, Nov. 5, 1966, 1281.

23. "The Peace Corps Leaves Guinea," Nov. 1966, compilation of newspaper clippings, PCL; *Horoya*, Oct. 31–Nov. 1966; Jack Keyser, "Guinea: Exit Smiling," in *The Peace Corps Reader*, 63–74; *La Presse du Cameroun*, Nov. 9–16, 1966.

24. "The Peace Corps Leaves Guinea," PCL.

25. Gerald J. Bender, James S. Coleman, and Richard L. Sklar, eds., *African Crisis Areas and U.S. Foreign Policy*, 171, 195, 328. In an unrelated incident, Idi Amin detained a plane that carried Peace Corps volunteers who were returning to the United States. After the volunteers were searched and locked up, they were eventually allowed to depart the country. For more on this particular incident see "Amin Heard 'Peace Corps' and Ordered Plane Brought Back," *New York Times*, July 9, 1973, 4:4, 5:7.

Sekou Touré died on March 26, 1984; Peace Corps volunteers returned to Guinea in 1985. For dates of entries and exits of Peace Corps volunteers to the different African countries, see Rice, *Peace Corps in the 80's*, 40.

26. Responses to questionnaires.

27. John G. Stoessinger, *Crusaders and Pragmatists: Movers of American Foreign Policy*, 137; Herbert S. Parmet, *JFK: The Presidency of John F. Kennedy*, 354.

28. Less than 2 percent of the returned Peace Corps volunteers who completed my questionnaire are working with an agency that deals with foreign policy.

Bibliography

Primary Sources

Private Collections

Julius Amin, Interviews conducted in Cameroon, December 1987–
    January 1988
Responses to questionnaires completed by returned Peace Corps vol-
    unteers from Cameroon, Ghana, and Guinea
Carl Denbow
Roy P. Fairfield
Mikell Kloeters
Freeman T. Pollard
Art Sherin
Eric Swenson
Richard Weber

Public Collections

Lyndon Baines Johnson Library, Austin
    White House Central Files, Subject Files Boxes 144–47.
    White House Central Files, Confidential Files, Boxes 25,
        75, 129.
    House Aide, Bill Moyers, Boxes 14, 15, 42, 76–77.
    National Security Files, Box 76.
    Vice-presidential Security Files, Box 1.
    Oral History, G. Mennen Williams.
John F. Kennedy Library, Boston
    Edwin Bayley, personal and organizational papers.
    Gerald W. Bush, research materials, personal and
        organizational papers.
    Samuel Hayes, organizational papers.
    William Josephson, copies of his Peace Corps chronological files
        1961–66.
    National Security Files, Boxes 27, 28, 102, 284.
    Oral Histories: William Attwood, Alhaji Sir Abubaker Tafawa

Balewa, Charles Darlington, Bradley Patterson, Leopold Sedar Senghor, Harris Wofford.
Peace Corps, nine rolls of microfilm (portions of rolls 1, 3, 4, 5, 7, 9 are still closed).
President's Office Files, Boxes 37, 85, 99, 111.
White House Subcentral Files Box 670.
National Archives, Buea, Cameroon
American Aides and Peace Corps Files, 1961–66.
Ministry of National Education Files, 1961–66.
Secretary of State for Interior, Application for Peace Corps Files, 1961–66.
Speeches of John Ngu Foncha Files, 1961–66.
West Cameroon Press Releases, 1963.
National Archives, Washington, D.C.
Peace Corps Evaluation Reports.
Reports on Peace Corps Termination Conference.
Williams, G. Mennen. Records of G. Mennen Williams, 1961–66, RG 59, General Records of the Department of State.
Peace Corps Library, Washington, D.C.
Interviews of Foreign Leaders.
Peace Corps Documents on Cameroon.
Peace Corps Evaluation and Quarterly Reports.
Shriver, Sargent. Speeches.
Wiggins, Warren. Speeches.
Special Collections, Ohio University, Athens, Ohio
Peace Corps Documents on Cameroon.

Newspapers and Periodicals

Accra Evening News 1961–66
Africa Concord 1987–89
Africa Digest 1961–70
Africa Report 1961–70, 1987–90
Africa Today 1961–65
Annals of the American Academy of Political and Social Science May 1966
Cameroon Times 1961–70
Cameroon Tribune 1986–90
Cameroun Tribune 1986–90
Christianity Today 1964
Ghanaian Evening News, 1962–66
Ghanaian Times 1961–66
Horoya 1961–70
Jeune Afrique 1963–68

New York Times 1961–73
La Presse du Cameroun 1961–68
Time 1961–62
U.S. News & World Report 1961
West Africa 1959–70, 1987–90

Government Documents

Kennedy, John F. *Public Papers of the Presidents of the United States.*
    2 vols. Washington, D.C.: Government Printing Office,
    1962, 1963.
Landrum, L. M. *The Role of the Peace Corps in Education in
    Developing Countries: A Case Study.* Washington, D.C.:
    U.S. Peace Corps, 1981.
McPhetres, Sam, and Eric Stevenson. "Completion of Service
    Conference, Cameroon V and VI." Yaounde, July 7, 1967.
Peace Corps. *Annual Report.* Washington, D.C.: Government
    Printing Office, 1963–66.
———. *Peace Corps Volunteer.* Washington, D.C.: Government
    Printing Office, 1962–66.
———. *The Peace Corps Reader.* Washington, D.C.: Office of Public
    Affairs, Peace Corps Office, 1968.
Rice, Gerard T. *Peace Corps in the 80's.* Washington, D.C.:
    Government Printing Office, 1986.
———. *Twenty Years of Peace Corps.* Washington, D.C.: Government
    Printing Office, 1982.
Truman, Harry S. *Public Papers of the Presidents of the United States.*
    4 vols. Washington, D.C.: Government Printing Office, 1948,
    1949, 1950, 1952.
U.S. Congress. *A Bill to Establish a Peace Corps.* 86th Cong.,
    2d sess., 1960.
———. Committee on Foreign Relations. *The Peace Corps. Hearings
    on S. 2000.* 87th Cong., 1st sess., 1961.
———. *Congressional Quarterly Almanac.* 87th Cong., 1st sess.,
    Vol. 17. Washington, D.C.: Congressional Quarterly
    Services, 1961.
———. *Congressional Record.* 87th Cong., 1st sess., Vol. 107, pt. 14.
    Washington, D.C.: Government Printing Office, 1961.
———. Foreign Affairs Committee. *Mutual Security Act of 1960.
    Report on H.R. 11510.* 86th Cong., 2d sess., 1960.
———. *The Peace Corps. Hearings on H.R. 7500.* 87th Cong.,
    1st sess., 1961.
———. *The Peace Corps. Report on S. 2000.* 87th Cong., 1st sess.,
    1961.

————. *Peace Corps Act. Conference Report on H.R. 7500.* 87th Cong., 1st sess., 1961.

U.S. Subcommittee on *Freedom of Communications.* Part 1. The Speeches, Remarks, Press Conferences and Statements of Senator John F. Kennedy, August 1–November 7, 1960. 87th Cong., 1st sess. Washington, D.C.: Government Printing Office, 1961.

————. Part 2. The Speeches, Remarks, Press Conferences and Study Papers of Vice President Richard M. Nixon, August 1–November 7, 1960. 87th Cong., 1st sess. Washington, D.C.: Government Printing Office, 1961.

U.S. Department of State. *Foreign Relations of the United States, 1950: National Security Affairs; Foreign Economic Policy.* Vol. 1. Washington, D.C.: Government Printing Office, 1977.

————. "GFRC Criticism of Peace Corps in Cameroon," Dec. 30, 1965.

————. "Memorandum for Mr. Kenneth O'Donnell." Nov. 18, 1961.

————. "Note of Thanks for Peace Corps Assistance." Aug. 20, 1963.

————. "Text of the Diplomatic Note from the Foreign Ministry." Nov. 2, 1965.

————. "Text of Embassy's Note to Foreign Ministry." Nov. 22, 1965.

————. *United States Treaties and Other International Agreements.* Vol. 13, pt. 2. Washington, D.C.: Government Printing Office, 1963.

United States Statutes at Large. Oct. 26, 1951, 82d Cong., 1st sess., Vol. 65. Washington, D.C.: Government Printing Office, 1952.

————. Sept. 22, 1961, 87th Cong., 1st sess., Vol. 75. Washington, D.C.: Government Printing Office, 1962.

Secondary Sources

Ambrose, Stephen E. *Eisenhower: The President.* Vol. 2. New York: Simon and Schuster, 1985.

————. *Eisenhower: Soldier, General of the Army, President-Elect, 1890–1952.* Vol. 1. New York: Simon and Schuster, 1984.

————. *Ike's Spies: Eisenhower and the Espionage Establishment.* New York: Doubleday, 1981.

————. *Rise to Globalism: American Foreign Policy since 1938.* 4th ed. New York: Penguin Books, 1985.

Ashabranner, Brent K. *A Moment in History: The First Ten Years of the Peace Corps.* New York: Doubleday, 1971.

Austen, Ralph A. "Slavery among Coastal Middlemen: The Douala of Cameroon." In *Slavery in Africa: Historical and Anthropological Perspectives*, edited by Suzanne Miers and Igor Kopytoff. Madison: Univ. of Wisconsin Press, 1977.

Barnet, Richard. *Intervention and Revolution: The United States in the Third World*. New York: World, 1968.

Bender, Gerald J., James S. Coleman, and Richard L. Sklar, eds. *African Crisis Areas and U.S. Foreign Policy*. Los Angeles: Univ. of California Press, 1985.

Burner, David. *John F. Kennedy and a New Generation*. Boston: Scott, Foresman/Little, Brown College Division, 1988.

Bush, Gerald W. "The Peace Corps as a Value-oriented Movement." Ph.D. diss., Northern Illinois Univ., 1968.

Carey, Robert. *The Peace Corps*. New York: Praeger, 1970.

Cerf, Jay H., and Walter Pozen, eds. *Strategy for Peace for the Sixties*. New York: Foreign Policy Clearing House, Praeger, 1960.

Chafe, William H. *The Unfinished Journey: America since World War II*. New York: Oxford Univ. Press, 1986.

Cheema, Shabbir G., and Dennis A. Rondinelli, eds. *Decentralization and Development: Policy Implementation in Developing Countries*. Beverly Hills, Calif.: Sage Publications, 1983.

Chinweizu. *Decolonising the African Mind*. Lagos, Nigeria: Pero Press, 1987.

——— . *The West and the Rest of Us*. New York: Random House, 1975.

Chukwumerije, Ibezim. "The New Frontier and Africa, 1961–63." Ph.D. diss., State Univ. of New York at Stony Brook, 1976.

Coquery-Vidrovitch, Catherine. *Africa: Endurance and Change South of the Sahara*. Translated by David Maisel. Berkeley: Univ. of California Press, 1988.

Cowan, Paul. *The Making of an Un-American*. New York: Viking Press, 1970.

Curti, Merle. *American Philanthropy Abroad*. New Brunswick, N.J.: Rutgers Univ. Press, 1963.

DeLancey, Mark W. *Cameroon: Dependence and Independence*. Boulder, Colo.: Westview Press, 1989.

——— . "The U.S. Peace Corps Program for Credit Union and Cooperative Development in Cameroon, 1969–1976." *Studies in Comparative International Development* 17 (Fall/Winter 1982): 92–123.

Destler, I. M., Leslie H. Gelb, and Anthony Lake. *Our Worst Enemy: The Unmaking of American Foreign Policy*. New York: Random House, 1984.

Donovan, Robert J. *Conflict and Crisis: The Presidency of Harry S. Truman. 1945–1948.* New York: W. W. Norton, 1977.

———. *Tumultuous Years: The Presidency of Harry S. Truman, 1949–1953.* New York: W. W. Norton, 1982.

Drimmer, Melvin. *Issues in Black History: Reflections and Commentaries on the Black Historical Experience.* Dubuque, Iowa: Kendall/Hunt, 1987.

Dwyer, David J. *An Introduction to West African Pidgin English.* East Lansing: African Studies Center, Michigan State Univ., 1969.

Eisenhower, Dwight D. *Mandate for Change, 1953–1956: The White House Years.* New York: Doubleday, 1963.

———. *The White House Years: Waging Peace, 1956–1961.* New York: Doubleday, 1965.

Ekiti, E. A. "Basel Mission Education Development in Cameroon since Reunification." *West Cameroon Teachers' Journal* 2 (Dec. 1964): 36–42.

Everett, Richard. "Cushioning the Stock." *Africa Report,* May–June 1986, 77–81.

Ezickson, Aaron J., ed. *The Peace Corps: A Pictorial History.* New York: Hill and Wang, 1965.

Fairfield, Roy P. "Ohio Volunteers Render Service beyond Community." *Ohio Alumnus,* Apr. 1964, 16–17.

———. "The Peace Corps and the University." *Journal of Higher Education* 35 (Apr. 1964): 189–201.

Fairlie, Henry. *The Kennedy Promise: The Politics of Expectation.* New York: Doubleday, 1973.

Ferrell, Robert H. *Harry S. Truman and the Modern American Presidency.* Boston: Little, Brown, 1983.

Fitzgerald, Merni Ingrassia. *The Peace Corps Today.* New York: Dodd and Mead, 1986.

FitzSimons, Louise. *The Kennedy Doctrine.* New York: Random House, 1972.

Friedan, Betty. *The Feminine Mystique.* New York: Norton, 1963.

Gaddis, John Lewis. "The Emerging Post-revisionist Synthesis on the Origins of the Cold War." *Diplomatic History* 7 (Summer 1983): 171–90.

———. *Strategies of Containment: A Critical Appraisal of Postwar American National Security Policy.* New York: Oxford Univ. Press, 1982.

———. *The United States and the Origins of the Cold War, 1941–1947.* New York: Columbia Univ. Press, 1972.

Gallup, George, ed. *The Gallup Poll: Public Opinion, 1935–1971.* Vol. 3. New York: Random House, 1972.

Gann, L. H., and Peter Duignan, eds. *Colonialism in Africa, 1870–1960*. Vol. 1 of *The History and Politics of Colonialism, 1870–1914*. Cambridge: Cambridge Univ. Press, 1969.

Gardinier, David E. *Cameroon: United Nations Challenge to French Policy*. London: Oxford Univ. Press, 1963.

Garrow, David J. *Protest at Selma: Martin Luther King, Jr., and the Voting Rights Act of 1965*. New Haven, Conn.: Yale Univ. Press, 1978.

Gavshon, Arthur. *Crisis in Africa: Battleground of East and West*. New York: Penguin Books, 1981.

Geary, Christraud M. *Images from Bamum: German Colonial Photography at the Court of King Njoya, Cameroon, West Africa, 1902–1915*. Washington, D.C.: Smithsonian Institution Press, 1988.

Gifford, Prosser, and William Roger Louis, eds. *Britain and Germany: Imperial Rivalry and Colonial Rule*. New Haven, Conn.: Yale Univ. Press, 1967.

———. *Decolonization and African Independence: The Transfer of Power, 1960–1980*. New Haven, Conn.: Yale Univ. Press, 1988.

———. *France and Britain in Africa: Imperial Rivalry and Colonial Rule*. New Haven, Conn.: Yale Univ. Press, 1971.

Goldman, Eric. *The Crucial Decade—And After: America, 1945–1960*. New York: Random House, 1960.

Halberstam, David. *The Best and the Brightest*. New York: Random House, 1972.

Hapgood, David, and Meridian Bennett. *Agents of Change: A Close Look at the Peace Corps*. Boston: Little, Brown, 1968.

Harbutt, Fraser J. *The Iron Curtain: Churchill, America and the Origins of the Cold War*. New York: Oxford Univ. Press, 1986.

Harper, Paul, and Joann P. Krieg, eds. *John F. Kennedy: The Promise Revisited*. New York: Greenwood Press, 1988.

Hayes, Samuel. *An International Peace Corps: The Promise and the Problem*. Washington, D.C.: Public Affairs Institute, 1961.

Hilsman, Roger. *To Move a Nation: The Politics of Foreign Policy in the Administration of John F. Kennedy*. New York: Dell, 1967.

Hoopes, Roy. *The Complete Peace Corps Guide*. New York: Dial, 1966.

———, ed. *The Peace Corps Experience*. New York: Clarkson N. Potter, 1968.

Howe, Russell Warren. *Along the Afric Shore: An Historic Review of Two Centuries of U.S.-African Relations*. New York: Barnes and Noble, 1975.

Humphrey, Hubert H. *The Education of a Public Man: My Life in Politics*. New York: Doubleday, 1976.

Hunt, Michael H. *Ideology and U.S. Foreign Policy*. New Haven, Conn.: Yale Univ. Press, 1987.

Jackson, Henry F. *From the Congo to Soweto: U.S. Foreign Policy toward Africa since 1960.* New York: William Morrow, 1982.

Johnson, Williard R. *The Cameroon Federation: Political Integration in a Fragmentary Society.* Princeton, N.J.: Princeton Univ. Press, 1970.

Jones, Charles Clyde. "The Peace Corps: An Analysis of the Development, Problems, Preliminary Evaluation and Future." Ph.D. diss., West Virginia Univ., 1967.

Kennedy, John F. *Profiles in Courage.* New York: Pocket Books, 1963.

——— . *The Strategy of Peace.* New York: Harper and Row, 1960.

Kinsey, Winston Lee. "The United States and Ghana, 1957–1966." Ph.D. diss., Texas Tech Univ., 1969.

Kirkendall, Richard S. *The Truman Period as a Research Field: A Reappraisal, 1972.* Columbia: Univ. of Missouri Press, 1974.

Kofele-Kale, Ndiva, ed. *An African Experiment in Nation Building: The Bilingual Cameroon Republic since Reunification.* Boulder, Colo.: Westview Press, 1980.

LaFeber, Walter. *America, Russia and the Cold War, 1945–1984.* 5th ed. New York: Knopf, 1983.

——— . *Inevitable Revolutions: The United States in Central America.* New York: W. W. Norton, 1983.

Lederer, William J., and Eugene Burdick. *The Ugly American.* New York: W. W. Norton, 1958.

Lele, Uma. *The Design of Rural Development: Lessons from Africa.* Baltimore: Johns Hopkins Univ. Press, 1975.

Leuchtenburg, William E. *Troubled Feast: American Society since 1945.* Boston: Little, Brown, 1983.

Le Vine, Victor T. "Calm before the Storm in Cameroon?" *Africa Report,* May 1961, 3–4.

——— . *The Cameroon Federal Republic.* Ithaca, N.Y.: Cornell Univ. Press, 1971.

——— . *The Cameroons: From Mandate to Independence.* Los Angeles: Univ. of California Press, 1964.

——— . "A Reluctant February Bride? The 'Other Cameroons.' " *Africa Report,* Feb. 1961, 5–6, 12.

Lisk, Franklyn, ed. *Popular Participation in Planning for Basic Needs: Concepts, Methods and Practices.* New York: St. Martin's Press, 1985.

Liston, Robert A. *Sargent Shriver: A Candid Portrait.* New York: Farrar, Straus, 1964.

Lowther, Kevin, and C. Payne Lucas. *Keeping Kennedy's Promise: The Peace Corps, Unmet Hope of the New Frontier.* Boulder, Colo.: Westview Press, 1978.

McGuire, Edna. *The Peace Corps: Kindlers of the Spark.* New York: Macmillan, 1966.

McKay, Vernon. *Africa in World Politics.* New York: Harper and Row, 1963.

Mahoney, Richard D. *JFK: Ordeal in Africa.* New York: Oxford Univ. Press, 1983.

Meisler, Stanley. "Peace Corps Teaching in Africa." *Africa Report,* Dec. 1966, 16–20.

Mengot, Ako D. "Are West Cameroonians' Educational Standards Falling?" *West Cameroon Teachers' Journal* 2 (Dec. 1964): 9–23.

————. "Pressures and Constraints on the Development of Education in West Cameroon." *Africa Today* 14 (Nov. 2, 1967): 18–20.

Miroff, Bruce. *Pragmatic Illusions: The Presidential Politics of John F. Kennedy.* New York: David McKay Co., 1976.

Moumie, Félix Roland. "Dr. Moumie and M. Ahidjo." *West Africa,* Jan. 2, 1960, 14.

O'Donnell, Kenneth P., and David F. Powers, and Joe McCarthy. *"Johnny, We Hardly Knew Ye": Memories of John Fitzgerald Kennedy.* Boston: Little, Brown, 1972.

Parmet, Herbert S. *JFK: The Presidency of John F. Kennedy.* New York: Penguin Books, 1984.

————. *Jack: The Struggles of John F. Kennedy.* New York: Dial Books, 1980.

Paterson, Thomas G. *On Every Front: The Making of the Cold War.* New York: W. W. Norton, 1979.

————, ed. *Kennedy's Quest for Victory: American Foreign Policy, 1961–1963.* New York: Oxford Univ. Press, 1989.

Ranelagh, John. *The Agency: The Rise and Decline of the CIA.* New York: Simon and Schuster, 1986.

Ray, Ellen, William Schaap, Karl Van Meter, and Louis Wolf, eds. *Dirty Work 2: The CIA in Africa.* Secaucus, N.J.: Lyle Stuart, 1979.

Redmon, Coates. *Come as You Are: The Peace Corps Story.* New York: Harcourt, 1986.

Reeves, T. Zane. *The Politics of the Peace Corps & VISTA.* Tuscaloosa: Univ. of Alabama Press, 1988.

Reuther, Victor G. *Goals for the United States Peace Corps.* Washington, D.C.: United Auto Workers, 1960.

Rice, Gerard T. *The Bold Experiment: JFK's Peace Corps.* Notre Dame, Ind.: Univ. of Notre Dame Press, 1985.

Rubin, Neville. *Cameroon: An African Federation.* New York: Praeger, 1971.

Rudin, Harry R. *Germans in the Cameroons, 1884–1914: A Case Study in Modern Imperialism.* New York: Greenwood Press, 1968.

Schlesinger, Arthur M., Jr. *Kennedy or Nixon: Does It Make Any Difference?* New York: Macmillan, 1960.

———. *Robert Kennedy and His Times.* Boston: Houghton Mifflin, 1978.

———. *A Thousand Days: John F. Kennedy in the White House.* Boston: Houghton Mifflin, 1965.

Seligson, Mitchell A., ed. *The Gap between Rich and Poor: Contending Perspectives on the Political Economy of Development.* Boulder, Colo.: Westview Press, 1984.

Sitkoff, Harvard. *The Struggle for Black Equality, 1954–1980.* New York: Hill and Wang, 1981.

Shriver, Sargent. *Point of the Lance.* New York: Harper and Row, 1964.

Smith, Mary-Ann Tirone. *Lament for a Silver-eyed Woman.* New York: William Morrow, 1987.

Snyder, J. Richard, ed. *John F. Kennedy: Person, Policy, Presidency.* Wilmington, Del.: Scholarly Resources Imprint, 1988.

Sorensen, Theodore C. *Kennedy.* New York: Harper and Row, 1966.

Stanford Research Institute. *Education and Manpower.* Vol. 2 of *The Economic Potential of West Cameroon—Priorities for Development, Prepared for the Government of the Federal Republic of Cameroon and the Government of the Federated States of West Cameroon.* Menlo Park, Calif., 1965.

Steel, Ronald. *Walter Lippmann and the American Century.* New York: Vintage Books, 1981.

Stein, Morris I. *Volunteers for Peace: The First Group of Peace Corps Volunteers in a Rural Community Development Program in Colombia, South America.* New York: John Wiley, 1966.

Stoessinger, John G. *Crusaders and Pragmatists: Movers of American Foreign Policy.* New York: W. W. Norton, 1979.

Thompson, Scott W. *Ghana's Foreign Policy, 1957–1966: Diplomacy, Ideology and the New State.* Princeton, N.J.: Princeton Univ. Press, 1969.

Thomsen, Moritz. *Living Poor: A Peace Corps Chronicle.* Seattle: Univ. of Washington Press, 1969.

Truman, Harry S. *Memoirs: Year of Decisions.* Vol. 1. New York: Doubleday, 1955.

———. *Memoirs: Years of Trial and Hope.* Vol. 2. New York: Doubleday, 1956.

Ungar, Sanford J. *Africa: The People and Politics of an Emerging Continent.* New York: Simon and Schuster, 1985.

United Nations. *Statistical Year Book, 1962–1973.* New York: Publishing Service, United Nations, 1963–74.

Viorst, Milton, ed. *Making a Difference: The Peace Corps at Twenty-five.* New York: Weidenfeld and Nicolson, 1986.

Walton, Richard. *Cold War and Counter Revolution: The Foreign Policy of John F. Kennedy.* New York: Viking Press, 1972.

Wingenbacti, Charles E. *The Peace Corps: Who, How and Where?* New York: McGraw Hill, 1963.

Wilson, Vincent, Jr., ed. *The Book of Great American Documents: With Inaugural Addresses of Jefferson, Lincoln, Kennedy.* Brookeville, Md.: American History Research Associates, 1982.

Wofford, Harris. *Of Kennedys and Kings: Making Sense of the Sixties.* New York: Farrar, Straus, 1980.

Wright, Gordon. *The Ordeal of Total War, 1939–1945.* New York: Harper and Row, 1972.

Zalba, Serapio R. "The Peace Corps—Its Historical Antecedents and Its Meaning for Social Work." *Duquesne Review* 11 (Fall 1966): 125–37.

Zimmerman, Robert F. "Peace Corps/Philippines: Image or Performance." Ph.D. diss., American Univ., 1968.

Zuniga, Ricardo Burmester. "The Peace Corps as a Value-oriented Movement." Ph.D. diss., Harvard Univ., 1968.

Index

The Peace Corps in Cameroon was composed in 10/13 New Baskerville on a Xyvision system with
Linotron 202 output by BookMasters, Inc.; printed by sheet-fed offset on 60-pound Glatfelter
Natural Smooth acid-free stock, Smyth sewn and bound over binders boards in Holliston Roxite
B cloth with 80-pound Rainbow Antique endpapers, wrapped with dustjackets printed in two
colors on 80-pound enamel stock and film laminated by Braun-Brumfield, Inc.; designed by
Ed King; and published by The Kent State University Press, Kent, Ohio 44242.